FORECASTING COMMODITY MARKETS

Using Technical, Fundamental and Econometric Analysis

Julian Roche

Probus Publishing Company

London, England
Burr Ridge, Illinois

First published in 1995 by
Probus Publishing Company
Lynton House, 7-12 Tavistock Square, London WC1H 9LB, England

Designed and typeset by Nick Battley, London, England

ISBN 1 55738 899 7

Printed in the United Kingdom

Contents

'Forecasting in business is like sex in society, we have to have it, we cannot get along without it; everyone is doing it, one way or another, but nobody is sure he is doing it the best way.'

G W Plossl, Manufacturing Control—The Last Frontier for Profits

Introduction

The authors of one of the most well-known introductions to technical analysis warn: 'When you enter the stock market, you are going into a competitive field in which your evaluations and opinions will be matched against some of the sharpest and toughest minds in the business. You are in a highly specialized industry in which there are many different sectors, all of which are under intense study by men whose economic survival depends on their best judgement. You will certainly be exposed to advice, suggestions, offers of help from all sides. Unless you are able to develop some market philosophy of your own, you will not be able to tell the good from the bad, the sound from the unsound.' Exactly the same applies to commodity markets, and the more so within derivative markets which are geared: a given percentage change in price can produce a much larger change in profit or loss.

Commodity forecasting is vital for industry practitioners. At the AMCOT Annual Sales Conference in Nashville in 1994, for example, the most frequently asked question was: 'What are our prospects in Europe?' The most commonly asked question to brokers in any commodity from their clients is inevitably: 'Which way is the price headed?' Most business conferences are exactly the same. Forecasting is equally important within industries that use commodities in one form or another. Commodity price and volume forecasts are necessary for managers who need to buy sugar for confectionery manufacture or coffee for supermarkets, even if the impact on their personal bottom line is a little more indirect. Commodity prices have a wide and substantial impact throughout the range of retail and industrial businesses that constitute the majority of any developed country's industry. Commodity prices are equally important for the public sector: the cost of fuel for the armed forces, of heating for government offices, of food for hospitals and prisons. Such prices feed into every business plan throughout the developed world. Commodity markets and the production processes on which they are based have evolved quickly in the past twenty years, and are continuing to do so. But the ability to predict the evolution of relevant aspects of the commodities markets has not—nor does it show any signs of doing so in the future, and this despite extensive research and many different approaches to the issue.

Forecasting is difficult, as forecasters tell decision-makers constantly, whatever market is being forecast. Commodity markets are complex, interrelated and subject to intense shocks which are especially difficult to predict. The roles of production processes, the weather, politics and economies in general are all crucial in determining price, demand, supply and stocks. The relative influence of each factor varies between commodities.

Different methodologies are clearly based on very different assumptions, and there are some important methods of distinction between them. Firstly, does the method seek to explain the variable to be forecast, and then to predict it, on the basis of the behaviour of its causes? This is what a data-hungry econometric model does; and it is also what fundamental analysis seeks to do. An econometric model is really a mathematical exposition of the ideas of fundamental analysts, so there is no contradiction between the two. Or does it seek to predict the variable from its own previous behaviour, generalizing from the behaviour of other similar variables? That is what time series analysis and technical analysis do. There is more in common between these two disciplines than their advocates would usually concede and that, judging from the language, the terminology and the limited communication between the disciplines one might ever glean. This book tries to make a comparison between econometric and technical analysis possible by using language and concepts that apply to both. Secondly, is the outcome to be expressed usually in annual numbers or in daily ones? Is it a short-term forecast designed primarily for trading purposes, or a long-term one for policy-makers? Is the forecasting process continuous and updated, or is it a one-off exercise? Thirdly, are they funded publicly and therefore probably publicly available or private, the result of a commercial operation's need for a forecast? Are they expensive and custom-built or forecasts derived from cheap, mass-produced software?

The book tries to be both comprehensive and wide ranging. It seeks to draw comparative forecasting experience from not only a wide variety of commodities, but also from the financial markets where forecasting techniques are more developed, more readily applied and, owing to the larger scale of the markets, more important in financial terms.

This book is practically orientated. It does not dwell, except where necessary, on the often complex mathematics of forecasting. Single examples are given where econometricians would blanch at not giving six. Rather, it tries to go straight to the point of how to use the results of forecasting, when to use forecasting, and what is necessary in order to carry out forecasting. It goes into the pitfalls of forecasting and the errors to which commodity forecasting is prone. It includes many historical examples of forecasting and many parts of guides to software and descriptions of systems; software packages for forecasting, such as *SPSS, STATPACK, Forecast Pro, Forecast Plus* and *MicroTSP* are discussed along with the numerous specialist forecasting packages which are available for commodity and other derivative forecasting. All this might suggest that the compilation of a comprehensive analysis of commodity forecasting is a relatively straightforward task. It is not. There is no one discipline, the practitioners are split by continent, by market sector, and, it seems, by attitude to forecasting and preferred approach.

There is one part of the book that I would especially have liked to have been much longer, and that is the comparative evaluation of different forecasting systems—the 'right way' that G.W. Plossl suggests all users of forecasts would like to see and which the editors of academic journals evidently would also like. The degree of accuracy of the results is the most important feature of a forecast—*not* how it was derived or constructed. Ideally this book should contain accuracy tables comparing different systems and approaches with specific reference to particular commodities over defined time periods, but also comparisons across a wide range of commodities. Evidence from researching this book, however, suggests that there is a woeful lack of detailed, especially systematized, comparative evidence on the success of different forecasting methodologies and published forecasts in terms of their ability to predict what actually happens.

The absence of such work throughout the literature is so marked as to draw the conclusion that there are clear institutional pressures operating against it. There is a vital conclusion to draw from this. Potential forecasters seeking to choose between methodologies for themselves, or amongst different software should, wherever possible, commission research on the background logic, but to a much greater extent, on the accuracy of different methods in predicting *precisely* the variables in which they are interested before committing themselves to a forecasting methodology. Such research could be commissioned from a management consultancy such as Arthur Andersen in the USA or one of the economics companies that does not specialize in forecasting, such as London Economics in the UK, most of which would be exceptionally well-placed to do this kind of work.

This may be a time-consuming and probably an expensive task, but the alternative—of using forecasts that are not as accurate as they could be—could easily be far more costly in terms of foregone commercial opportunities. Customized analysis of the effectiveness of forecasting packages and options is an overdue element of consultancy practice.

Chapter 1

What is a commodity market?

Economists, who do most forecasting, define a commodity as a portion of physical wealth, usually to be distinguished from money in all its forms as well as from free goods and manufactures. Commodities satisfy human wants and needs, from shelter to food to clothing; they are essential materials for manufacturing processes. They are restricted in supply and hence have an exchange value as well as a use value. Traders and commodities analysts have a rather narrower sense of the word commodity, and it is in this sense that this book considers the concept. 'Commodities are natural substances, perhaps processed, which have economic value and can be perceived using human senses, can be quantified and measured for quality, and can—at least in theory—be owned.'[1]

Very approximately—the division is a historical one rather than based on absolute physical delineations—commodities can be divided into the categories of:

- Softs
- Metals
- Energy
- Others

Softs include the traditional commodities of the London futures markets, such as coffee, cocoa, sugar and rubber, and those of New York and Chicago such as cotton, soya and pork bellies—but they also include those that are traded either mainly or exclusively on spot/auction markets such as tea and spices, rice, fish, vegetables, fruit, soya, and the grains—although these are sometimes separated into another category, as well as fruit and vegetables.

Metal commodities are defined by their geological formation and chemical composition. Within the general category of metals, there is a

[1] *Roche, CLD p1.*

relatively well-defined subdivision of precious metals, predominantly gold and silver, but this also includes uranium, platinum, palladium and other similar metals.

Energy commodities are principally oil and gas and their derivatives, such as partially-refined oil products. Electricity has become an over-the-counter product traded in London, and other energy commodities are: nuclear power, coal, hydro-electric power, wind, geothermal and wave energy—although these latter are clearly difficult to quantify except in terms of the electricity that they produce.

The 'Other' category sweeps up a widely disparate number of different commodities and there is no agreement as to its boundaries. Those traded on exchanges as futures contracts, at least, have ranged from insurance to property, and exchanges have considered lumber, computer chips, ammonia and phosphates. Other commodities include precious stones, building materials and the difficult-to-isolate area of intellectual property, software and expertise. In theory, almost any identifiable object could become a commodity if it is traded, and the old 'physical' tag to commodities is receding into the past. In practice, a commodity in this category is created when there is a market for it and futures markets could, theoretically, trade manufactured or semi-manufactured goods.

Commodities—principally, but not necessarily, softs—can also be aggregated to form indices, the price evolution of which can be regarded as typical of the sector as a whole. Of these, there are five especially worth noting. These are the IMF index, the Economist index, the UNCTAD index, the World Bank index and the Goldman Sachs Commodity Index (GSCI). The composition of these indices is based on different percentages based on consumption figures from traded commodities. Each index has its rationale, its advocates, advantages and disadvantages. All can be traded, and many are.

Practically the only distinction worth noting now is that between commodities on the one hand, and financial products on the other. Financial products involve media of exchange; commodities are the subjects of exchange. That is about the only meaningful rule-of-thumb, and a contract like insurance must be said to lie in-between the two. Almost all traded commodities are also economic commodities. Scarcities differ and so do production costs between regions and ultimately nations, so trade in commodities has been part of human life for as long as records exist and archaeologists can discover. Trade, whether between villages or between nations, inevitably in turn gave rise to markets. The main characteristics of a market are a set time or period, a regular occurrence, a definite and limited place of assembly, the existence of regulations governing the exchange of commodities, and the maintenance of order. In such markets, prices for the exchange of commodities have been set and exchanges made.

The complex international commodity markets of the late twentieth century are the direct descendants of the rural markets which themselves persevere throughout the world. They are also the precursors of the international electronic integrated global commodities markets for which the world has been waiting for decades and which now do not seem likely for decades more.

Types of market

Markets vary enormously. The most important distinction is not size or physical location, although these vary enormously, but in categories between spot (or physical, or actual, or current) markets on the one hand, and derivative markets on the other. Derivative markets are where those wishing to divest risk—hedgers—come together with speculators—those who wish to take it on. All the commodities derivative markets are based on a physical commodity or an index. The market to buy and sell the physical commodity for immediate delivery is the 'spot' market which is contrasted to a derivative market. When a pearl is bought for $200,000, in derivative market terminology the underlying product has been traded for $200,000 on the pearl spot market. Such physical commodities markets differ enormously. The international spot market for crude oil, for example, is both very liquid (it is easy to buy or sell the amount you want without moving the price) and complex. There are many different sub-markets, each particular in its participants, its structure and its location. For example, the Rotterdam spot market has dozens of participants, most of them in major oil and trading companies. The European naphtha market, by contrast, consists of the commodity in transit to Europe with fewer than a dozen traders in major oil and trading companies; the global rice market is dominated by fewer than a dozen companies with historical links to producer and consumer countries. It is certainly the case that physical markets for commodities do tend towards being tightly-organized clubs. Trading problems that still exist include:

- Problems in determining accurate prices, although this is slowly changing as IT makes concealment less easy;
- Administrative problems involved in finding counterparties, there being no centralized marketplace;
- The default issue;
- The price risk.

The main practical distinction in international commodity markets is between organized futures markets on the one hand and all other markets on the other. Forward markets are however a form of derivative market. All agreements made now for delivery in the future are called 'forward' agreements, so futures markets themselves are a type of forward market. But one definition of a forward contracts is 'a commitment between two parties to exchange a specific product or service at a specific price at a specific date'. The Pearl Company Inc.'s promise to buy a specific pearl, price agreed at $200,000, in three months' time is a forward contract. The Pearl Company Inc.'s agreement to sell the same pearl to a jeweller at $250,000 in three months' time is also a forward contract. The two together would be the much sought-after 'back-to-back' contracts: guaranteed profit and little or no involvement with the physical commodity itself. As might be imagined, exact fits like this are rare, although some oil cargoes may be sold on ten or more times before they reach their destination, for example between the Gulf and Rotterdam.

Like physical/spot contracts, forward contracts are subject to national laws and regulations. In many cases international obligations are involved and there may be counterparty risks of *force majeure*, or worse, delay in payment or default in payment, exacerbated by long chains of sellers and buyers, with the inevitable concomitant of expensive and lengthy arbitration and litigation; or forward contracts may not be available at all because of the difficulty in matching buyer and seller and then in agreeing mutually acceptable terms within a cost-effective time frame. These risks helped futures markets to develop in the first place. Unlike exchange-traded futures and options contracts, forward contracts are not standardized in any particular way and are negotiated privately. Hence forward markets, bereft of organized exchanges and accurate price reporting, are often as impenetrable to price discovery as physical spot markets, but both forward and spot markets are usually principal-to-principal and brokers are not usually involved in the same way which reduces overheads and complexity. Many commodities, such as rice, are frequently sold in forward markets.

In futures and options markets, all market users are called players. Brokers buy and sell on behalf of market players. When players buy or sell in derivative markets they take, and then hold, a position in the market. They are consequently 'exposed' to a risk of price movement in the market, the extent of which is known as their exposure. Exposure is either being long of the market or short. If you buy a pearl, in derivative market terminology, you are long pearls. If you have agreed to sell a pearl next month at an agreed price, without having bought the pearl yet (a common trading practice) you are short pearls. It is possible to buy the physical commodity and sell in the futures market, levelling out the risk and becoming—if the amounts are the same and the qualities equal—neutral to price change. This characteristic of traded markets of being able to sell before buying is very important as it means that large numbers of market participants—not just manufacturers who depend on keeping commodity costs down—will suffer when commodity prices rise.

Futures contracts

These are standardized forward contracts. The quantity, grade, delivery points and type of the commodity are all known in advance. Only the price is left to fluctuate. A typical definition is: 'A legally binding agreement on a nationally-recognized exchange to make or take delivery of a specified instrument, at a fixed date in the future, at a price agreed upon at the time of dealing.' The exchange (in Japan) or the associated so-called 'clearing house' (in the USA and UK) carries the risk of default and, in exchange, insists on a deposit (the *initial margin*) and the payment of variation margins on a daily basis (which fully cover the change in price of the contract that day—minimizing the exchange or clearing house's risk). It is this aspect of futures contracts—the high level of gearing generated by the deposit system—which has rightly created the impression that futures contracts are risky instruments. With a deposit of 10 per cent, a price movement of just 10 per cent can wipe out (or double) the initial investment. This gearing makes accurate price forecasting of shattering importance for futures markets.

Futures contracts' characteristics are usually described in a list as follows:

i) The size of the contract. This can be so many kg or tonnes, or it can be in terms of the number of dollars per index point. Not every futures contract ends in physical delivery—some are cash settled. Too large a size, and to trade becomes too risky and liquidity falls; too small, and traders become irritated at the exchange levy on every contract and at associated brokerage charges.

ii) The minimum price change of the contract, also known as the tick size. Too large a tick size and the contract moves only slowly and becomes unattractive and unrepresentative of the spot market; too small and no trade of any size can be executed before the market moves again. Sometimes exchanges impose maximum price movements for a single day's trading, which are called *limits*.

iii) The traded months, e.g. January, June and October, nine months forward quoted at all times (i.e. in July 199X, the last month quoted would be June 199(X+3).

iv) The hours that the contract is traded. These are either a fixed period in the morning and afternoon, as with most soft commodity futures markets outside Japan, or a series of specific ring calls, as with the London Metal Exchange and Japanese futures markets.

A futures exchange, such as the Chicago Board of Trade or the MATIF, is an organized central marketplace for the trade of futures and options contracts. There are now over 50 futures exchanges worldwide trading hundred of commodity futures contracts and each country has its own specific regulations for their operations. It is worth noting, however, that since at least the early 1980s, commodities have been overshadowed by financials in respect of volumes traded and new contracts emerging onto futures markets. The London International Financial Futures and Options Market (LIFFE) now dwarfs the London Commodity Exchange, whilst the International Petroleum Exchange and the London Metal Exchange stand in between in terms of volume traded.

The predominant explanation as to why some extremely important metals do not have futures markets is that their price is stable, determined by long-term contracts signed either at an international level, or between major companies. This has traditionally been the case for iron and steel, for example. History, mainly, explains the case for softs and textiles: tea, for example, has traditionally been sold at auction, whereas coffee traders have used futures markets. Some markets, such as rice, are difficult to pin down in terms of a specific type of rice and delivery locations for traders to agree on for use as a futures contract. Cotton has always been very actively traded in a futures markets, whereas silk has been an auction market. Rapidly-evolving tradition is responsible for similar divisions in the energy markets: oil uses futures markets, whereas some of its derivative markets, such as naphtha, resist the intrusion of open pricing that futures markets entail.

Option contracts

These exchanges also trade options based upon many of their contracts although, many more options are traded over-the-counter (OTC) between firms than are traded on exchange floors. A commodity option is the right, but not the obligation, to buy (a call option) or sell (a put option) a specific quantity and quality of a commodity at a specific price, known as the 'strike' price.

This price can be:

- at a specific time, known as a *European option;*
- before or at a specific time, known as an *American option;*
- an average over a period. This is increasingly popular in commodities and known colloquially as an *Asian option.*

Those who buy options are said to be *takers, buyers* or *holders,* whilst sellers are also called *writers* or *grantors.*

Options contracts on physical commodities are written either to be completely specific to the two companies involved or to be tradeable. 'Traded options' refer to those which are actually traded on exchanges and are options on futures contracts themselves, rather than physical commodities. Option writers usually quote for a variety of different strike prices and expiry dates. The premiums vary significantly over time according to complex formulae that are related to the price of the underlying futures contract. Options are either worth exercising, in which case they are said to be *in-the-money*—or not (*out-of-the-money*), in which case they will expire worthless if this remains the case until expiry. A call option is out of the money when the strike price is below the current futures price, and vice versa. The opposite applies to a put option. The intrinsic value of an option is the amount by which it is in the money: it will cost more than that to buy, because it may become more valuable as its expiry time approaches—although it may also become less valuable. Buying options is generally recognized as a less risky strategy than direct involvement in the futures market, as loss is limited to the initial investment and the forecasting task is of the yes/no type: Will the option expire worthless or not? (This depends on whether the price reaches or falls to a particular level or not). Writing options, however, is a more risky strategy as prices can, of course, rise or fall to a theoretically unlimited degree. Exchange-traded options contracts can demonstrate a surprising lack of liquidity and have yet to equal exchange-traded futures contracts' volume, except in a limited number of cases.

Participants in markets

In most physical or spot commodity markets worldwide, the dominant participants are international trading companies of a vast variety of sizes and types. Some of them, such as BP or Continental Grain, trade both futures and physical contracts in a wide variety of different markets, but usually in related commodities. Others, such as Marc Rich, Cargill or Goldman Sachs/ J Aron, are involved in a much wider variety of different commodities. Departments exist to trade specific commodities and the company may have employees in many different locations worldwide. Other companies may trade only in a few commodities such as sugar or rice and may have only a very limited and occasional involvement with any futures contracts at all. There are nevertheless very few trading companies, however small, that do not have reason to become involved in forward contracts from time to time and which go short and long in particular markets on occasion. These companies are governed by the laws of their country of origin. These include laws relating to unfair terms of trade, the offering of defective goods for sale, unfair descriptions of products, civil remedies for default in contracts and other related legislation. Legal action across borders, especially by companies in the developed world against developing country companies, where there are very different traditions and where laws, especially trading laws, may not be so rigorously enforced, is often near nigh impossible in the case of defaults. Similarly, when large Western trading companies do collapse with significant debts, resource considerations simply preclude small creditors in developing countries from obtaining adequate recompense.

In the futures markets, participants are more clearly identified and divided into categories. Applicant companies seeking full membership of exchanges (and perhaps more importantly therefore, of clearing houses) are thoroughly vetted in respect of their net worth, their management reputation, their type of business and administrative efficiency. This vetting procedure has become steadily stricter throughout the world since the early 1980s when some futures markets participants took advantage of lax regulations to encourage in many cases unsuitable risk taking participation in futures markets by individuals and small funds. Every exchange throughout the world has its own membership requirements and application procedures. For example, to be considered for membership of the London Clearing House—which clears for the commodities futures markets and for LIFFE—an applicant must provide this information:

- Latest audited accounts;
- Memorandum and Articles of Association, Certificates of Incorporation;
- Details of group structure, including the audited accounts of the parent company;
- Identity of any major shareholders;
- Names of directors and relevant senior executives;
- Business and senior personnel profiles.

All clearing members must sign a standard clearing member agreement which establishes the legal nature of the relationship between the two parties. Clearing members may either trade the futures and options markets on their own accounts, which some occasionally do, or broke on behalf of their clients. They may also clear for non-clearing members of the exchange. Their clients are usually other brokers further down the retail chain, individuals of high net worth who have accounts with them, or—most likely—funds and companies. The funds are either using the futures market to hedge physical positions, or they can be using the futures market as part of a diversified investment strategy. Increasingly, there are funds which are wholly devoted to investment in the futures markets. The terms under which these funds can invest specifically include whether they are allowed to go short in the market as well as go long.

Manufacturing and other non-trading companies using the futures markets should really be doing so in order to hedge physical positions. Managers of such companies should resist the temptation to speculate on the futures markets, however successful in the short term such speculation might be, and the companies' shareholders in their wiser moments should certainly concur. The problem is that futures market operation tends to be concentrated in the treasuries of such companies and other executives do not necessarily know or understand the distinction—important also for tax purposes—between speculation and hedging. Admittedly this distinction can be difficult to establish. The company is almost inevitably likely to be short and long of a specific commodity at varying times. Most transactions can therefore be presented as hedging within the context of a large company.

The world's top commodity contracts

Contract	Exchange	1993	1992
Crude Oil	NYMEX	24 868 602	21 109 562
Copper	LME	14 855 430	7 338 242
Soybean	CBOT	11 649 333	9 000 169
Corn	CBOT	11 462 618	10 356 632
Aluminium	LME	10 083 342	8 225 792
Gold	BM&F	9 406 163	7 932 576
Gold	Comex	8 916 195	6 002 009
Brent Crude	IPE	8 852 549	6 172 155
Gold	Tocom	8 764 441	4 193 775
Heating Oil	Nymex	8 625 061	8 005 462
Unleaded Gasoline	Nymex	7 407 809	6 674 757
Crude Oil	Nymex	7 156 518	6 562 163
Red Beans	TGE	6 353 667	7 804 868
Platinum	Tocom	4 984 480	4 631 724
Silver	Comex	4 855 924	3 016 339
Soybean Meal	CBOT	4 718 095	4 145 397
Soybean Oil	CBOT	4 612 229	4 282 678
Sugar No 11	CSCE	4 285 945	3 667 481
Zinc	LME	4 167 832	4 023 223
Live Cattle	CME	3 306 952	3 319 618
Coffee C	CSCE	2 489 223	2 152 383
Palladium	Tocom	2 275 843	404 091
Cocoa	CSCE	2 128 384	1 397 235
Nickel	LME	2 118 170	1 442 536
Raw Sugar	TGE	1 934 293	1 279 354
Cotton Yarn	TOCOM	1 865 469	2 330 029
Cocoa	LCE	1 849 126	1 384 873
Cotton	NYCE	1 603 027	1 701 258
Live Hogs	CME	1 401 754	1 556 092

Cont.

(cont.)			
Coffee	CSCE	1 022 017	860 943
Sugar	CSCE	916 170	848 750
Coffee Robusta	LCE	885 940	837 190
Pork Bellies	CME	698 799	784 152
Live Cattle	CME	500 664	561 058

Figure 1.1 The world's top commodity contracts

Although Figure 1.1 may look impressive at first sight, it is worth recalling that in 1993 and 1992, the Nymex crude oil contract was only the fifth largest traded futures contract in the world. Between it and the second largest traded commodities contract—the LME copper contract—lay fifteen financial contracts. However commodities contracts show stronger in the second fifteen of worldwide futures contracts, with the CBOT soyabeans contract coming in at No.22 and the IPE's Brent Crude contract at No.30. Further information on world commodity contracts may be found in Appendix 3.

Chapter 2

The importance of forecasting

Economists have always wanted to forecast commodity prices, for their practical importance and their potential attractiveness for quantitative analysis, as well as for the equally important institutional reasons that forecasting adds to their work, status and budgets. They can rightly argue that forecasting commodity prices *is* important. 'For implementation of stabilization policy in individual countries, it is important to have timely analysis of the measurements of primary commodity prices denominated in the country's own currency units.'[1] Most commodity modelling, as opposed to forecasting in particular, has grown out of the needs of national and international agencies to determine the impact of particular policies on commodity markets and to develop price forecasts as a background for policy. Indeed, the inherent instability of agricultural markets, combined with their continued importance for national populations, is usually cited as the reason why governments intervene so frequently and so actively in agricultural markets. This is far from saying that if the markets were predictable they would not do so; but it is to demonstrate the importance of forecasting within governments. One problem has always been that the financial resources and expertise for forecasting has been concentrated in locations and organizations for whom price change is not a life or death matter. That is slowly changing, as better forecasting becomes available more cheaply, but it remains the case as far as specialist expertise is concerned.

Energy forecasting, for example, expanded its importance dramatically after the oil price shocks of 1973-74. Since 1945, oil and related products such as plastics and man-made fibres have increased in relative importance compared to coal and wool. Crude oil prices remain important indicators of other energy prices, such as natural gas and refined oil products and on through coal and electricity. Although oil price shocks have become progressively less frequent throughout the 1980s and 1990s, with relative price stability even throughout the Gulf War, there is no certainty that this

[1] *ICMM, p. xxi.*

will continue indefinitely. The importance of energy in general and oil in particular to Western economies assures energy modelling of a continuing high status.

To take another example, at a microeconomic level, commodity price forecasts are used within firms as contributions for sales forecasts, for purchasing plans and for profit analysis. If the need for expenditure on commodities is likely to increase in the short term, this may in turn have financial implications that will require analysis and planning. Commodity price forecasts are vital for capacity planning, planning for sales and market share, financial planning and budgeting, planning for research and development, and top management's strategic planning. The theoretical objective is to secure all the commodities required by the company at the lowest possible costs, but this will never be entirely possible because products combine commodities, and there are storage costs and opportunity costs in halting production. The maintenance of low costs is always a juggling act, but clearly operating in an environment where the future cost of specific inputs to the production process is known improves the company's chances of long-term profit maximization. For a well-run company, long-term forecasts of price will also tend to become part of the long-term calculation of the viability of specific activities and their profitability.

Any involvement in the commodity business itself, whether as a trader or a broker, inevitably brings the practitioner up against the need to forecast market variables, especially price. Certainly, most traders follow the majority of published forecasts for their commodities. Peter Scott, former European representative of the major US cotton export company AMCOT, put his needs slightly differently: 'At its simplest, we need to be able to estimate total cotton consumption in each of the countries to which we export, and project US market share. I follow the Cotlook, USDA, ICAC and other forecasts. I need to know about supply and demand for cotton and competing fibres, economic cycles, fashion trends, global demographics, and government policy, not necessarily in that order.'[1] Similarly, for fund managers, the theory of asset allocation does suggest, for example, that all assets will perform similarly in the long term, but the asset manager's skill is in selecting out-performing short-term assets—and that means calls and puts which work, and futures positions that show a net profit. Trading profits usually depend on accurate forecasts as much as on effective cost control. Probably the most important aspect of economics

[1] *Letter to the author, 23 August 1994*

work in commodities is forecasting, although the institutional difficulty that it involves individuals becoming responsible for their pronouncements militates heavily against it.

Although forecasting techniques do differ, they all share certain features and assumptions. Many of these have been substantially criticized and they explain certain problems, and why forecasts are—to put it bluntly, but honestly—so often wrong. Firstly, to state the obvious, the future and the relationships between variables that it contains are unknown. Forecasting therefore relies upon known relationships between variables in the past or hypothetical ones. The accuracy and structure of the history of the variables is crucial in determining the forecasts. Therefore any break in the sequence of data causes a deterioration in the accuracy of the forecast. This can occur for example when the data-issuing organization changes the methodology that it uses to produce the data, resulting sometimes in two separate sets of data, the old and the new, and sometimes in spliced series that satisfy no one, but which may be unavoidable.

Secondly, forecasts are inevitably seriously flawed, and those forecasting in the commodity arena would acknowledge this as readily as those in other sectors. The message to companies using forecasts is that there are heavy risks to be run in using them. It is worth accepting the maxim that profitability should be possible subject to the bottom end of the range of forecast possibilities. To make profitability depend on the accuracy of just one forecast is an exceptionally risky move for any company. Caution about forecasts is part of the general theory of portfolio management. This applies to a company's assets as much as to investment management. Linked to this inaccuracy is the fact that almost all forecasts tend to reduce their accuracy as time goes on. If you take the wrong direction at the first turn, you can be 1 km away from your destination after two minutes, and you will get further away as time goes on—because of the wrong turning at the first opportunity. The ripples from a stone are the usual example. It is exactly the same for forecasts. More can go wrong over a longer period, and that is why long-term forecasts tend to be more unreliable than short-term ones. This is not always the case—long-term forecast ranges may be accurate, but the approach to them in great doubt. It does, however, tend to be so. None of this is to suggest in any way that to work in the complete absence of any forecast at all is remotely sensible; indeed, when planning and trading decisions have to be made it is in practice impossible not to act on the basis of a forecast, even if not made explicit.

The importance of forecasting: worked examples

There should be little doubt in anyone's mind that in trading especially, but also in retailing and manufacturing, an accurate forecast of commodity prices can mean all the difference between profit and loss. For a trader, too many inaccurate trades will lead to high losses and eventually, the culprit will—almost inevitably—be made redundant, and find it difficult to get another one trading the same commodity as word will have spread. The dramatic and ironic exception to this rule is where so large a physical stock of a commodity has been acquired by a dealer that the company needs to keep him on so he can use his connections in the physical business to sell it off, however high the losses. This is mercifully rare.

A company's trading profit is determined by the price change in the commodity, carrying costs, fixed charges and transactions costs. This applies whatever the type of market, but there are important differences between them, as outlined below:

Spot or physical trading

Here the important forecast period is between the price at the time at which the commodity is bought—the present moment, in the case of a spot market—and the time that the commodity is to be sold. The commodity may be able to be stored, in which case the storage costs can be factored into the profitability equation for the commodity.

Suppose a pearl is bought by the Pearl Trading Co. on 1 January for $5000. The forecast carried out by the traders of the Pearl Trading Co. is for pearls of this type to rise by 10 per cent in the period to 1 June. Carrying costs for six months are a fixed $50 and amortized overheads divided over all trades $100. The forecast profit is therefore $350. Because the carrying costs are low relative to the value of the commodity, a price rise of only 3 per cent will allow the company to break even. Less than 3 per cent will result in a loss. The forecast can therefore go 70 per cent under in its estimation and there will still be a profit. Suppose that the distribution of confidence levels is normal (a bell shape) about the 10 per cent forecast level, or that at least, if not a normal distribution, then it is at least a calculable one. Then it is possible to go straightaway further. It is possible to say what distribution of confidence levels about the 10 per cent level would affect the decision as to whether to buy, given the desired risk profile of the company and the institutional and internal pressure to trade upon it.

Had the company forecast a 2 per cent rise in pearl prices, the trade would not have been entered into, pressure to do so apart, and a significant profit opportunity would have been lost. Had the company forecast a 20 per cent rise and been disappointed, the significance of this disappointment would have depended on the actions that the company had taken on the basis of the assumed profit, such as announcing a dividend, refurbishing its offices or taking further speculative risks.

Forward trading

In this case, the crucial difference for profitability is clearly that between the price agreed at the time of purchase and the price obtained at the time of sale. The price agreed at the time of purchase is unlikely to be the current price, but is a current reflection of the future spot price, which bears a relationship both to the current spot price plus cost of carry and expected future fresh supply.

Suppose, on 1 January, the Pearl Trading Co. agreed to pay $5000 for a pearl in six months' time. Its forecast is for a 10 per cent price rise and a strong demand for pearls. With no carrying costs to consider, only the administrative overheads (say $100 per deal) need to be factored in, leaving a profit of $450 on the deal. If the forecast is wrong, demand may prove very elastic with respect to price. The company is forced to take delivery of the pearl and to pay $5000, but it may not be able to sell it except at a distress level of perhaps $4000. Together with administrative overheads, this means a loss of $1100 on the deal. The forecasts that are relevant to this kind of trading, which still typify many commodities markets—especially those without active futures markets such as rice, silk and hemp—involve confidence measures regarding not only price, but also the level of trading in the market. For such commodities, the headline levels of price that are quoted, for example on the Bangkok rice spot market—say little about the amount of the commodity that can be off-loaded at any price. Arguably real estate and insurance are markets that work in this way. Similarly, with a futures market, the depth of the market at any given price is just as important as the price level that is being indicated.

Futures trading

In this case, there are additional considerations for the forecaster of the trading company to consider and state a view upon. It is not just a question of forecasting a price at a certain point, but of the evolution of prices over the entire period between the taking of a position on the futures market and its equalization. It is important to remember that on a futures market it is possible to 'short' the market—i.e. take a position which entails that you make money to the extent that the futures market expectations of future prices fall, rather than rise. This equalization therefore occurs through the buying back of a contract if one has sold first and vice versa. Of course, in almost any futures market there are 'day traders' or 'scalpers' whose forecasts as a matter of policy never run overnight, but these are the exception rather than the rule. Even most personal traders on their own account have positions that run for several days and usually longer.

Suppose, on 1 January, the Pearl Trading Co. buys $5000 worth of October pearl index futures. This is called *going long* and entails profit on a price rise and loss on a fall. A pearl index has been assumed in order to avoid the question of delivery and minimize the significance of carrying costs in this example. The contact expires, we further suppose, on 25 October. This date in October will be fixed by the rules of the exchange contract. The company intends to sell back the futures in June. Now it could be that the futures position has been taken as a hedge—to protect in this case against the need to buy $5,000 worth of pearls in June and therefore to lock in the price of $5,000 now, for planning purposes. Either the pearls will cost less than $5,000 and there will be an equivalent loss on the futures position, or vice versa, and in any event the $5,000 cost has been locked in—a way of using the futures market to eliminate the need for forecasting. The hedge may in the event either be very imperfect—perhaps because the pearl index used for the contract does not very accurately reflect the type of pearl that the company needs to buy—or because the company is straightforwardly using the futures market to speculate, as many do. In these cases, the forecast will be exceptionally important. Any position on the futures market is 'marked to market' every day—i.e. losses are called for and profits paid for every open position showing a gain, depending on what the futures price has done that day. Futures prices in turn will depend on/create spot prices. Forecasts are therefore important even when there is a hedge.

Suppose the contract is $100 per index point, that the futures price for October of the index stands at 50 on 1 January, and that interest rates are at 12 per cent per annum. The price of an October contract on 1 January is therefore $5000. The Pearl Trading Co.'s forecast is for a 20 per cent rise in October prices to June, but for a fall thereafter. The simplified forecast is for the increase to occur in two steps, one on 1 February of 10 per cent and then another on May 1st of 9.1 per cent (10 per cent of the 1 January price). If this is followed, the October quote would climb to 55 in February and 60 in May. Five x $100 would be deposited into the company's bank account in February, earning $25 interest in the period to the end of June, and five x 100 in May, earning an additional $10 interest. This is in addition to the capital gain—profit—of $1000. It is easy to see that a fall in the value of the contract during February, if sustained for several months, would overthrow the benefit of eventual price gains. This will be especially true at a time of high interest rates. Capital would be tied up in the position on the futures market in the process. Suppose, for example, that the contract fell by 40 per cent on 1 February—a very large fall, but not inconceivable. The company's brokers would immediately demand a cash injection of $2000. This would have to be sustained at a cost of $100 in the period to the end of June. This cost of carrying the negative position in the market would then have to be set against the eventual profit. If the market reversed itself and recovered all the way to the original 20 per cent rise this would be easy. The total profit would still be $1000 - $100 = $900. It is however clear that with narrower margins and increased volatilities, profits in futures markets from eventual positions, confidently forecast from, for example, fundamental trends in the commodity, can be eaten away quickly by the cost of maintaining adverse positions with brokers. There is also the significant administrative cost of maintaining and monitoring the position and arranging covering funds for adverse positions. The implication of this is clear: those firms using the futures markets must have a smooth inter-temporal forecast and not just one that operates between points of time.

Options trading

This final example liberates the firm from the responsibilities of paying up margins to brokers, because the purchase of an option or the money from selling it is a one-off transaction. Both seller and buyer of an option will stand to gain and lose as the price fluctuates over time towards the expiry of the option. Option pricing depends on how long the option has to expiry and the closeness of the strike price of the option to the current level of the futures price. The degree of profit made by the buyer and seller of the option will depend very precisely upon the accuracy of their forecasts. It is no use for the seller of an option to have an excellent forecast of the price of the commodity at the time that the option is last available to be exercised if the price of the option soars in the meantime. Given that the seller has granted it anyway, he or she has foregone the potential profits that would have been available had the sale been held off until later. The exception is a European-style option, rather unusual in any exchange or even in off-exchange trading.

Suppose the Pearl Trading Co. buys an option to sell a pearl in three months' time at $500 and pays $15 for the option. It forecasts that the pearl price at that time will be below $500. Note that in this example an exact forecast is not required: an above/below judgement is what is required. If the price fails to fall to $500 the $15 will be lost. The extent of its fall below $500 will determine the extent of profit. The market will have its own view of the probability of this occurring, and will have priced the option accordingly; profitability in options trading depends upon the accuracy of forecasting price change.

Aspects common to all forecasts

Firstly, forecasts generally assume that the past will be similar to the future, or else they become scenario assessments—conditional forecasts which are often derived via similar means. Forecasters are keen on conditional forecasts and like to present a range of alternatives to senior decision-makers. To the angst and consternation of the forecasters themselves, decision-makers usually cut through the ranges and scenarios presented to them by forecasters to the mid-point when making political or trading decisions. Secondly, forecasts are rarely accurate. One very senior forecaster once observed dryly that the one thing he could absolutely guarantee about his forecasts is that they would not be true. Another macroeconomic forecaster who had spent his career with one major company observed that after twenty years he had reviewed his US forecasts—his GNP estimates in current $ were half the reality. But forecasts do indicate likely trends, and at best they do that job very well. In most cases, too, as noted above, forecast accuracy decreases as the time horizon lengthens, although this is a much more contentious argument and the real point is that the likelihood of 'sudden shocks' increases as the time horizon lengthens, so that trends which may still be quite accurate are superimposed on dramatically-altered baselines.

Finally, forecasts for groups of things, for example for a range of different types of rice or grain, does tend to be more accurate than forecasting specifics. Industry forecasts, claim Shim, Siegel and Lieu[1] similarly, are more effective than forecasts of individual companies, although this may not be entirely accurate in the case of commodity indices which contain a balance of some supporting and some conflicting price directions.

How to carry out a forecast

First of all the required scope of the forecasts must be determined, and not by the forecasters themselves. Left to their own devices they will forecast and, more particularly, scenario model more and more, longer and longer term. Their output will be of progressively less interest to senior decision-makers and consume progressively more resources whilst the forecasters progressively work further away from committing themselves to a firm view of the future. An accurate summation of the objectives of the forecast, together with strict limits on expenditure and the variables to be forecasted, will ensure that the process does not get out of control in this way. This should be counterbalanced by the point about 'modelcide': that the wheel is often reinvented even within the same institution as a result of

[1] *In 'Strategic Business Forecasting'.*

forecasting projects falling into abeyance after the need has passed. This happens even more frequently between organizations, adding needlessly to long-term costs. Secondly, the time horizon of the forecast must be established and commensurately, how long the forecast itself is to take. A one-year forecast that takes six months to produce is of little use although it is still far from unknown. The next stage is to choose the model's forecasting technique. Much of what follows in this book is about that choice and its implications. The data for the model must then be gathered, the model tested, and finally the forecast produced. If the need for the forecast is to be continual and some institutional pressure can be generated to recognize the long-term benefit of continued investment, some sort of feedback needs to be introduced so that the forecast can be continually improved through the identification and elimination of its weaknesses. There is a great deal of such improvement which can occur with most forecasts. Unfortunately, insufficient forecasting need is perceived as continuing for many models to be thus improved. In other words, identifying the future need for forecasting within an institution is an important part of the initial stage of the forecasting process as a whole.

Chapter 3

Qualitative forecasting

Professional forecasters are apt to claim—rightly—that, 'Though they may not realize it, all such individuals [those involved with commodity markets] derive their opinions from models of the markets in which they are interested'.[1] These models are informal, however, carried in their heads rather than written down, programmed into a computer or drawn down from software, They are subjective, based on experience, casual observation and anecdote. They are also Gestalt models, simultaneously solved for the most part. All this neatly opens the way for professional forecasters to claim that as such they must 'obviously' be limited to varying degrees. Professional forecasters point to probable limitation in the extent to which they can account for all the relevant price, supply and demand factors, their relative importance, and the complexity of the relationships between them in any consistent way. Professional forecasters will usually assert this without appearing to justify the assertion, and they must be challenged.

From the standpoint of the professional econometric forecaster; whose livelihood depends on the development of complicated econometric or technical models, reference to qualitative forecasting is almost always met with polite deprecation. 'In many cases, it is only the kind of consistent, explicit, descriptive and analytical framework of a quantitative model which can provide a satisfactory basis for the study of complex markets.' one comments with evident satisfaction[2]. There are no readily available studies of how effective the casually sought opinions of individual experts are about the future direction of prices for a particular commodity compared to more complex models. This argument must therefore remain unproven. The complexity and causal linkages of a model ought not to be ends in themselves for a forecaster. What matters is results, now and in the future. On the whole those experts who are intuitively good at forecasting market direction, especially in those commodities with active futures

[1] *Hallam, p2*
[2] *Hallam, p2*

markets, tend to keep their opinions to themselves, and there is no mechanism for finding and tracking their honest opinions. In many cases, they may be sufficiently influential to have a role, however small, in influencing price direction themselves. Forecasters must be right in that in zero-sum games like futures markets, except for hedgers, there must be a range of accuracy in the forecasts used. Not every trading company or indeed trader is as accurate as every other, let alone accurate all the time, even though, in many cases on futures markets, there is a substantial percentage of hedge trades.

Now it is true that the polite deprecation, if the professional forecaster is pushed, will usually extend to an admission that qualitative forecasting is useful in the short term and in 'supplementing' projections based on quantitative methods. Professional commodity traders would certainly put the argument exactly the other way round: that models of commodity prices and demand may usefully supplement information provided by first-hand experience of the market and a strong sense of the direction in which it is headed, but they are not to be the determinants of trading activity. They would say the same about the more complex methods of qualitative forecasting. In both cases, their assertions must be questioned and can only be justified by results.

Three of the better-known qualitative forecasting methods are expert opinions, whether of brokers, traders, merchants, retailers or producers, the Delphi method, and PERT-derived forecasts. In practice, traders' personal judgement forms a fourth method, and it is more frequently used than all the others combined, but is the least possible to quantify and examine.

Expert opinion

Subjective opinions can be sought from a variety of sources and averaged. The main advantage of this method is that it is quick, cheap and methodologically uncomplicated. The forecast maker usually provides an unweighted average of the answers received. No complex statistics are required and the only equipment required is a telephone and a directory of experts.

The method has very important disadvantages too, especially when applied to commodities. Firstly, finding the experts who are willing to provide an opinion may be difficult. They may be unwilling to state their opinions. Some companies specifically request their traders and other employees not to do so, on the grounds that, if quoted, these opinions may unfairly move the market themselves. What may become a short-term profitable move could be injurious to the long-term reputation of the firm. Those experts who might be willing to contribute to the survey might be abroad, a particular problem with commodity forecasting. It may prove difficult to pin experts down to more than a general rise or fall forecast. Finally, experts may only be prepared to state their views if provided with a 'carrot' of information—perhaps the replies of other individuals. Experts may therefore simply repeat these views back or subtly alter them, rather than answering questions truthfully.

Secondly, every organization which needs a forecast has a position in the market, and so such organizations are often wise to obtain information from experts— often competitors—using another company name or at least in as casual way as possible. This is especially important given that all experts in the commodity markets, with the exception of full-time analysts in organizations not directly involved with the market, such as Cotton Outlook, the ICAC or ABARE, work either for themselves or for companies which have positions in the market. It is always in the interests of a company which has a position for the price to rise or fall, just as in stockbrokers' research reports. It is therefore quite likely that the official forecasts released by companies, or even the 'off-the-record' comments released to journalists or clandestine pollsters seeking to amalgamate expert opinion, will themselves be biased. Even the quasi-autonomous organizations which have no market position themselves are faced with occasional pressure to be less than totally honest about the future direction of prices. This applies especially when prices are likely to fall extremely steeply or rise as steeply, upsetting market positions and reducing profits.

These criticisms apart, sampling expert opinion may still be the best method available for a given commodity where data is scarce or models have not been built and, before making a major investment decision, it always makes sense to talk to the experts first. Some of the problems above can be overcome by building a good professional relationship with the experts, by discounting those with known positions and by weighting different answers to different degrees. It is therefore important to have as effective as possible an intelligence system about what those positions really are. This is done in the sampling process for obtaining spot prices for a number of commodities, for example the Baltic Freight Index and the Cotlook indices which are obtained this way. The same applies to forecasts.

A refinement of this survey approach is known as the *Delphi Technique*. The technique stresses the importance of speaking to the experts individually about their views on the future. No group meeting is allowed and no information about others' opinions is passed. Forecasters then summarize the information provided and ask the experts further questions. This method is thought to be useful for long-term forecasting.

■ An example of the use of the Delphi Method:

Price in $	Midpoint	No of panellists	Weight (per cent)	Average
250-226	-	0	0	0
225-201	213	2	10	21.3 (*x*)
200-176	188	4	20	37.6
175-151	163	7	35	57.05
150-126	138	4	20	27.6
125-101	113	2	10	11.3
100-76	88	1	5	4.4
Total:		*20*	*100*	*159.25*

Figure 3.1

In this example, 20 panellists responded and the survey bunched their answers into $25 ranges. Both the size and number of the ranges, if altered, would change the overall result. For such a small number of respondents, however, it would be equally sensible to add all their answers and divide by twenty. This form of sampling is known as *qualitatively unweighted,* with the ranges being introduced partly to compensate for this. Had individuals been regarded as more trustworthy, or closer to the scene of the action than others, then the sampling organization would have been likely to weight their answers more highly. In the example above, suppose that the two panellists who answered in the 225-201 range were top traders who were known to have a good track record in predicting prices. The sampling organization might choose to weight their answers as six times as significant as others. The new number in the table above at (*x*) would be 85.2 and the new overall average forecast, now weighted according to the greater significance attached to the key traders, would be 177.16—not 223.15, which would be the result of the obvious error of failing to adjust downwards the significance of the other panellists to ensure that the weightings still amounted to 100 per cent.

Some companies involved in the commodity markets seek access to a wide variety of professional opinion in making forecasts. The distinction in retail sales forecasting between expert opinion sought amongst the sales force and amongst others does not really exist in wholesale trade markets such as those for commodities, as there is no professional sales force as such. Actual use of the Delphi method in commodity trading internationally seems sufficiently rare as to be out of sight and, most would probably say, rather impractical except within large teams such as the USDA or Merrill Lynch.

A technique called PERT (Programme Evaluation and Review Technique) has been useful in other fields in obtaining results from expert opinions. This methodology requires experts to provide three estimates—pessimistic, most likely and optimistic. PERT theory then suggests that these can be combined to get the best forecast by using the formula: $\{P + 4 \times (ML) + O\}/6$ with a specified standard deviation (likely range of probabilities) equal to $\{b - a\}/6$. So, for example, if an expert is asked the price of pearls in three months time, and says 'within the 200-250 band, but my best guess is towards the top end of that range, say 240' then PERT suggests that the actual forecast is $\{200 + 960 + 250\}/6 = 235$ and that the standard variation will be $\{250 - 200\}/6 = 4.2$. Advocates of PERT in other fields suggest that it is often easier and more realistic to ask the expert to give such an opinion than to specify a particular price.

Secondly, PERT includes an element of probability in the standard deviation which means that confidence levels can be discussed. For example, the expert above can be incorporated into a forecast or a presentation on it with the statement that he or she is 95 per cent confident that the results will fall within $8.4 (two standard deviations) of $235 per pearl. Again, commodity trading moves faster, and traders' time is more precious, than the usual users of PERT techniques, so the technique is unknown in the markets and would be regarded as impractical.

Professional forecasters naturally insist that qualitative forecasts are not as accurate as their (much more expensive) quantitative versions—that they are, in particular, too optimistic. On the other hand, very little expertise is necessary to administer, understand or explain qualitative forecasts. Apart from Delphi and PERT techniques, they can be assembled quickly. They often have institutional clout in a way that econometric models tend to lack. Sophisticated econometric models are also virtually unintelligible to all but the most experienced and competent theorists, and this undoubtedly accounts for much of the suspicion surrounding them. Of course, what really matters is how effective the methods are comparatively in forecasting commodities, and on that there is little evidence.

Chapter 4

The concept and history of technical analysis

Two radically different forecasting and analysis methods have evolved for examining markets: the technical and the fundamental. These have led to two methods in the assessment of both stocks and futures markets (both commodity and then financial), and to a lesser extent spot markets, to determine future prices: fundamental analysis, and technical analysis.

Conventionally, an introduction to technical analysis starts from a differentiation between these two—just two—different approaches: 'The first is that financial market prices ultimately reflect fundamental values in the economy. On this view, financial prices are determined by actual and expected developments concerning these values, and forecasting financial prices is therefore a matter of forecasting fundamentals'.[1] Fundamental analysis therefore depends on statistics, mainly economic ones. In stocks, the fundamental analyst looks at companies' overall performance in equities and, in commodities, at the supply and demand situation as noted above. Of course, no fundamentalist entirely ignores the performance of the price itself over time.

Technical analysis, on the other hand, refers to the study of the behaviour of the market itself as opposed to the study of the goods which are transacted on the market. Can the two be distinguished? Yes. Technical analysis itself is 'the discipline of recording, usually in graphic form, the actual history of trading such as price changes or volume of transactions, in a certain stock [commodity] or in 'the averages' in a particular form. Technical analysis then deduces from that pictured history the probable future trend'.[2] By contrast to fundamental analysis, technical analysts see the market as already incorporating all relevant fundamental factors already. Every price, therefore, implicitly contains a market estimate of forecast developments in fundamental values. Technical analysis (in its purest form, at least) can therefore completely ignore fundamental factors.

[1] *Plummer, p55.*

[2] *Plummer, p6.*

Forecasting fundamentals is a matter of economics, the interaction of demand and supply. Technical analysis, clearly, does not rely on an understanding of the specific market. Proponents of technical analysis argue that it takes into account the simultaneous hopes, fears, guesses and moods of all investors. Technical analysts point out that most economic theory is based on the presumption that individuals make their decisions independently of one another. Technical analysis places by contrast to fundamental analysis therefore a great deal of stress on the activity of human beings acting in markets as being in crowds. 'A crowd is essentially part of the hierarchical structure of nature, and each crowd can be defined in terms of its processes rather than its physical characteristics.'[1] Crowds have life-cycles and are subject to shocks. Numerous markets can be observed in which such crowds operate.

What all this implies is that price movements in commodity markets just as much as in financial markets, are predictable. Technical analysts say that: 'We see the same forecasting patterns developing on the charts today that we have seen over and over again for the past twenty years'[2] and for that matter for the past four hundred years. It would be even longer, technical analysts say, if price charts were available. Prices, technical analysts say, move in trends. Trends tend to continue until something happens to change the supply/demand balance. Such changes are usually detectable in the action of the market itself. Certain patterns or formations, levels or areas, appear on the charts which have an implication. These can therefore be interpreted in terms of probable future trend development. They are not infallible, it must be noted—conveniently no one claims that—but the odds are definitely in their favour. Time after time, as experience has amply proved, they can be more prescient than the best informed and most fundamental analysis. Yet, it is worth observing *en passant*, some find the idea of predicting the price whilst not even knowing what lies behind it 'abhorrent'—and claim that it is playing with lives.

Charts are the working tools of the technical analyst. There are many different types of chart, frequently derived from the objective of getting a representation of a particular index which forecasts trend changes. Most basic commodity technical analysis ideas involve some of the simplest forms of chart: a record of the price range, high and low, closing price and the volume of shares traded each day. These can be supplemented by weekly and monthly charts. On the x axis is time and y axis is price. The

[1] *Plummer, p41-42.*
[2] *Edwards and Magee, Preface.*

key figures are the highest and lowest price in a day, the closing and opening price and turnover. The opening price seldom, if ever, has any significance in estimating future developments. The close, however, is vital. It is interesting that technical analysts do not seem to concentrate on daily averages although, as will be seen, great attention is paid to averages of other types. In the past, there has always been an important question of scales for the charts, although now software will recalculate charts on all scales immediately. Examples of the scales used are the original plain, semilog (equal distance—equal per cent) 1/1 2/2 3/4, etc. Percentage relations have always been recognized as important in trading—the semilog scale permits direct comparison, for example, of high- and low-priced stocks and eases choice of high per cent profit. This facilitates stop-loss orders.

The history of technical analysis is, at least in the West, relatively recent. Magee and Edwards clarified and expanded the work of Charles Dow. He laid the foundation for modern Western technical analysis in 1884 by developing the 'averages'. Richard Schabacker, former editor of *Forbes* magazine in the 1920s showed how signals, considered important in averages, were applicable to stocks themselves.

It is noteworthy that, as it developed, technical analysis focused primarily on stocks and shares, and indexes of stocks and shares, not on commodities. Magee and Edwards are typical in conceding quite late on in their well known work and almost reluctantly that 'It should be possible, in theory, therefore, to apply our principles of technical analysis to any of the active commodity futures (wheat, corn, oats, cotton, wooltops, cocoa, hides, eggs, etc. (for which accurate daily price and volume data are published. It should be, that is, if proper allowance be made for the intrinsic differences between commodity future contracts and stocks and bonds'. It is clear that these authors—and they are typical amongst technical analysts—do not concentrate on commodities as a first priority. The differences they acknowledged between commodities and share markets are still potential problems for the application of technical analysis to commodities. They are therefore worth noting in advance of the consideration of technical analysis itself.

They first make a highly historical point which nevertheless still has relevance to a wide number of current commodities markets. It will, with the increasing relative economic power of a number of countries whose governments, such as Thailand, are still very much wedded to interventionist practice as far as agriculture is concerned, continue to be. In 1947, investors were told that, generally, commodity charts were not useful. The markets had been dominated after 1941-42 by government regulations, loans and purchases. They were so completely subject to the changing and often conflicting policies and acts of the various government agencies concerned with grains and the other commodities that the normal evaluative principles of the market had been seriously distorted. Undoubtedly this was very true. The best forecasts for future prices were only short term and made by the government. At that time, radical reversals of trend could and did happen overnight without any warning as far as the action of the market could show. The normal fluctuations in supply-demand balance, although often radical, which create significant definite patterns for the technician to read were simply absent in most cases or giving false signals. And while fortunes were made (and lost) in wheat, corn and cotton futures during the World War II period, Magee and Edwards say it is safe to say that they were not made from the charts. After 1950 or so, it is further suggested, the charts once again became useful. Their argument is that subsequently, 'The effects of present government regulations have apparently resulted in "more orderly" markets without destroying their evaluation function'[1]. Allowing for the various essential differences between commodities and securities, they claimed that basic technical methods could therefore be applied to commodity markets. This reasoning must be questioned for a number of different markets. What is probably largely true is that the markets where such intervention is at its strongest do not normally possess accurate enough long-term price reporting to enable such charts to be constructed. It is very doubtful, for example, whether traders use technical analysis now, or ever have done, to decide on whether to buy or sell Bangladeshi jute or Vietnamese rice. Cotton and rice are more interesting intermediate examples.

It is certainly right to elucidate some of the differences that are said to exist between stocks and commodities. This will help to place in the context of technical analysis the different traits of commodity charts. Firstly, undoubtedly one of the most important differences is that commodities futures contracts for future delivery have a limited life (see Chapter 1), exactly like financial futures. For example, the October rice contract for any given year has a trading life of about eighteen months. It comes 'on the board' as 'a new issue', is traded in, with volume increasing more or less constantly throughout the period and then becomes a long or short physical position as it expires on delivery. In a way, therefore, each futures contract is a distinct commodity all of its own, separate from all other rice contracts. Practically, of course, it seldom gets out of line with other rice contracts and spot rice prices—but the effect is that long-term support and resistance levels have no meaning whatever for a rapidly-expiring commodity

[1] *Magee and Edwards, p328.*

contract, even though the contract will become a physical position (or an equivalent cash one) on expiry. This does not apply to spot markets in commodities.

Secondly, there is no doubt that a large percentage of transactions in commodity futures are hedging rather than speculation. In some cases, this could be as high as 50 per cent, but it varies between markets. Traditionally it has been argued that hence even near-term support and resistance have less meaning than with stocks. However, stocks are now used themselves to hedge FTSE and S&P futures holdings, so this argument is less strong than it used to be. It must, however, be conceded that since hedging is, to a considerable degree, subject to seasonal factors, there are definite seasonal influences on all commodity price trends. The commodity speculator must bear these in mind, even if only to weight the meaning of their apparent absence at any given period.

Technical analysts sometimes concede one more important difference between stocks and commodities. Certain kinds of news—news about weather, drought, floods, etc., that affect the growing crop, if we are dealing with an agricultural commodity, can change the trend of the futures market immediately and drastically. They are not, in the present state of our weather knowledge, foreseeable. Analogous developments in the stock market, technical analysts suggest, are extremely rare. Takeover bids and the sudden emergence of technological breakthroughs would, however, at first sight appear to be exactly comparable developments. Such caveats do bridle for pure fundamental analysts, who insist on reminding the technical analysts that their original starting point was that the spot or futures price incorporates all these fundamentals anyway. In practice, what this amounts to is a recognition that both methods of price forecasting are useful, since both go together in practice to constitute the price. That is a welcome admission.

Technical analysts point to a third difference in the matter of volume. The interpretation of volume for stocks is relatively simple. By comparison, the interpretation is greatly complicated for futures contracts in commodities as in financials because there is in theory no limit to the number of contracts that could be sold in advance of delivery date. The open interest may exceed supply—quite legitimately—although in practice the times when open futures contracts exceed the available supply for a particular month are very few indeed. However the fundamental analyst (and cynic of technical analysis) may legitimately ask: 'Yes—so what? Why should this necessarily pose a problem for the technical interpretation of volumes?' More relevant is that volume tends to be reported a day late which may upset calculations.

Technical analysis amounts to the creation of rules about the behaviour of price. Magee suggested three principles: 'Stock prices tend to move in trends; volume goes with the trend; a trend, once established, tends to continue in force.' Just about every notable technical analyst has put forward a similar set of aphoristic nutshells. All are agreed that considerable attention should be paid to patterns that develop when the trend is reversed. The problem is detecting the trend. Magee preached care in individual stock selection irrespective of where the 'market' as a whole was headed. A similar principle is applicable to commodity market trading, where each commodity reflects a separate market. This remains true even if general trends in the commodity markets as a whole and sub-groups such as textiles can easily be discerned.

The famously-quoted examples of *head and shoulders,* and *basic trendlines,* are both figures found in basic chart analysis. Trendlines are somewhat better defined and more useful than for stocks. Some analysts have claimed that those figures associated in stocks with short term trading or with group distribution and accumulation, such as *triangles, rectangles,* and *flags,* appear less frequently in commodities and are far less reliable as to either direction or extent of ensuing move. Support and resistance levels are less potent in commodities than in stocks, it is argued. Sometimes they seem to work to perfection, but just as often, they fail to do so. For similar reasons, gaps have less technical significance. All these militate against the use of technical analysis as a forecasting tool in commodity markets to anything like the same extent that is possible for financial markets.

The basic theory

Dow Theory is the oldest technical analysis theory. It is derived from Charles H. Dow, who was also the founder of Dow-Jones industrial index. Long before Dow, it had been obvious that stocks went up and down in price together, as indeed, do commodities, on the whole. Exceptions are rare and did not persevere. Dow therefore stressed the general market trend. Dow expressed this in terms of the average of market trends. The basic theory says that, firstly, the averages discount everything. Secondly, there are three fundamental types of trends—primary, secondary 'corrections' and minor trends. This allows the interpretation of markets as being either bull and bear (up or down). The investor should aim to buy as early as possible in a bull market and sell when the bear market begins. The secondary trend will retrace between 1/3 and 2/3 of the advance—over three weeks—but in the theory this is just a statement of probabilities. It is generally recognized that the secondary trend is the most difficult to spot. The third, minor, trends are brief, with normally a period of up to 3 weeks. Primary and secondary trends cannot be manipulated by central organizations such as central banks, the US Treasury etc., but minor ones can. This is practically a circular point of definition. Frequently cited in the early development of technical analysis was the sea analogy: the tide represents major trends, waves are intermediate trends, and wavelets and ripples are the minor trends. This comparison has been used since the earliest days of Dow, but of course the ocean is more regular than the commodity or stock markets. There are, after all, no tide tables of cotton or rice prices.

Every bull market, the theory suggests, has phases. First, there is accumulation and a steady increase in price and volume. Then, late investors get involved. In the last stage, prices and volumes still rise but 'air pockets' start to open; low-priced stocks of no investment value are whipped-up, but top grade issues refuse to follow. Much the same applies to commodities: specialized markets may continue to rise but the mainstream agricultural, textile, energy and other commodity markets refuse to rise with them. In the so-called distribution period, far-sighted investors offload their holdings. Then there is the inevitable panic and prices slide. Then the final stage is concentrated in high value holdings. Clearly, it is a continuous flow of trade rather than specific periods. It is all more complex in some respects with commodities because of seasonality, stocks, delivery dates and hedgers as well as fund holdings in futures markets. No two bull or bear markets are exactly alike and no time limits can be set. In the original development of the Dow Theory there were an industrial and a rail average which had to conform. The commodity equivalent of the rail average is perhaps the textile sector. There is always a question of confirmation of whether the trend has actually reversed. Lines may substitute for secondaries—a sideways movement in which prices run within 5 per cent or less of their mean. An advance is bullish and vice versa. The longer the line and the more compact it is, the greater the significance of a breakout from it is. A line may develop in one average (or commodity) whilst another is typically secondary. Dow Theory only uses closing prices, not extreme highs and lows. Rapid disagreement evolved about the significance of the overcoming of previous closes. All agree that a trend should be assumed to continue in effect until such time as its reversal has been definitely signalled. But this just states a probability. The corollary is that a reversal in trend can occur at any time after that trend has been confirmed.

The alleged defects of the theory is that it represents second guessing. It re-interprets events in the light of experience rather than giving trading signals in advance. 'Too late' means that investors are only given the ability to deal with the 'middle' of a bull or bear, and that may be too late to make a profit. The chance of being totally accurate is slim, and it may be that an investor can catch only half the movement if the principle is strictly followed. However, the accurate use of the principle increases investors' money far more rapidly if successful, even with transactions costs, than just one buy and sell over the whole period. The theory left much to be desired. The investor had little certainty, specific stocks were not recommended, and only later did it prove possible for investors to buy and sell a diversified portfolio or an index commodity such as the GSCI.

It is now appropriate to consider some of the basic chart formations which were the essence of the original forms of technical analysis. Detailed expertise over technical analysis requires more than the study of one or more books, however. There are courses available, and they are necessary.

Reversals

A reversal produces a characteristic area or pattern on the chart—a reversal formation. Some are quick, whereas others take weeks. The greater the reversal area—the wider the price fluctuations within it, the longer it takes to build, the more contracts exchanged during its construction—clearly the more important its implications. There can be, for example a one-day reversal. Groups can buy quietly and are then faced with the need to off-load even more quietly, which may prove impossible. It is difficult to measure the percentage offload of the total daily volume. In practice there is some debate as to the extent that it matters whether transactions are the result of the highly-organized operations of a single group of insiders or of an investment syndicate or, as is more often the case, with the quite unorganized activities of all the investors variously interested in a contract. The patterns of distribution are called *tops*. Most of the same pattern forms appear also as *bottoms*, in which manifestation they signify accumulation not distribution.

The head and shoulder formation is said to be the most reliable of all the reversal patterns. It is certainly the pattern most typically associated with technical analysis. There needs to be the following for a head and shoulders formation to exist:

- A strong rally, ending a more or less substantial advance. Trading volume is high, followed by a minor recession in which volume runs at a considerably reduced level than during the days of rise and at the top.
- Another high volume advance which reaches a higher level than the top of the left shoulder, and then another reaction generated by less volume. This takes prices down to somewhere near the bottom level of the preceding recession, somewhat lower perhaps or somewhat higher, but in any case, below the top of the left shoulder. This is the *head*.

- A third rally, but this time on decidedly less volume than accompanied the formation of either the left shoulder or the head. This does not reach the height of the head before another decline sets in. This is the *right shoulder*.

- Finally, a decline of prices in this third recession down through a line (the *neckline)* drawn across the bottoms of the reactions between the left shoulder and head, and the head and right shoulder, respectively, and a close below that line. The amount of the close is sometimes said usually to be about 3 per cent of the price. This is the *confirmation* or *breakout*.

Each and every item is essential to a valid head and shoulders. The lack of any one casts doubt on the forecasting value of the pattern. It is only possible to recognize that they all exist after the pattern has been demonstrated, at which point the forecasting value is, of course, zero.

Exactly the same applies to a *head and shoulders bottom*, and the price pattern is reversed:

- A decline, climaxing a more or less extensive downtrend, on which trading volume increases considerably. This is followed by a minor recovery in which volume is less than during the final decline and at the bottom.

- Another decline, which carries prices below the bottom of the left shoulder, on which activity shows some increase as compared with the preceding recovery. This usually does not equal the level attained on the left shoulder. It is followed by another recovery which continues to above the bottom level of the left shoulder and on which trading volume may pick up, and at any rate exceed that on the recovery from the left shoulder. This is the head.

- A third decline on markedly less volume than accompanied the making of either left shoulder or head, which fails to reach the low level of the head before another rally starts. This is the right shoulder.

- Finally, an advance on which activity increases considerably, which pushes up through the neckline and closes above by an amount allegedly approximately equal to 3 per cent of the price, with a conspicuous burst of activity attending this penetration. This is the confirmation or breakout.

Technical analysts say that the essential difference between top and bottom patterns lies in their volume charts. Activity in a head and shoulders bottom formation begins usually to show uptrend characteristics at the start of the head and always to a detectable degree on the rally from the head. It is even more marked on the rally from the right shoulder. It must be present on the penetration of the neckline, or else the breakout is not to be relied upon as a decisive confirmation. In other words the formation is slightly different. Bottoms are generally longer and flatter. They take more time in relation to the pattern of points than do tops, especially when occurring at reversals in the primary trend.

Multiple head and shoulders are known as *complex formations*. These are head and shoulders reversals in which either the shoulders or the head—or both—have been doubled or modulated into several distinct waves. They appear more often at bottoms than tops. A common form consists of two left shoulders of approximately equal size, and then two right shoulders, again of approximately even size and balancing the two on the right. Another is made up of two heads with two or more shoulders on either side. Still another, of which there is frequently more than one good example at any significant market turn, consists of double shoulders on either side of a head which is itself composed of a small, but quite distinguishable, head and shoulders development. Complex head and shoulders bottoms are even more likely to show symmetry. Technical analysts insist that it is just as possible to discern the trading signal from multiple head and shoulders as from single ones, but this is difficult to agree with. It is indeed too easy to come to the conclusion that they have produced a false signal. Although they may be as reliable as a single head and shoulders bottom, except in respect of the extent of the move, they may be impossible to recognize.

If the process is further developed it becomes a *rounding turn*, which can be pictured plainly. It is defined as a gradual, progressive and fairly symmetrical change in the trend direction, produced by a gradual shift in the balance of power between buying and selling. For example, if buying has been stronger than selling for some time past, the price of the commodity will have shown a general upward trend. As long as the buyers of the commodity—whether a future or, in theory at least, a spot commodity—remain more numerous, more aggressive, more powerful than the sellers, that former upward trend will continue. The trend evens off gradually and eventually reverses. There may be a long advancing trend slowly beginning to round off, holding in apparently stationary suspense for a time, and then commencing a retreat, reversing the previous upward movement into a new and accelerating downward trend. *Rounded bottoms* have been commonly referred to as *bowl* or *saucer* patterns. *Rounded tops* are sometimes called *inverted bowls*. Neither type appears as frequently as head and shoulders bottoms. Rounded bottoms occur most often in low priced commodities, in an extended flat-bottomed form which usually takes many months to complete. These can appear during extended price rises. Rounded tops are very rare amongst the lower and medium price ranges but are found occasionally. As to volume, in a rounded bottom it gradually decreases. Demand is still weak but pressure on it is less, so, while prices still decline, the rate of decline is slower and the trend tends to curve more and more to the horizontal. At the bottom, with the two forces technically in balance, relatively few transactions are recorded. Then demand begins to increase, and as the price curve turns up, trading becomes more active. Volume accelerates with the trend until often it reaches a climactic peak in a few days of almost vertical price movement on the chart.

The points of the low-volume lines traced out on a chart, when connected, will describe an arc which often roughly parallels the price bowl above. These patterns, when they occur after an extensive decline, are of outstanding importance, for they nearly always denote a change in primary trend and an extensive advance yet to come. Very occasionally, the entire major move is completed in a few weeks, but usually the uptrend which follows the completion of the pattern itself tends to be slow and subject to frequent interruptions. This might bore the impatient trader but eventually yields a substantial profit to the patient one. Sometimes, although trading volume does reach an extreme low at the bottom of a bowl, after prices have passed dead centre and begun their first gradual climb, something in the nature of a premature breakout may occur. Without warning an outbreak of buying may send prices up almost vertically up for a couple of days' trading. Prices then fall back into their former trading range.

In the *dormant bottom* pattern there is extended flatness, which is seen characteristically in flat commodity markets. The total number of open contracts is quite small. Eventually there is a sudden and usually quite inexplicable flurry of activity. This may either be premature, or it may be the first lift in a sort of step up process with shorter and shorter intervals between each step until finally a consistent uptrend develops. With relatively few contracts outstanding, and only an occasional lot put up for sale 'at the market', investors (perhaps only insiders connected with the company) would succeed only in running the price up out of reach if they started to buy commodities. So they simply 'hold a basket under it' as the saying goes, quickly picking up anything that is offered but never reaching for it, until eventually the tree is shaken clean. Then they may raise their bids a point or so. If that seems to bring out a lot of selling interest, they go back to their waiting tactics.

The volume pattern is seldom as clearly defined as at bottoms. It tends to be high and irregular throughout the entire rounding-over movement in prices. Under close scrutiny, one can usually see some signs of a change from bullish to bearish activity in the minor fluctuations after the peak has been passed, but the volume warnings do not become conspicuous in most cases until the downtrend has begun to accelerate toward the vertical. Rounded tops cannot be counted upon to produce a greater move than the preceding price swing in the opposite direction—but they almost never deceive. Their implications can be roughly estimated from the magnitude of the trends which led to them and the length of time they take in the rounding over-process. The rounded tops which often appear on weekly and monthly charts therefore carry major import.

Technical analysts note that all these formations appear in monthly and weekly charts with identical significance. However the volume activity may be more difficult to trace; head and shoulders tops are especially frequent on monthly charts.

The problem is that all these signals, as with original Dow Theory, tend to give signals after the event. If an investor sells a commodity future exactly when a head and shoulders top has been completed on its chart may cash in on no more than half of the total decline from its extreme high to extreme bottom. This is because by the very terms of the measuring formula, the first half of the decline can have taken place before the top reversal formation was finally confirmed. Someone, of course, sold at the top. In general, however, the more experienced the investor, the less concerned he or she is with selling precisely at the top. No one can be absolutely sure that they are selling at the top—and putting a bottom under a major commodity futures contract or a diversified spot contract is beyond anyone's power, as the attempt at a silver monopoly attempt showed. Tops are indicative of consolidation—terminating an up or down movement only temporarily and setting the stage for another strong move in the same direction later on. Sometimes they do develop at times of major trend change, and these are the points which it is most essential for investors to realize. The most commonly observed form of top is composed of a series of price fluctuations, each of which is smaller than its predecessor. Each minor top fails to attain the height of the preceding rally, and each minor recession stopping above the level of the preceding bottom. The result is a sort of contracting Dow Line on a chart—a sidewise price area or trading range whose top can be a more or less accurate application of geometry. This forms an acute triangle, although it is not necessary that its top and bottom boundaries are of equal length or make the same angle with the horizontal axis. This is also referred to as a *coil*. While this is going on, trading activity exhibits a diminishing trend, perhaps irregularly.

There are a number of other well-known formations, for details of which it would be necessary to consult detailed technical analysis works. These include:

- Right-angle triangles
  ('Ascending' and 'descending' are the bullish and bearish manifestations)
- Rectangles, double and triple tops and bottoms
- Broadening formations
- Orthodox broadening top—no broadening bottoms
- Right angled broadening formations
- The diamond
- Wedge formations
- One-day rehearsal
- Selling climax

Consolidation formations

- Flags and pennants
- Rectangular consolidations
- Head and shoulders consolidations
- Scallops—repeated saucers

Technical analysts suggest that patterns of the compact, strictly defined sort such as rectangles and right-angled triangles are less common than they were fifty years ago. Symmetrical triangles are apt to be somewhat looser than they were in the 1920s and early 1930s and not as clean cut and conspicuous on the charts. Typical profit-taking patterns such as flags and pennants continued to be as common as ever, while 'normal' trend pictures, including those formations associated with normal trend development such as head and shoulders, rounding turns, etc. became even more common. The reasons for these changes are fairly apparent; all of the following have played a part in the evolution:

- Commodity Futures Trading Corporation (CFTC) regulations in the USA, and their equivalents in other countries. Regulatory rules and market rule enforcement have severely reduced the flagrant price manipulation aimed at taking advantage of naive investors;
- Higher margin requirements;
- Greater public sophistication and a more conservative—we might better say more pessimistic—approach to the problems of investment and commodity trading generally.

It remains possible, of course, for insiders to hold back for a limited time, or to release prematurely, news announcements of a good or bad portent with regard to the affairs of a particular corporation, in order to serve their personal strategic purposes. Even government agencies have been accused of this. But the futures purchases and sales of officers, directors and principal owners of agricultural companies are now too closely watched to permit of a good deal of skulduggery. Nevertheless, the average investor had better still be somewhat sceptical as to the probability of any great advance in the market following publication of a poor crop report.

Moving averages

The MAA (Moving Average Analysis) theory is based on the fact that a price cannot deviate from its moving average for more than a short time. When comparing the average to the current price, high and low prices, and the price change from various other prices, the MAA can detect relevant deviations to predict the probability of a continued price move in a previously indicated direction. According to this theory, a price can only be either close or at its average, too far away or in between. This seems unremarkable and not much of a trading signal, but the theory further suggests that as the price drops below its average, the likelihood for the price to rise back to its average increases. Similarly, the further the price rises above its average the more chance there is for it to fall back towards it. And the closer the price is to its average beyond that elusive mid-point at which it will turn, the more likely it is to move away from it. This is a theory incorporated into much commercial software, for example that of *TBSP*.

However there is little doubt that short-term moving averages can be of great assistance in trading commodities. One simple moving average technique which has historically been utilized is to plot ten-day highs, lows and closes. After ten days, the averages of the three series can be plotted on a separate chart, beginning a second chart on the 11th day covering the prices on days 12-22 etc. Clearly it is possible to plot a three-day average after plotting four days of fluctuation. There are a theoretically infinite number of different periods over which a moving average can be taken, although only a few combine trading usefulness with sufficient scope. The mechanical trading rule normally used in conjunction with such moving averages is that wherever the short-term average line moves below the long-term average line, a sell signal is given. When the short term line moves above the long-term line, a buy signal is given. For this, it is usually the case that judgement is added from a number of other indicators such as those based on the volume of contracts traded, the price pattern being formed, descending triangles, rectangles etc., and the waterfall effect.

The significance of moving averages

Technical analysts say that moving averages, when used correctly, are one of the most powerful tools available to the technical analyst. But in fact any technical tool, used correctly, is powerful. 'Unfortunately, the decision as to how many averages, what type and especially what periods to use, makes moving average analysis really quite difficult'[1]. The problem is that although the indicator works quite well in a trending market, when the market is trading within a small range, jumping back and forward, then the results can be disastrous with a number of so-called *whiplash* movements occurring which can take away daily profit margins very quickly. Hence technical analysts have developed the more complex exponential moving average which attaches a greater weight to recent figures.

■ *Waterfalls*—an example of a technical analysis trading rule
The waterfall rule restricts trading interests only to futures contracts which have undergone a sustained and major uptrend or downtrend. It is a very cautious rule. In the latter case, the properly scaled arithmetic chart shows a nearly vertical decline for several weeks or even months—the waterfall pattern. A period of price congestion then develops, after which the three day moving average crosses the ten-day moving average from below. This is often said to be a preliminary buy signal and may be acted upon. Those advocating trading on the basis of such a signal usually suggest that under these circumstances a protective limit should be placed just below the previous low closing price in the downward price movement. A similar short sales signal is given after sustained uptrend when the three-day moving average crosses the ten day moving average from above. Once the waterfall buy or sell signal has been given, it is considered to be in effect until the protective limit is penetrated by a new closing low. A considerable backing and filling may occur with a three-day moving average actually moving below the ten-day moving average after a buy signal. The presumption in this case is that an immediate trend reversal has been signalled, possibly a major trend reversal. Whatever the outcome, it is suggested, follow up technical analysis should be used.

Point and figure movements

These facilitate the study of pure price movement; there is no consideration of the time element and only price changes are recorded. On such charts, '*X*'s show a trend and an '*O*' marks a reversal. Reversal moves the columns along one on the point and figure chart and can be varied by changing the value of the box, or by changing the reversal criteria, or the number of

[1] *Hexton, p27.*

boxes needed to create a reversal. A support line is used to connect upward to the right from under the last column of *Os* and vice versa. The 45° line connects rally tops or reaction lows. In a bullish market the support line is drawn at a 45° angle upward to the right from under the last column of *Os*. As long as the prices remain above that line the major trend is considered to be bullish. In a downtrend, the bearish resistance line is drawn at a 45° line downward to the right from the top of the highest column of *Xs*. As long as prices remain below that trend line, the trend is bearish.

Trend channels

Position traders study longer-term trends than day traders, but both look at the ranges in which the commodities in which they are interested are trading. Trend channels occur when a line is drawn parallel to the main trend line and the price bounces off and between these two parallel lines. The break out can often be determined by the closer proximity of the price to the upside of the parallels, when an upside break out usually occurs, or vice versa when the price begins to draw closer to the lower parallel and a downside break-out generally occurs. Some analysts use the width of the trend channel to measure the distance of the anticipated break-out. Nearly all minor and most intermediate trends follow nearly straight lines. But in fact not only the smaller fluctuations but frequently also great primary swings of several years' duration appear on the charts as though their courses had been plotted with a straightedge ruler.

If a similar ruler is applied to a number of charted trends, we quickly discover that the line which most often is really straight in an uptrend is a line connecting the lower extremes of the minor recessions within those trends. In other words, an advancing wave in a commodity market is composed of a series of ripples. The bottoms of each of these ripples tend to form on, or very close to, an upward slanting straight line. The tops of the ripples are usually less even. Sometimes, they also can be defined by a straight line, but more often, they vary slightly in amplitude, and so any line connecting their upper tips would be more or less crooked. On a descending price trend, the line most likely to be straight is the one that connects the tops of the minor rallies within it, while the minor bottoms may or may not fall along a straight edge. These two lines—the one that slants up along the successive wave bottoms within a broad up move and the one that slants down across successive wave tops within a broad down move—are the basic trendlines.

It is perhaps unfortunate that a more distinctive name for them has never been devised than 'line'. The point is to decide which breaks (penetrations by a price movement) are of important technical significance and which are of no practical consequence, requiring possibly only a minor correction in the drawing of the original trendline. There are no 100 per cent certain, quick answers to this problem, as can be expected. The significance of some penetrations cannot be determined as soon as they appear, but must await confirmatory indications from other chart developments. In a great majority of instances, however, an important break—one that requires a prompt review and possibly a revision of trading policy—is easy to recognize.

It is necessary to have top reversal points to fix a down trendline and two established bottom reversal points to fix an up trendline. The boundary lines of triangles and rectangles, as well as necklines of head and shoulders formations, are simply special types of trendlines. Commercial technical analysis programs often use these types of trendlines. The *Swing Catcher* system, for example, identified *swing lows*, defined as 'a low day with higher prices both in front and behind the low day, thus forming a swing low'[1] whilst a *swing high*, conversely, is defined as 'a high day with lower prices both in front and behind the high day forming a swing high' (ibid.). It has been claimed that the straightforward technique 'is being used by the most successful large traders'.

An obvious conclusion is that when the trendline is broken, i.e. when prices drop down through it in decisive fashion, it signals that the advance has run out. It calls time for the intermediate-term trader to sell that commodity, and look for reinvestment opportunities elsewhere. When a small top reversal pattern forms on the chart of an issue well up and away from that commodity's intermediate up trendlines, so that there apparently is room for the downside implications of the reversal formations to be carried out before the trendline is violated, then the intermediate trend trader may well decide to ignore the small reversal pattern. He or she may perhaps hold on as long as the trendline holds. It is an expensive practice to switch out of every commodity as soon as there is evidence of a minor setback, provided that the chance of further intermediate advance exists because of transactions costs. The problem is that to determine this it is necessary to find and draw the line that accurately defines the intermediate-trend, and then to recognize when that line has broken in decisive fashion.

What is certain is that sooner or later, trends change. They may change by reversing from up to down to up. They may also change direction without reversing, as, for example, from up to sideways and then perhaps to up again, or from a moderate slope to a steep slope, and vice versa.

[1] *Trend Index Trading Company, Special Report 1*

Profits are made by capitalizing on up or down trends, by following them until they are reversed. The investor's problem is to recognize a profitable trend at the earliest possible stage of its development and then later to detect, again as quickly as possible, its end and reversal. The reversal of any important trend is usually characterized, as we have already seen, by the construction of some sort of joint price and volume pattern—in brief, of a reversal formation.

Other issues connected with trends are, firstly, how may they best be plotted on the charts which are constructed to make technical analysis work? Trendlines can be plotted on an arithmetic versus log scale—straight arithmetic on semilog produces a curved line which rises at first and then gradually rounds over. Straight on semilog will produce an accelerating curve on arithmetic. Secondly, how can they be used to reinforce or supplement the technical forecasts derived from other chart formations and support/resistance studies? Tests of authority for trends can be created. The larger the number of bottoms that have developed at (or very near) a trendline in the course of a series of minor up waves, the greater the technical importance of that line. With each successive 'test', the significance of the line is increased. A first and tentative up trendline can, for example, be drawn as soon as two bottoms have formed. But none of this is wholly reliable.

Moving average crossover divergence (MACD)

The MACD was developed by Gerald Appel. It is an oscillator comprised of the difference between two exponential moving averages of the closing price. Appeal's original work used an exponential moving average of 12 periods and 25 periods. Trading signals were generated by overlaying a 9-period exponential moving average on this oscillator. Clearly, both can be altered.

Price detrend oscillator

This is calculated as the close price less the smoothed value of the close price. It is another way of examining a simple moving average crossover system.

Amendment of trendlines

An example of the development of the concept of channel is Lambert's Commodity Channel Index or CCI. Don Lambert developed this indicator in the 1970s and it was first written about in *Commodities* magazine in October 1980. It was designed to help identify cycles in commodity prices—a timing system that is best applied to commodities which exhibit seasonal or cyclical characteristics. The CCI does not determine the lengths of the cycles, it is designed rather to detect when such cycles commence and finish, using statistical analysis which incorporates a moving average and a divisor of mean deviation which reflects both possible and actual recent trading range.

Price action line

This is the running summation of the close minus open divided by the high minus low.

Price change line

This indicator looks at the difference between today's opening price and yesterday's closing price as a function of true range. True range was defined by Welles Wilder as the largest of the following: the distance from today's high to today's low, the distance from yesterday's close to today's high, and the distance from yesterday's close to today's low.

On balance price

This indicator looks only at the relative change in close price from day to day. It is calculated as $SUM(Sgn(C-\{CT-1\})$ where *CT-1* is yesterday's close and *Sgn* denotes only that the value is 1, 0 or -1, if the value is positive, zero or negative, with no regard to magnitude.

Double momentum oscillator

This is the sum of two price percentage changes which is then smoothed twice to eliminate whipsaws. The period selected is used to determine two momentum periods. The first is the selected period plus 20 per cent and the second is the selected period minus 20 per cent.

Linear trend oscillator

The linear trend oscillator is based on the change in slope of a linear least squares fitted line; the number of periods can be varied. As the least squares method fits the data around a line with the minimum deviations around them, the slope is expressed as an angle of the least squares line, multiplied by 100, which means that the range will lie between -100 and +100.

The Bollinger Oscillator

John Bollinger, of Bollinger Capital Management, developed this indicator to show Bollinger Bands in a slightly different light. This indicator shows where the closing price is relative to the upper and lower Bollinger Bands, shown as a percentage. As an example, if the value of this was zero, then it would entail that the close for that day was on the lower band. Similarly if the value were 70, then the close was 70 per cent above the lower band or 30 per cent below the upper band. When the closing price is greater than the upper band the commodity can be considered to be overbought. This is not necessarily a sell signal until it comes back down through the upper band. If the threshold values are set at 0 and 100, these thresholds would represent the bands.

The Welles relative strength indicator (RSI)

The concept behind this is to determine when a particular market is in a trending mode. J. Welles Wilder developed the RSI in the late 1970s. It has been a popular indicator with many different interpretations. It is a simple measurement which expresses the relative strength of the current price movement as increasing from 0 to 100. In essence it averages the up and the down days, with reference to the day's close relative to the previous day's close. Wilder favoured the use of the 14 period measurement because it represented half a natural cycle. He also set the significant levels of the indicator at 30 and 70. The lower level is indicative of an imminent upturn and the upper level of a downturn. A plot of RSI can be interpreted using many of the typical bar chart formations, such as head and shoulders. Divergence with price within the period used for the calculation of the RSI works well, if the divergence takes place in the upper or lower regions of the indicator. Many chart services show RSI with 14 periods used for its calculations; others use 9, and some allow the investor to alter the period to suit, for example, the dominant cycle of the commodity's own price data.

Overbought/oversold (OB/OS)

This indicator shows the percentage by which the price is above or below the moving average selected, allegedly saying when this greatly accelerated momentum of buying or selling cannot be sustained. The OB/OS line is again a trend, only when the OB tops out or bottoms out that a secondary reaction or period of consolidation can be expected.

Fan formations

Widely-used in technical analysis are fan formations which are created by taking, for an uptrend, a major low point and connecting the trend line with the first major correction. The same low point is taken and the next trend line is connected with the next secondary line, and again, until there are four trend lines drawn one below the other. The concept is that once the closing price falls through the primary trend line this is a warning signal that the uptrend is in difficulty. On the downside, breaking through the secondary trend line means that long positions should be closed out, or at the very least, protected by writing calls against the commodity or purchasing put options. By the time the price has fallen through the third trend line it is usually too late and a major new downtrend is in existence. Sometimes, however, there is a 'second chance' to bail out on the penetration of the third trend line in the fan formation, and then the fourth trend line really is the last opportunity to escape loss as the price falls.

Support and resistance

Support can be defined as a price level that attracts buyers into the market and stops any further price declines. Resistance is the opposite. An upward break out of channel is signalled by prices moving away from the lower parallel and making temporary breaks through the upper trend line. Another similar definition of support is buying, actual or potential, sufficient in volume to halt a downtrend in prices for an appreciable period. Resistance is the antithesis to support. It is selling, actual or potential, sufficient in volume to satisfy all bids and hence, to stop prices from going higher for a time. Support and resistance, as thus defined, are nearly—but not quite—synonymous with demand and supply respectively. They are kinks in demand and supply.

A support level is a price level at which sufficient demand for a stock appears to hold a downtrend temporarily at least, and possibly reverse it. A resistance zone, by the same token, is a price level at which sufficient supply of a commodity is forthcoming to stop, and possibly turn back, its uptrend. In theory, there ought always to be a certain amount of supply and a certain amount of demand at any given price level. In practice, this is nearly always true. The relative amount of each will vary according to the circumstances and determine the trend. But a support range represents a concentration of demand and a resistance range represents a concentration of supply. Estimating support-resistance potential, in particular the location of precise levels, is difficult. However any analytical study of the chart records will quickly show that it is much easier for prices to push up through a former top level than through the resistance set up at a previous volume bottom. With a decline, of course, the opposite is true. It is generally the case that a little selling may come in at a former high, but usually only enough to cause a brief halt rather than the more or less extensive reactions or consolidations which develop when the trend comes up against a real resistance zone.

A more detailed examination of these issues would confront, for example:

- The round figures
- Repeating historical levels
- Pattern resistance
- Volume on breaks through support
- Support and resistance in the averages

Stochastics

George Lane originally developed stochastics. These are oscillators which measure the relative position of the closing price within the daily range. Stochastic indicators are based on the premise that closing prices tend to accumulate near tops of each period's trading range during price uptrend and vice versa. The stochastic curve is calculated on the following basis using the formula:

$$\frac{\text{latest price} - \text{period low}}{\text{period high} - \text{period low}}$$

plotted in a range of 0 to 100.

For the short-term measure, a moving period of 14 days and a smoothing period of three days is often used or alternatively a 21-day moving period and a three-day smoothing period. In simple terms, the close relative to the range of prices over the last x number of periods ago is being measured and 14 periods is a frequently used value for x.

These formulae are based on the observation that closing prices tend to cluster near the day's high prices as an upward move gathers strength and vice versa. For example, when a market is about to turn from up to down, it is often the case that the highs are actually higher, but the closing price settles near the low. This differentiates the stochastic oscillator from most others, which are normalized representations of the relative strength, the difference between the close and a selected trend.

To interpret stochastics it is necessary to have familiarity with the way the indicator reacts in specific markets. The usual initial trading signal occurs when the 3 period moving average of the stochastic oscillator crosses the extreme bands (75-85 on the upside and 15-25 on the downside). Some advocate that in using this system the actual trading signal should not be made until the stochastic indicator itself crosses its own moving average. The argument for this is that, although the extreme zones help to assure an adverse reaction of minimal size, the crossing of the two lines acts in a way similar to dual moving averages.

Speed resistance lines

These measure slope, which is effectively the speed of price change over time. Speed lines of 1/3 and 2/3 indicate a slope which is that percentage of the initial trend. Yes but where do you start from to get the original trend? Speed lines should not be used as buy or sell signals in the market, but rather as identification of support and resistance levels and warning signals that previous trends are in jeopardy.

Gaps

A gap, in technical analysis, represents a price range at which (at the time it occurred) none of the commodity or futures/options changed hands. This is a useful concept to keep in mind, because it helps to explain some of their technical consequences. Gaps on daily charts are produced when the lowest price at which a certain commodity is traded on any one day is higher than the highest price at which it was traded on the preceding day. This can happen weekly and monthly but this is obviously rarer.

Another definition is a day's trading which takes place at a price level which, at no point, touches the range of the previous day's trading. On a daily bar chart, a gap will appear between the first day's trading and the second. Although arbitrage can cause a gap, it is usually caused by lack of sellers overnight. The next day the price opens higher or sometimes lower if there is a lack of buyers.

There are some specific types of gap:

- *Breakaway* - Occurs in thinly-traded markets. Often signals the commencement of a strong market move and often occurs on heavy volume, breaking away from a congestion area.

- *Runaway gap* - After prices have been moving ahead for some time, usually in the middle of the move, another runaway gap, sometimes known as a measuring gap, appears. Volume is usually moderate and if the market is still trending upwards, this gap is a sign of continued strength in the market. It is often referred to as the measuring gap simply because it usually occurs at the half-way point in the trend
- *Exhaustion gap* - Here the supply of sellers is exhausted and the remaining buyers get their commodity at a substantially higher price, hence the gap. The exhaustion gap appears towards the end of the market move and is usually accompanied by heavy volume. The final pattern that should be noted is the island reversal. This usually occurs after the exhaustion gap, when prices trade in a fairly narrow range for a couple of days and then gap down, leaving the price curve looking like an island surrounded by space.

Open interest (OI)

The open interest of a futures or an options contract is defined as the total number of outstanding long contracts. When a new contract starts trading, the total OI is zero. When a buy and sell order are matched, the OI rises to one. It continues to rise whenever a new buyer buys from a new seller and decreases when an existing long sells to an existing short. OI does not change when a new buyer purchases from an existing long or a new seller sells to an existing short. It is often said that a sharp decline in OI following an extended sideways or declining market may reflect commercial short covering and hence presage an impending rally. Similarly, a sharp rise in OI following an extended advance might be interpreted as a bearish signal. In general, OI tends to rise during a trending period in the market.

The importance of volume

In original Dow Theory it was said that volume goes with the trend—that trading activity tends to increase as prices move in the direction of the prevailing primary trend. The same applies to a lesser extent, for secondary trend too. Technical analysts said that volume simply affords collateral evidence which may aid interpretation of otherwise doubtful situations.

In chart analysis, volume is conventionally shown as a histogram (bar chart) going from 0 to the maximum volume for the number of periods plotted. Volume shows the daily trading activity in the commodity. Trends in this level of activity are useful indicators, more so than a single period's volume. Some market periods involve historically low volume, such as the days before and immediately after a major holiday, the summer months generally, and whenever trading is stopped at an exchange because of some unforeseen event such as a terrorist alert. These events and considerations should be taken into account when incorporating volume into technical analysis, hence the usually used method of moving averages. A large number of indicators for technical analysis that incorporate volume have therefore been developed.

Examples of such indicators are as follows:

On-balance volume

This was developed and popularized by Joseph Granville in 1963. OBV produces a volume line curve which can be used to either confirm the current trend, or to anticipate a reversal of the current trend, by diverging from the price curve itself. Total volume for each day is assigned a plus or minus value depending on whether prices are closing higher or lower for the day. A higher close causes the volume indicators to be assigned a plus value while a lower close would give the volume indicator a negative value. A running cumulative total is then deduced by adding or subtracting each day's volume based on the direction of the market close. If the trend is up, the OBV should also be making higher tops and bottoms, i.e. trading up. When it stops but the price continues up, divergence suggests impending reversal. And vice versa.

Chaiken-Williams-Granville

Chaiken's indicator, developed by Marc Chaiken, is the running summation of the close price minus the mid-point of the day's range *(H-L)* times volume. *Williams' accumulation/distribution*, developed by Larry Williams is the running summation of the close minus open divided by the high minus low times volume. Granville's *on-balance volume*, which is a running sum of volumes, is calculated as $SUM(Sgn(C-\{CT-V\}V))$, where *Sgn* denotes only that the value is +1, 0, -1 if the value is positive, zero or negative, with no regard to magnitude, and CT-1 refers to yesterday's close.

Current volume strength (CVS)

The CVS (current volume strength) theory is based on the fact that fluctuations in supply and demand (changes in volume) indicate the direction of a price. The calculations are based on cumulating the daily volume: adding the daily volume to the cumulative volume if the price rose, and subtracting it if the price fell. The resulting number is then compared to the price to determine if the new CVS is a momentum up or down point.

■ An example of a CVS plot

Price	Vol	CVS	S/R
40	125	+125	-
41	150	+275	-
43	135	+410	Res
42	200	+210	-
39	150	+60	-
40	125	+185	-
39	200	-15	Sup
44	175	+160	-

Figure 4.1

A line is drawn to this point from the latest three consecutive CVS down points. If the new point falls below this line, it is a new support point. If not, it is compared to the three latest consecutive up points. If it is above this line, it is a new resistance point; the CVS is disregarded in all other circumstances. Next, the software program using CVS determines whether the CVS points and the corresponding prices line up. If they do, the support and resistance lines are compared to each other in order to calculate each other's slope. The trend is rising if both lines have negative slopes or falling if both lines have negative slopes. All other combinations produce no clear indication of price direction. Some commercial systems, such as TBSP, utilize this principle as one of prime importance in generating signals.

Money flow index

Related to this is the idea of the money flow index. This takes the up closes, multiplies by the daily volume and smooths the values over the selected number of periods, which is usually 14. Secondly it takes the down closes, and does the same thing. Then it normalizes the data to produce an indicator always between 0 and 100. Extreme areas of 20 and 80 indicate areas of oversold and underbought respectively.

Volume spread analysis

It is worth mentioning this idea, originally developed in the 1900s by Richard D. Wyckoff. The idea is to distinguish 'strong', mainly professional, holders, from 'weak' ones, mainly individuals. 'The basic underlying premise of VSA philosophy is that a bull market starts when there has been a complete transfer of holdings from weak holders to strong holders, generally at a loss to the weak holders.' And vice versa.

Equivolume analysis

In fact, there are innumerable different technical analysis indicators and systems, each concentrating on a different aspect of the market. Just as conventional technical analysis focuses on price signals, so the equivolume analysis principle developed by Richard Arms focuses on volume. This is a method which incorporates both volume and price into one charting component, a box, which represents one day. Whereas in most conventional charts time is placed along the x axis, equivolume places it along the y axis with price along the x axis. A tall thin box represents a day when the stock, or commodity, is running into little resistance and is moving easily. A wide box means resistance has appeared and movement has become more difficult.

In equivolume charting, the ratio of mid-point movement to box size is called *ease of movement*. It is a numerical method used to quantify the shape of a box used. The ratio can also be described as that of the volume to the price range. Heavier volume with the same price range as the day before yields a wider box which represents difficulty of movement. Therefore, a higher box ratio indicates more difficult movement and a lower box ratio represents easier movement. Arms suggests that the mid-point of the day's trading range gives a better representation of the day than the closing price, which is really just the last trade. The mid-point, by contrast, is the sum of the high price of the day and the low price of the day divided by two. Comparing intra-day change in the mid-point gives movement (M), and the box ratio (B) produces the ease, which when taken as M/B gives the ease of movement. These figures almost invariably have to be smoothed by using a moving average instead of the raw values, possibly best a 13-period average. This reduces the sensitivity of the index sufficiently to eliminate the whipsaws in sideways movements. It is noticeable that these indicators are more usually applied to stock than commodity movements.

Fibonacci numbers and associated technical analysis

Another important constituent element of technical analysis is that based on the existence of certain basic, numerical, cycles in nature which are reflected in the prices of stocks and commodities. Advocates of such principles suggest that human nature is affected by lunar phases and that it is plausible to develop a cyclical theory based on astrological considerations. Fundamentalists might readily concede that the weather is to a large extent determined by the relative position of the moon, certainly, but the astrological cycles are far more abstruse than that. The famous Fibonacci numbers are the best example of such forecasting aids. These numbers are believed to be able to be used to forecast the exact magnitude of predicted moves in a wide range of markets. Advocates suggest that there is a 46-year Uranus-Saturn cycle, a 14-year Uranus-Jupiter cycle, a 20-year Jupiter-Saturn cycle, Sun spot cycles, eclipses and many others.

Static cycles have long been used by technical analysts to forecast future turning points in the markets. Static cycles are characterized by a fixed interval between events. Set national holidays, seasons and full moons are all examples of events that occur with regular intervals. Such cycles when reflected in the commodity markets, advocates of these theories contend, are usually the result of natural events. There are many commodities which oscillate in price in this fashion: the price of soyabeans changes regularly with the seasons, for example, such that *ceteris paribus* the price is lower during the wet months and higher during the dry months. Likewise the price of rice on the Bangkok spot market depends on the crop, proving that it does not take an active futures market to create the necessary conditions for natural cycle oscillation. In fact, virtually all agricultural crops follow this type of annual routine. Forecasting commodity prices is almost assumed, in trader parlance, to mean reading accurately the scale of such changes, their timing, and the other market factors superimposed on such seasonal fluctuations.

However, many such static cycles have proved ineffectual in predicting commodity prices because, advocates of the theory claim, of the intervention of irregularly timed cycles which appear and then disappear regularly. These irregular cycles are often caused by 'dynamic' forces, which if understood, the advocates of the theory suggest, will enable the trader to forecast trend changes well in advance of the facts. This means that such a theory entails a concept of dynamic numbers which makes them predictable but not with a fixed interval between events. They are distinguished by a 'constant of proportion'.

The logarithmic spiral is an example of an expanding form based on a constant of proportion. This is where Fibonacci numbers can be introduced. Fibonacci was a thirteenth century Italian mathematician who discovered the constant proportion number sequence to which he gave his name. 1, 1, 2, 3, 5, 8, 13, 21, 34, 55, 89, 144, etc. The first and second number adds to the next number and so on. The ratio of any number of the next approaches 0.618 after the first four numbers. The ratio of any number to the lower number next to it is approximately 1.1618. The ratio of alternate numbers approaches 2.618 or its inverse 0.382. This proportion was known as early as the millennium before Christ in the times of the Ancient Greeks and is identified in the theory by the letter *phi* (Φ). The Fibonacci fan lines are constructed automatically by defining a high and a low point or vice versa in the evolution of price. The slope of the trend between these points in calculated and the three Fibonacci lines are drawn, reflecting the slopes which are 0.618, 0.5 and 0.382 of the original trend. The fan lines are therefore not simple retracements from the defined high and low but are retracements from an 'imaginary' high or low which would have been achieved had the original trend remained in place.

Phi, the theory claims, can be found throughout nature, from, the design of Nautilus sea shells to the structure of the galaxy. Phi also appears, advocates claim, in human nature too, in music, art, architecture, biology—in the relationship between leaves and stems, for example—and also in the markets. Dynamic rectangle numbers are said to be 'the primary building blocks for nature's designs'[1]. They appear in the markets because the collective emotions and behaviour of all those participating either directly or indirectly in the markets reaches a point when a trend has gone on simply too long and the price is not appropriate any more. The trend trend changes. The periods between the points, and the associated prices, are in many cases related to phi. This is 'crowd psychology' applied to the dynamic cycles underlying such markets. 'A crowd has its own energy and collective mind. It can be viewed as a dynamic system and as such, it is governed by the same laws that exist throughout nature. Since a crowd is a dynamic system, and since financial and agricultural markets exhibit crowd behaviour, it follows logically that Fibonacci relationships should be found operative in all liquid markets.'[2] Cycle theory states that these markets, including commodity markets, comprise composite cycles. These are small, medium and large cycles which, when combined, shape the price actions and reactions that determine prices in markets. Even fixed cycles of different amplitude and frequency when combined will produce some very apparently irregular patterns, it is certainly true. Viewed over a sufficiently long period of time, however, advocates claim that it is genuinely possible to see the repetition of the cycles.

In reality, identifying trend changes, especially during the accumulation, distribution or consolidation phase, is not as clear cut as it ought to be on the basis of theory. The price high and lows do not always correspond with the cycle high or low. What the theory's advocates contend is that 'noise' or

[1] *Ed Kasanjian and Brad Swancoat, 'New Techniques, in Technical Analysis of Stocks and Commodities', 1992.*

[2] *Fibnode marketing literature.*

'incidental price spikes' often cloud the ability of technical analysis to quantify time and price cycles. But the theory's advocates do believe that by calculating future data points from both static and dynamic cycles, technical analysis of this kind can forecast not only trend changes but also price swings, market retracements, extensions and support and resistance levels.

The method of the analysis is as follows. To project a trend change for any particular market using dynamic ratios, it is first necessary to identify the significant changes in trend (pivot) points, and then as with econometric analysis to go back at least 100 data points. This is, again, a similar number of data points to that preferred by econometricians. Next, it is necessary to calculate the time between each combination of pivot points. Then each time interval must be multiplied by the ratios in the dynamic spiral (phi, square root 2, square root 3, square root 5) and the results added to the end of that time interval. The analyst must mark where the result lands on the time line in the future. Each time interval must also be multiplied by the static ratios and the results marked. As the line is marked, the results will cluster around certain periods, which the theory declares are harmonically related to the previous trend changes and where future trend changes can be expected to occur. Quite logically, the higher the concentration of projected data points, the more confidence that one can have in the forecasted trend change. The analysis also requires careful noting of the types of spirals from which the clustered projections originated. Multispiral clusters, Kasanjian Research has suggested, are more powerful. These are derived from different spirals, where some data points in the cluster are in proportion to previous pivot points by the phi ratio, others by square root 2 and others by other dynamic spiral numbers.

Many analysts have applied these concepts to the markets, including commodity markets. Some of the most famous were W. D. Gann, R. N. Elliot, E. Gould and R. Prechter. Their theories and published works are highly respected still amongst traders and are beyond the scope of this book although well worth investigation. Some trading software, such as *Ganntrader 2*, incorporates many of these principles which are unique to each individual system. There is evidence that detailed knowledge of these systems can repay with accurate forecasts of commodity price movements: but the understanding itself is a colossal task.

Ratios of 0.618 and 0.382 are important to Elliott Wave theorists, who look for the price to correct from the original trend by these amounts. There are three aspects of wave theory. In order of importance, these are pattern, ratio and time. The pattern refers to the wave pattern of formations that comprise the most important element of the theory. Ratio analysis is useful in determining retracement points and price objectives by measuring the relationship between the different waves. Finally, time relationships also exist and can be used to confirm the wave patterns and ratios.

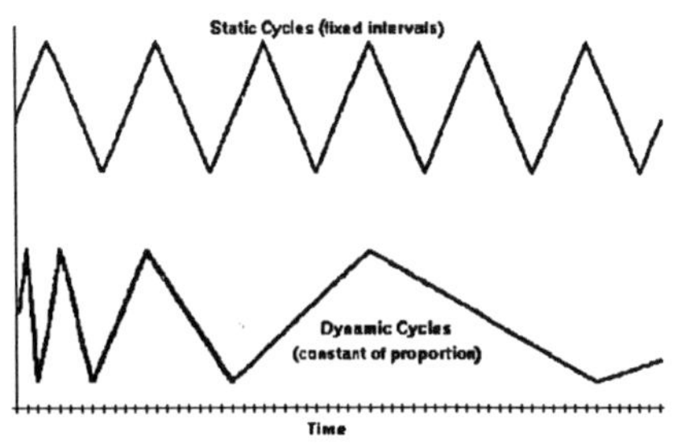

STATIC CYCLES VS. DYNAMIC CYCLES

Static cycles will have intervals between peaks, while dynamic cycles will have a constant proportion between peaks.

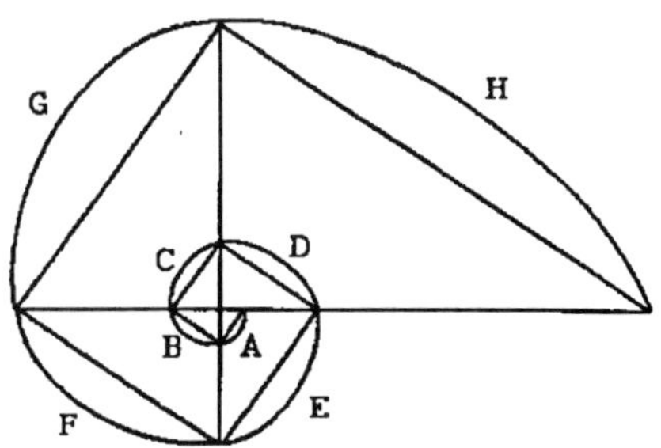

GOLDEN RATION EXPRESSED AS A LOGARITHMIC SPIRAL

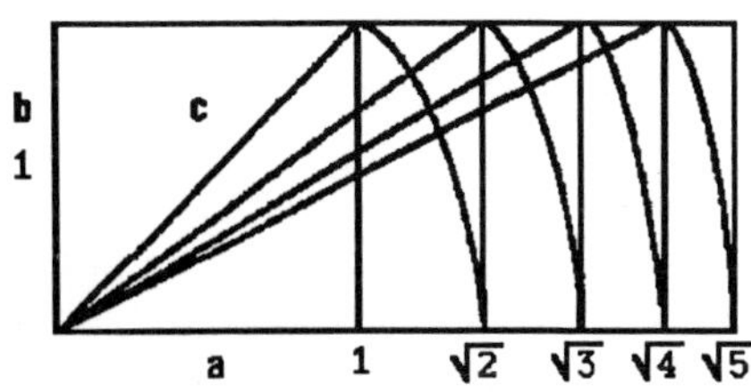

DYNAMIC RECTANGLES

Dynamic rectangle ratios are based on the diagonal of the rectangle. For example, the diagonal of the 1 x 1 rectangle is used as a base for the next rectangle.

0.250 = 1/4
0.333 = 1/3
0.500 = 1/2
0.667 = 2/3
0.750 = 3/4
1.000 = 1/1
1.250 = 1-1/4
1.333 = 1-1/3

STATIC RATIOS

Static ratios are whole numbers plus 1/4s and 1/3s or 1/4, 1/3, 1/2, 2/3, 3/4.

Φ	$\sqrt{2}$	$\sqrt{3}$	$\sqrt{4}$
$0.618 = \sqrt{\Phi}^{-1}$	$0.707 = \sqrt{2}^{-1}$	$0.577 = \sqrt{3}^{-1}$	$0.447 = \sqrt{5}^{-1}$
$1.618 = \sqrt{\Phi}^{1}$	$1.414 = \sqrt{2}^{1}$	$1.732 = \sqrt{3}^{1}$	$2.236 = \sqrt{5}^{1}$
$2.618 = \sqrt{\Phi}^{2}$	$2.000 = \sqrt{2}^{2}$	$3.000 = \sqrt{3}^{2}$	$5.000 = \sqrt{5}^{2}$
$4.236 = \sqrt{\Phi}^{3}$	$2.828 = \sqrt{2}^{3}$	$5.196 = \sqrt{3}^{3}$	$11.180 = \sqrt{5}^{3}$

DYNAMIC PROGRESSION OF RATIOS IN FINANCIAL MARKETS

Figure 4.2 Key Gann trading concepts

Another similar ratio is that of 'dynamic rectangles' where the diagonal of one rectangle is used as the base for the next rectangle. Then there are 'Gann' methods named after the famous trader (see Figure 4.2). The major Gann methods that a potential Gann trader must learn are the geometric angles, division of the range, 7 times the base, squares of the high, low and range and the natural squares of 52, 90, 120, 144 and 360. Also, the study of the planet time cycles and aspects is an important part of Gann's work and should not be overlooked.

But although these theories may shed some light on certain market changes, they are far from infallible guides to market changes—evidenced by the fact that software based on them does not always trade every contract to profit—far from it. That is not because the software reflects the trading strategy implied by Gann or Elliott inaccurately—not at all. One reason is that there are almost certainly a number of different dynamic cycles in operation in a market at any one time. It is difficult to isolate them. Another is that predicting the changeover between different cycles is difficult. That is precisely where the major profits and losses are to be made.

Conclusions

Many software packages provide most of these indicators, but it is important to note that, at any one time, different indicators can show quite different expected price movements. They are not all infallible guides: of course not, or else there would be no losers (except those not using any indicators at all, and they would be a diminishing group) in what is after all a zero-sum game. A typical software resume of the signals generated by different indicators is shown in Figure 4.3, which illustrates the age-weighted consensus of the signals as displayed by the *CandlePower* system which uses them as back-up. The reason why the rating shown is higher for the buy than the sell signals is because they are more recent. The 'Avg per cent Gain' gives a 'quality' rating for each indicator, which is the average percentage gain or loss of that indicator. ESP is a representation of the filtering concept used by *CandlePower*. (See the section on candlestick analysis later in this chapter.)

Technical analysts have in the past suggested that successful speculation in commodities requires far more specialized knowledge, demands more constant daily and hourly attention, than that for stocks and share markets. It was argued that ordinary individuals could hope to attain a fair degree of success in investing in securities by devoting only their spare moments to their charts, but they ought to shun commodity speculation entirely unless they are prepared to make a career of it. This was before the days of financial futures, and still the shorting of equities markets is unusual, but

MCD Age-Weighted Consensus

300 Periods

Indicator	Signal	@	Date	/	Age	Avg % Gain
ESP(5)	Sell	@	931208	/	16	1.65
CCI(14)	Buy	@	931228	/	3	0.15
%B(20)	Buy	@	931228	/	3	0.27
RSI(14)	Sell	@	931103	/	40	2.19
%K(14)	Sell	@	931230	/	1	-0.21
%D(14)	Sell	@	931209	/	15	0.24
MFI(21)	Buy	@	931229	/	2	0.04
ROC(12)	Buy	@	931228	/	3	0.86
EMV(13)	Buy	@	931229	/	2	0.04
DMO(18)	Sell	@	931209	/	15	1.42
LTI(15)	Buy	@	931229	/	2	-0.30
WDI(14)	Sell	@	931209	/	15	1.14
PDO(21)	Sell	@	931231	/	0	0.83
MACD(7)	Sell	@	931208	/	16	0.20

Consensus: 6 BUYS = 56% 7 SELLS = 44%

Display Trading History? (Y/N):

Figure 4.3 CandlePower4: The age-weighted consensus of software signals
Source: CandlePower

still technical analysts need to justify why charts should not work as well for commodities as for stocks.

The going price, technical analysis enthusiasts say, already encompasses all the fundamental information that can be had, plus more of equal or greater import. What actually happens is that prices move in trends and trends continue until something happens to change the supply and demand balance. Everyone agreed that, in practice, the statistics that the fundamentalists study play a part in the supply-demand equation—that is freely admitted. But there are also many other factors affecting it, and there are certainly many, many occasions when fundamental analysts have to shrug their shoulders and admit that 'market psychology' is dominating the market. The market price reflects not only the differing value opinions of many orthodox security appraisers, but also all the hopes and fears and guesses and moods, rational and irrational, of hundreds of potential buyers and sellers, as well as their needs and their resources. In total these factors, which defy analysis and for which no statistics are obtainable, are nevertheless all synthesized, weighed and finally expressed in the one precise figure at which a buyer and a seller get together and make a deal (through their agents, their respective stock brokers). This is the only figure that counts.

Moreover, the technician claims with complete justification that the bulk of the statistics which the fundamentalists study are past history, already out of date and sterile, because the market is not interested in the past or even in the present. It is constantly looking ahead, attempting to discount future developments, weighing and balancing all the estimates and guesses of hundreds of investors who look into the future from different points of view and through glasses of many different hues.

Oriental candlestick analysis and its current applications

The candlestick method of technical analysis originated in the Japanese rice market of the 1600s and 1700s. It has become widely known in the West since then, although it is highly disputable as to how many Western trading companies actually use the method to trade commodities. Some, at least, use it as one of their forecasting methods. It is visually quite similar to conventional charting but some argue that it presents a visually more appealing picture. In essence, the candlestick is formed as follows. A day is represented by a tall, thin box, known as the *real body*, whose length is determined by the difference between the open and the close. If the closing price is above the opening price, the body is hollow, and vice versa. Small vertical lines, known as shadows, extend above and below the body and represent the high and the low for the day. The actual creation of a candlestick chart is therefore quite straightforward. Where candlestick charting becomes sophisticated is in the understanding of the various chart patterns that are made up of one, two or more days. There are reversal patterns with such names as *Tsutsumi* (engulfing pattern), *Kabuse* (dark cloud cover) and *Narabi Kuro* (upside gap two crows). Candlestick analysis has trend change indicator patterns, continuation patterns and miscellaneous patterns. Tsutsumi is a strong reversal indication, especially after a strong trend. A bullish engulfing pattern occurs when a solid body is followed by a larger hollow body that engulfs the previous day's body. *Hoshi* (stars) are reversal indicators. A star is a small body that made a gap following a long body; a morning star is bullish, and an evening star bearish. The third day of a morning star should be hollow and the close should be more than halfway above the solid body that preceded the star. *Doji* lines are where the open and close are about the same and indicate indecision. These lines can be used as areas of support and resistance. Merrill Lynch technical analyst and options strategist, Steve Nilson, has suggested that options traders could use them to mark opportunities to buy volatility. *Harami* is similar to an inside day. The market is at a point of indecision or trend change, and this is depicted as a small body within the previous day's larger body. *Kubitsuri* (hanging man) is bearish if it occurs after an uptrend. The body is at the upper end of the entire day's range with very little or no upper shadow, while the lower shadow is at least twice the length of the body. The *Falling Three Methods* is a rare but important pattern. It is made up of five lines: three small hollow bodies surrounded by two long solid bodies. It is especially bearish in a downtrend.

There are a large number of different candle patterns which are recognized and summarized in Appendix A of the *CandlePower* technical manual. The number of days required for each pattern appears after the name of the pattern.

- **Bullish reversals**

Hammer (1)
Inverted hammer (1)
Belt Hold (1)
Engulfing (2)
Harami (2)
Harami Cross (2)
Piercing Line (2)
Doji Star (2)
Meeting Line (2)
Three White Soldiers (3)
Morning Star (3)
Morning Doji Star (3)
Abandoned Baby (3)
Tri-Star (3)
Breakaway (5)
Three Inside Up (3)
Kicking (2)
Unique Three River (3)
Three Stars in the South (3)
Concealing Baby Swallow (4)
Stick Sandwich (3)
Homing pigeon (2)
Ladder Bottom (5)
Matching Low (2)

- **Bearish reversals**

Hanging Man (1)
Shooting Star (1)
Belt Hold (1)
Engulfing (2)

Harami (2)
Harami cross (2)
Dark Cloud cover (2)
Doji Star (2)
Meeting Line (2)
Three Black Crows (3)
Evening Star (3)
Evening Doji Star (3)
Abandoned Baby (3)
Tri-Star (3)
Breakaway (5)
Three Inside Down (3)
Three Outside Down (3)
Kicking (2)
Upside Gap two Crows (3)
Identical Three Crows (3)
Deliberation (3)
Advance Block (3)
Two Crows (3)

- **Bullish continuation**

Separating Lines (2)
Rising Three Methods (5)
Upside Tasuki gap (3)
Side by Side White Lines (3)
Three Line Strike (4)
Upside Gap Three Methods (3)

- **Bearish continuation**

Separating Two Lines (2)
Falling Three Methods 950
Downside Tasuki Gap (3)
Side by Side White Lines (3)
Three Line Strike (4)
Downside Gap Three Methods (3)
On Neck line (2)
In Neck Line (2)

The idea has been developed of a Candle Index which was a response to a perceived need to quantify the frequency of candle patterns. The basic Candle Index (as, for example, included in the *CandlePower 4* trading system) is based upon the number and frequency of candle patterns that occur in the data being analysed. It will oscillate above and below a zero line. Each bullish candle pattern is incorporated into the index at value 1 and the same for each bearish indicator. More sophisticated versions of the index must incorporate weights to different strengths of candle patterns and also to their timing; but the idea remains the same, that the values are summed and the result is a running summation of the candle pattern's value. A positive index number is a buy signal and vice versa.

Filtering concept

This was developed to assist the analyst in removing 'premature' candle patterns and to eliminate 'bad' patterns. Because candle patterns are intensely dependent on the underlying trend of the market, lengthy price trends will usually cause early pattern signals. An additional factor was required, similar to the use of confirming signals by other technical analysts. Most indicators have a buy and sell definition to assist in their interpretation and use. There is a point prior to a buy or sell signal that is normally a better place for a signal to be acted upon, but it is hard to define this. Most indicators, as advocates of cyclical wave theory rarely tire of pointing out, do lag the market. If an indicator's parameters are set too high, then the result will be too many wrong signals or whipsaws. *CandlePower* has therefore incorporated a 'pre-signal' area based on thresholds and indicator values. It is not possible to calculate how long an indicator will be in the pre-signal area, but advocates do claim that the longer an indicator is in its pre-signal area, the better the actual sell or buy signal is. For threshold-based indicators, such as the RSI, the pre-signal area is that between the indicator and the thresholds. For oscillators such as the moving average crossover, it is defined as the area after the indicator crosses the zero line until it crosses the moving average.

***CandlePower* analysis**

CandlePower charting with the software package is similar to the candlestick technique in that the body represents the difference between the open and the close, and the high and low are depicted as vertical lines extending above and below the body. Here, too, a solid body means the close was below the open and a hollow body means the close was above the open. If the opening price is not available, the previous day's closing price is used in place of the open. Through this replacement CandlePower can be used for any commodity for which there is no opening price. As in equivolume charting, the width of the body represents the day's volume: the wider the body, the greater the volume. The indicator displayed above the *CandlePower* chart is again the difference between the closing price at a 21-day moving average.

CandlePower™ 4

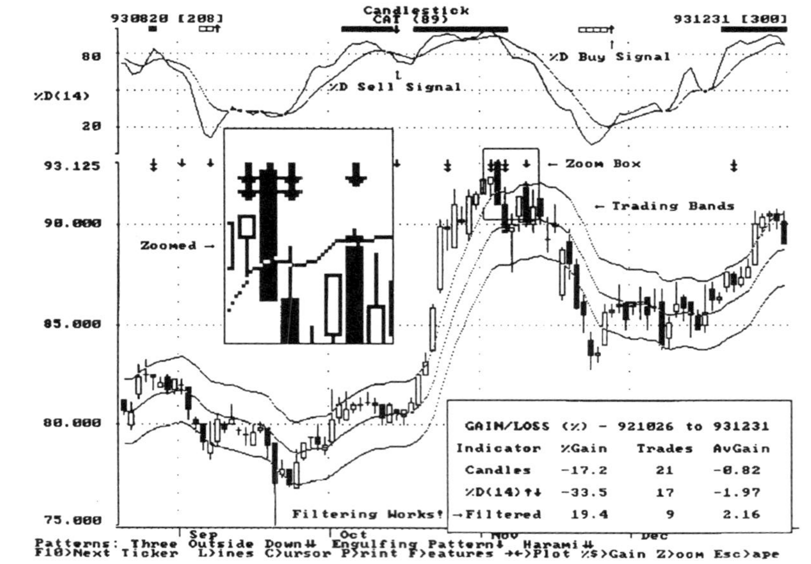

Figure 4.4 CandlePower 4: An illustration of candelstick patterns.
Source: CandlePower

In addition to the application of candlestick principles, the rules for equivolume trading apply also to *CandlePower* charting. For example, tall thin days represent days of easy movement, as it does with equivolume charting. Similarly, square days usually mean the movement has come into some resistance and in many cases mean the end of a move, either up or down.

Advocates of the *CandlePower* technique claim that it offers similar if not better information than either equivolume or pure candlestick charting and that the representations (see Figure 4.4) are as visually appealing as either of them.

Many of the same arguments applicable to technical analysis in general apply equally to candlestick analysis. Though undoubtedly useful as a forecasting tool, it would be an unusual trader or company that relied upon it exclusively, even in Japan.

Available services and software

A typical, indeed first class, Western charting service on paper is provided by Investment Research of Cambridge Ltd. (IRC) (An example of their charts is shown in Figure 4.5) The service contains all relevant chart information for a wide variety of commodities, and also the direction of the following indicators:

- Medium-term trend direction;
- Short-term trend direction;
- Resistance, defined by IRC as 'the area in which stops are recommended if trading from the short side, or the area targeted if trading from the long side';
- Support, defined as 'the area in which stops are recommended if trading from the long side, or the area targeted if trading from the short side. Resistance and support bands represent the upper and lower boundaries in a sideways trend'.

The net result of these calculations is a *Position Recommended*. This is either long, short or either with a query, which occurs if no strong recommendation is to be given, occurring when a target has been reached or if the signal begins to weaken, for example through the loss of momentum. The long or short recommendation remains so long as the trend remains in the same direction and reversal is not implied. The query will disappear if a new target is established. A star denoted a change from the previous issue, for example if support levels have moved up or a new position.

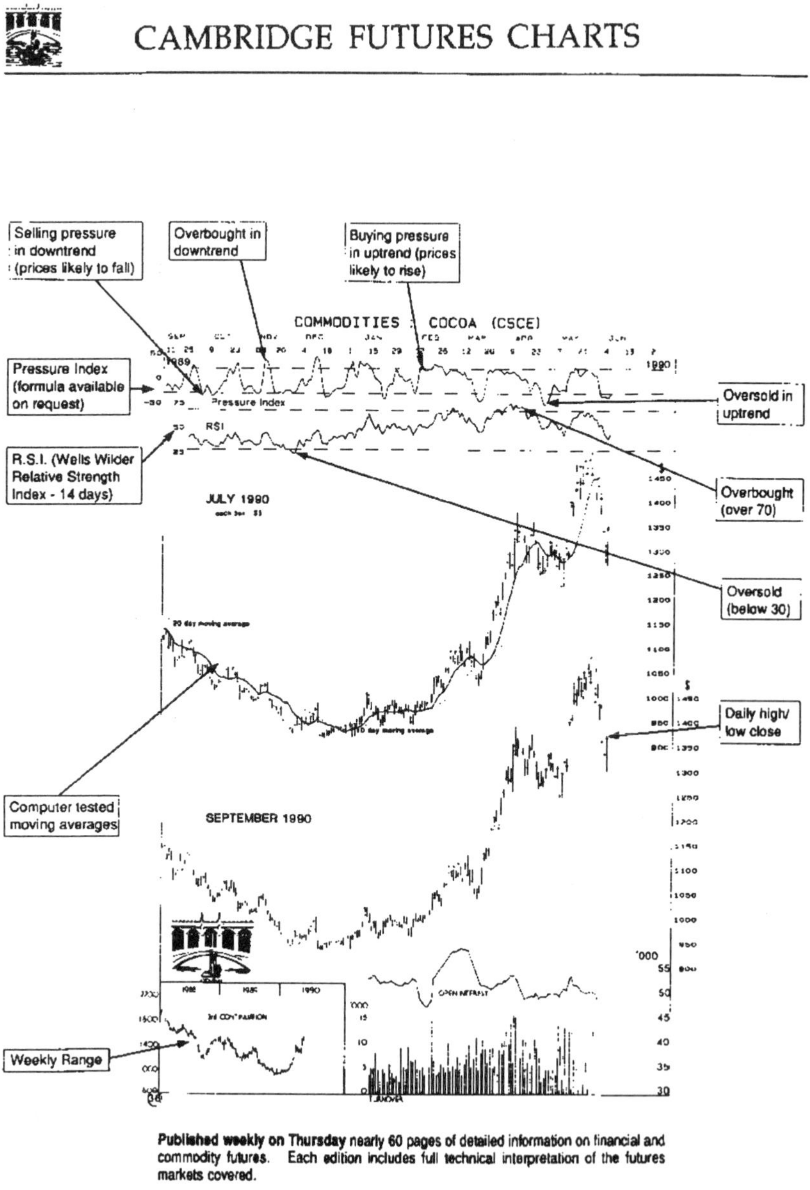

CAMBRIDGE FUTURES CHARTS

Published weekly on Thursday nearly 60 pages of detailed information on financial and commodity futures. Each edition includes full technical interpretation of the futures markets covered.

Figure 4.5 A Cambridge Futures Chart published by Investment Research of Cambridge Ltd.

Examples of the weekly recommendations that IRC gave its clients on 30 June 1994 were as follows:

> Cocoa (London Commodity Exchange): Sept #953. MMT: Sideways. STT: *Down R = *1400-1440, S = *1300-1250. P = *-. (i.e. neither a buy nor a sell recommendation. The associated comment was that 'Selling pressure is dominating and this has caused a breach of the initial support. Some further falls are possible—but the worst of the weakness may well have been seen'.

> Cotton (NYCE): Dec 71.95 cents. MMT: Up STT = *Sideways R = 77-78, S = *72-80, P=*- (again neither a buy nor a sell recommendation). The associated commentary here was: 'Support has been broken and the reaction currently underway could well extend. However, a major reversal would only come through if the 70 cent level were broken—and this is not currently implied'.

It was noticeable that IRC tended to give stronger signals about more illiquid markets such as the agricultural markets of the LCE, and more cautious remarks about the US agricultural markets. This may not be a regular feature of IRC publications, however. It was also a noticeable feature of the IRC publication that financial market recommendations were included in an exactly similar way to those of the commodity markets. Advanced technical analysis such as that of IRC does not make such a large distinction between commodity and stock or financial derivative markets as its predecessors in the earlier part of the century. Indeed, commodity markets appear to be suffering in general from one of Parkinson's Laws—that concerning the quality of the environment and support facilities being in inverse proportion to the dynamism and importance of the activity itself.

A different type of Western chart service, also based on charts, is provided by companies such as MESA. Their *3D for Windows* system computes profits on the basis of seven indicators and produces trading recommendations based on the crossing of the indicators. The display is in 3D and the system is claimed to be able to identify Trend modes and Cycle modes, pinpoint turning points and identify leading and lagging functions. *Metastock* is another example of such a program.

The equivalent Oriental computer application is typified by a system such as *CandlePower 4*. This system is claimed automatically to identify patterns that reliably pinpoint trend reversals. *CandlePower 4* is the latest version. It combines candlestick analysis with other indicators such as those of the equivolume system to produce 'filtered' buy/sell signals, which are those candle signals that occur when the chosen indicator also cuts in. 'There are three trading methods that are used by *CandlePower 4*...The first method is based on the "selected" candle patterns that the program automatically recognizes. The second method is based on the selected indicator, and the third method uses filtered signals as a basis for trading. Whenever a file is loaded, simulated trades are performed on all of the data, using all three methods. Testing has shown, using the AutoRun routines contained in the program, that filtered trading produces better results than either of the first two methods.'[1]

It is instructive to compare the operation of forecasting software with typical 'trading' software.

Right Time from TBSP is a leading example of trading software. TBSP says 'The programs first determine the Trend, either Rising, Falling or Unsure. Secondly, the Stock, Stock L/T and Mutual Funds programs find the Overall Market Direction. Next, the recommendation (Buy, Short, Hold, Close or Warning) is found. If the Recommendation is Buy or Short, the MAA is determined.' Another very well known trading software package is that produced by Essex, *Futures Pro.* Essex have been producing trading software for PCs since 1983, and *Futures Pro* combines the different systems which the company produced hitherto. The program can be used either as a trading system or a toolbox and comes complete with historical databases which it is set to update on a daily basis from most established data vendors, including being able to receive this data via a satellite connection. 'The Daily Signal Report is the essence of the *Futures Pro* trading system...After you enter the open, high, low and close prices from the prior day's trading session, the *Futures Pro* System takes over. It factors those prices into its proven parameter sets, logic and the historical database. A trading signal is then issued at a specific price for each of your enabled markets. Stop order placements are also generated, providing you with essential position management tools.' The program monitors the positions taken daily, through the data input, but as it is not real time trading software it cannot react immediately. There is no pyramiding, although some other trading software programs suggest this as a course of trading action. The program comes with high quality graphics and presentation. Essex says of the trading strategy underlying the program that empirical research has clearly shown that breakout strategies have significantly outperformed most other trading techniques. For example, the Gann-Elliot

[1] *CandlePower Demo Manual, p20*

approach seems to Essex to be excessively subjective; the more trendy ideas such as the Chaos Theory are not sufficiently useful trading techniques.

A good example of the type of technical analysis trading program—which by definition is a forecasting system, albeit one that in the limit will work—in the sense of making the user money—if it is accurate only in the matter of trend over the period that the investor is actually using—was *Swing Catcher,* now according to Futures Truth no longer commercially available. It is quite noticeable that the old distinctions between econometric models and forecasting methods and technical analysis have been translated into the software world—never the twain shall meet. *Swing Catcher* was rated very highly as a trading system by Futures Truth, and by users surveyed by *Futures* magazine in 1991.

What a program like *Swing Catcher* does is this. From the use of over 50 daily trading indicators of the type discussed above, all based on recent price relationships, the program weights them based on their historical effectiveness. The cumulative total of the indicators is called a Trend Index by the program, which is then used as a set up for all the signals, based on the cumulative sum of all the daily point values. Actual sell and buy signals are created based on the strength of the indicators' total point value together with several absolute program entries. The program uses the same fixed pattern recognition and price correlation technical indicators for all markets at all times. This accords with the whole approach of technical analysis, minimizing adjustments for specific markets. With *Swing Catcher,* only three major parameters are adjustable, representing just 5 per cent of the total number. Those responsible for such technical indicator based programs as *Swing Catcher* argue that the optimization of too many indicators, 'a system will become heavily curve fitted to the back-data it was tested with, and likely will not work in real-time trading.'[1]. With such a program, it is not necessary to monitor the market all day; the entire trade, including trade entry order, specific target price and stop-loss, can be submitted to a broker at one time, and before the market opens for the day. It is not even necessary for the trader to know the opening price. The program operates in two different trading modes, the reduce drawdown (conservative mode), which means that no more than one contract is open at any one time, and the Maximize Profits (Aggressive Mode) which trades one contract per individual entry signal, but has a limit of three or no limit on the maximum number of open contracts at any one time. The system does not make a large number of trading recommendations—in one test

[1] *Software literature for Swing Catcher*

suggesting twenty trades for a market in one year. This feature it has in common with a number of other technical analysis programs that build internal confidence levels to a certain point before releasing a buy or sell recommendation. Using *Swing Catcher*, never more than one contract is traded at any one time, a conservative method in itself.

Another typical system, which is marketed with a superb graphics demonstration disc, is the *PBS* system. The idea behind this system is that 'The difference between a day's high and low price is the day's point range. You simply subtract the low from the high for that period. Any period can be used. Once you have the range for one day, you can do the same calculation for any number of days in a row, and then take an average. If you want to look at the range over a 4-day period, you subtract the low from the high each day, and after 4 days you add up all four individual day's ranges, then divide by 4 to get the 4-day average range'[1]. If the gap is opening up the true range is the distance from yesterday's close and today's low and vice versa. This is averaged over any selected number of days to get the average range. As advocates of this system claim that almost every market swing is preceded by a spike or impulse day, the difficulty is in judging a true breakout. The system uses a volume adjustment to produce trading signals based on the average range. '*PBS* contains a totally self-contained mechanical volatility system as well as a full technical analysis charting program. You can stick to a 100 per cent mechanical approach to trading if you prefer. We have found that a little sprinkling of common sense with a few of the regular indicators can improve your results enormously.' (Ibid.)

There are also systems that are based predominantly on specific ways of looking at the market. *CandlePower* (see above) is an example of such a system, and so is *Nature's Pulse* from Kasanjian Research. This latter system builds in all the cycles that are indicated by Fibonacci numbers and static cycles: 'Our proprietary research has enabled us to discover the best methods for pivot and point dynamic ratio selection, and our noise filtering system eliminates unwanted signals.'[2]. There are five cycle indicators built into the software:

- **The A-Cycle**. This analyses static cycles within a market, enabling the user to select up to 100 pivot points and start a static cycle of any frequency length desired. Any point in the future where a dominant

[1] *From demonstration diskette.*

[2] *p7. Nature's Pulse marketing literature*

static cycle has repeated in the past are considered as a possible market turning point.

- **The B-Cycle** facility can be used to select up to 100 pivot points automatically. It can project either a series of static cycles or the Fibonacci number sequence.

- **The C-cycle** allows the user to choose up to 50 price swings and then multiplies the time difference between the beginning and the end of each swing by a set of multipliers chosen by the user. Several dynamic cycles coinciding on a particular date would indicate that a market turn is forecasted to occur there.

- **The D-cycle** lets *Nature's Pulse* calculate all possible combinations of price swings from up to 100 pivot points selected automatically and then multiplied by a set of multipliers inputted by the user. As many as 250,000 combinations can be produced, and again, a point in the future where several static and/or dynamic cycles coincide is a good indicator, the theory argues, to suggest that a change in trend will occur at that time.

- **The E-cycle** can be used to project a turning point in the price trend of a market.

A sophisticated technical trading package such as *Metastock,* which is one of the best known and most used by technical traders, incorporates a wide variety of different technical indicators. The sheer number of different indicators available is a demonstration of the difficulty in choosing between them and the problem that they can indicate quite contrary directions.

There are also numerous systems available from professionals who claim to have established reliable but unspecified methods for trading futures markets. For example, G & R Financial Services produce a *VCIP Day Trade System* which follows the following three criteria to generate trade recommendations every day: '1) Only one direction to trade and one time entry (i.e. no stop and reverse or enter again after stopped out of initial trade) 2) Concentration points (CPoints) and 3) Money management principles.' These tend to publish advice on the financial futures markets but there are some that pay attention to commodities.

Accumulation/Distribution
Accumulation Swing Index
Andrews' Pitchfork
Black/Scholes Price
Bollinger Bands
Channels
Chaikin Oscillator
Commodity Channel Index
Commodity Selection Index
Correlation Analysis
Cycle Lines
Delta
Demand Index
Detrended Oscillator
5 Directional Movement Indicators
Envelopes
Fibonacci Arcs
Fourier Transform
Gamma
Gann Angles and Grids
Herrick Payoff Index
Japanese Candlesticks
Linear Regression Lines
MACD
Mass Index
Median Price
Momentum
Money Flow Index
Moving Averages (5 methods)
Negative Volume Index
On Balance Volume
Open Interest
Option Life
Parabolic SAR
Percent Retracement
Performance
Point & Figure
Positive Volume Index
Price Oscillator
Price Rate-Of-Change
Price and Volume Trend
Quadrant Lines
Relative Strength Index
Speed Resistance Lines
Spreads
Standard Deviation
Stochastic Oscillator
Swing Index
Theta
Fans & Time Zones
Tirone Levels
Trade Volume Index
Trendlines
TriangularAverages
TRIX
Ultimate Oscillator
Vega
Vertical/Horizontal Filter
3 Volatility Indicators
Volume
Volume Oscillator
Volume Rate-Of-Change
Weighted Close
Williams' A/D
Williams' %R
Zig Zag

Figure 4.6 A comprehensive collection of technical indicators

'The question of why one would want to sell a system that works as well as *Nature's Pulse* comes up all the time. We are indeed considering taking it off the market sometime in the next year in order to prevent too many people having it. But also keep in mind that the number of people that presently have the program is so minuscule, that, collectively, we can never alter the course of the financial markets.'[1] But one is always left asking why these individuals, and even companies, bother to establish relatively labour-intensive advisory services with low profit margins when the option of trading markets using their own systems is available. It is almost a Groucho Marx situation—I wouldn't join any commodity trading club that would have me as a member....

[1] *Eddie Kwong, Kasanjian Research, letter to the author, 25 August 1994.*

Analysis of the programs

Traders constantly complain of two aspects of such technical trading programs. Firstly, that they just do not work. Even the most successful users of such programs as *Swing Catcher*, those featured in the marketing literature, have some winning and some losing trades—and of course the markets these programs trade in are zero sum games. For every one trader's forecast that was right, however made, another's was wrong. There is no detailed statistical information available—Futures Truth is the best—on the effectiveness of the different methods. One important reason for this is that the majority of trades are carried out using a forecast based on a combination of different methodologies. Secondly, many trades—especially on futures markets—are actually hedges against changes in the physical market, so they are not directly comparable to pure trading operations where the accuracy of the forecast can be empirically measured.

The second complaint frequently made about trading programs is that they are too complex. The problem is very much Catch-22 and, in fact, typical of any small business. To invest in a number of different forecasting systems such as *Swing Catcher* is, for the individual investor of even moderate means, not unfeasible. Data feeds on a daily basis are not expensive either—in the region of $100 per month or their sterling equivalent, and the individual numbers for specific markets are published in newspapers and individuals can enter them, although those serious about trading will obtain information systems such as *Metastock* or *Livewire.* But to make significant profits, especially on intra-day trading, sufficient to keep oneself through accurate forecasting of price trends, requires full-time participation in the markets—being actually on the trading floor where rumour is rife and large orders can sometimes be 'sniffed in the air'—which is called becoming a 'local' on the markets—or by taking very considerable risks with large amounts of cash at stake. Neither option is attractive to dentists in Ohio or bankers in London, and so the scale of their involvement and the extent of their profits and losses remains relatively low.

The application of the software

The UK Society of Technical Analysts has its own professional examinations and associated training courses. Leaders in the field in the UK are Investment Research of Cambridge Ltd. which manages its own unit trusts and advises institutions worldwide as well as publishing chart information and advice to clients about target prices and stop-loss levels.

As of 1994, however, it seems impossible to find a commercial trading operation trading commodities for profit that relies on such a software package or indeed wholly on technical analysis. That is not to say that they are particularly expensive: the Essex Trading Co. *Futures Pro* package, which is quite representative, costs $595 for each traded contract, and other such systems are available more cheaply than that.

Option pricing

The pricing of options is often thought to indicate forecasts of future prices, and more particularly, of their likely volatility. The science of options pricing is a huge subject in itself. Options pricing software is in widespread use, for example *Options Master* from the Institute for Options Research.

An example of the type of program that is available is that produced by the Optionomics Corporation. Their system includes:

- Real-time options analysis, with implied volatility, delta, gamma, vega and theta, trade settlement and posting to profit and loss accounts;

- Simulations of risk varying time and price parameters, arbitrage analysis, unlimited strike prices and contract months;

- Historical volatility and implied volatility information.

The program has a position analysis feature, allowing the construction of simulations for tracking the portfolio's current exposure and testing scenarios to project where the portfolio may be in the future. A current software program from Optionomics, *Strategist,* combines OTC with exchange-traded options within a portfolio. The program can produce accurate prices for options based on the well-known Black-Scholes formulae for options prices for a multitude of markets.

But these are not, strictly-speaking, forecasting systems. Even obtaining better than the 'correct' price for an option and providing additional information about it which may have correlated in the past with trading range is not the same as guaranteeing a profit. An example is the 'Alpha factor' concept which represents pure 'time value' and can be combined with implied volatility and the futures price to produce a factor important in determining trading range. All bettering the 'correct' option price means is that the seller of the option has a different risk profile or forecast of the evolution of future prices. Nor does the ability to run simulations mean the same thing as evaluating them in terms of prospective profitability or likelihood.

Chapter 5

Fundamental analysis

Many physical traders still say that they have a great respect for, but occasional distrust of, technicians and chartists. The widespread belief is that technical analysis still has a long way to go because some physical customers do not understand the principles involved. This is the case even in an industry such as cotton, where there is an extremely active futures market—with prices that can be accurately recorded and charted—and indeed a market in which the chartists are relatively active. One influential UK rice broker said that on the only occasion that he had listened in depth to what a chartist had to say about likely future developments in the rice contract on the Chicago Exchange, the chartist had been wrong, and he therefore did not propose to consider the matter further.

If physical traders look with distrust on technical analysis, but still need to forecast, whether intuitively or otherwise, what alternative methods are available? The most widespread is fundamental analysis. Economists believe that 'a technological understanding of the economic processes underlying each market is necessary. The agronomy of crop production, the techniques of crop distribution from harvest to end-use, the contributions of meteorology, the engineering of metallurgy, the engineering of processing factories, the combating of oil spills, the control of pollution and many other technological aspects of the different markets are essential for a good understanding of the forces at work in each case'.[1] Klein also refers to the importance of legal and political factors which are well understood by commodity traders.

International trade organizations tend to agree that prices are created through the intersection of supply and demand modulated by exactly these sorts of factors. For example the International Wheat Council (IWC) believes that 'It appears that money itself has become the major traded commodity. Fundamental events in grain markets are sometimes overshadowed by the intervention of speculative capital.' The IWC further

[1] *Klein, ICMM, p.xxi.*

believes that a decline in interest rates reinforces this trend. Earlier statements from the International Cotton Advisory Commission (ICAC) back this up: 'Since 1990, commodity markets have been subject to a series of impacts associated with lower world economic growth and relatively abundant supplies of certain agricultural commodities. Declines in prices were exacerbated by the disruption of world trade due to the war in the Middle East and, most important, the collapse of the Soviet Union and the subsequent integration of the former COMECON countries into the economy of the rest of the world. As a result, the IMF index of non-fuel commodity products declined 8 per cent in 1990 and a further 5 per cent in 1991.'[1]

The problems for fundamental analysis are many. Firstly, it is necessary to assemble all the relevant influencing factors: this may not be easy. Secondly, their influence needs to be ranked and rated, both in terms of what effect on price there already has been and in terms of their likely future influence. Thirdly, for forecasting purposes, an idea of how these factors will evolve in the future is necessary. All these are extremely difficult.

Services provided

One of the most important global commodity forecasting services is that provided by the Economist Intelligence Unit (EIU) in London. This service concentrates on the fundamentals affecting commodity markets. 'Every issue, six times a year, World Commodity Forecasts (WCF) assembles an unrivalled range of raw materials forecasting data. In separate publications on hard and soft commodities, it provides a succinct analysis of market trends and the forces of supply and demand shaping them—culminating in specific price forecasts up to 18 months ahead for 28 major commodities...Each issue of World Commodity Forecasts follows a standard format. [Along with historical data and market trends to date, every WCF contains] The macroeconomic context to our forecasts—covering trends in economic growth, industrial output, inflation, trade and exchange rates...For each commodity, in depth forecasts of production, consumption, trade, stocks and other relevant factors—with specific price forecasts up to 18 months ahead. Two tables summarize forecast trends for each commodity—supply and demand totals and quarterly and annual averages of daily (mainly spot) prices for the next 18 months.' In 1995, the subscription cost £348 per year, or it could be divided into two separate

[1] *C Valderrama, 'Modelling International Cotton Prices', ICAC, Washington DC, 1992, p2.*

publications, *Food, Feedstuffs and Beverages* and *Industrial Raw Materials*, each for £290. The former contains analysis of cocoa, coffee, barley, maize, rice, sorghum, wheat, coconut oil, copra, palm kernel oil, rapeseed oil, soyabeans, soyabean oil, sunflowerseed oil, sugar and tea. The latter monitors aluminium, copper, cotton, crude oil, nickel, rubber, tin, wool and zinc. In addition, the EIU publishes specific individual reports. That on cotton, *Cotton to 1995: Pressing a Natural Advantage* has certainly acquired an important status within the industry. Others have a similar position despite the fact that much of the statistical data in them has aged and the forecasts themselves are out of date as the fundamental factors influencing the market have changed.

Institutions such as the IWC, the ICAC and the Australian Bureau of Agricultural Research Economics (ABARE) are concerned primarily with the short-term outlook for their chosen commodities. The IWC publishes forecasts for the current market year in its published *Grain Market Report.* From time to time it also provides confirmation of data for inclusion in the forecasting models produced by other institutions such as the OECD, the Food and Agriculture Organization of the United Nations (FAO) and the World Bank. The resources available to the IWC and comparable organizations such as the International Wool Secretariat have tended to reduce since the 1970s. In particular, once substantial economics departments have been pruned. As the IWC says: 'The Council's last attempt at long-term forecasting was in 1988. Since then declining staff numbers and diminishing budgets have obliged us to concentrate on the near-term outlook.' Long-term forecasts for commodities, similar to the macro-economic forecasts that were popular at the same time, were demonstrated to be frequently overtaken by events—as the IWC also says 'Changes in basic assumptions can rapidly derail the most careful calculations.' In the main part such activities have been stopped. They never provided much of a trading advantage in themselves, as all traders knew about them and futures markets in particular tended to discount them. Their only real significance was frequently in moving the market short-term, and even in that regard short-term crop forecasts from the United States Department of Agriculture (USDA) have much more impact than long-term forecasts from anyone at all.

ABARE is the leading quasi-governmental organization concerned with the economics of agriculture in Australia. With 280 staff it has a powerful forecasting division, reflecting the very considerable importance of the agricultural sector to the Australian economy. ABARE provides short-term forecasts for most commodities three times a year and a medium-term forecast once a year. ABARE also currently conducts an annual conference known as OUTLOOK which communicates ABARE's forecasts and allows direct questioning by conference delegates. The cost of attendance is attractively low and the importance of the event in Australia is reflected by ministerial attendance.

There are also a wide number of organizations in the private sector, especially in the USA but also in Japan and to a lesser extent in Western Europe, which specialize in providing what are currently known—quaintly—as 'wire' services information on commodities, based primarily but not exclusively on fundamentals. Below are some completely hypothetical examples of the type of report that emerges from these organizations, whose services are often relatively expensive to purchase. The pearl markets referred to are non-existent, the data quite arbitrary, and the *Jewel Reporter* non-existent: but the style and approach are indicative of the type of fast moving overnight fundamental reporting that is typical of the markets which are covered by futures.

ASIAN PEARLS REPORT

FRIDAY 4 JUNE 1996

OVERNIGHT NEWS!

INDONESIA AND RUSSIA TO SIGN JEWEL EXPORT AGREEMENT AT 10.15 MOSCOW TIME TODAY. THE PACKAGE IS TO CONTAIN 25.9 MLN RBLS FOR PEARLS; 123 MLN FOR DIAMONDS; 43.7 MLN FOR RUBIES; 12 MLN RBLS FOR SAPPHIRES; 40 MLN DLRS FOR SET STONES; AND 5 MLN VARIABLE TO BE ALLOCATED BETWEEN STONES LATER

JEWEL REPORTER REPORTEDLY ANNOUNCES GLOBAL PEARL PRODUCTION AT 123,000 TONNES WITH 78,000 BLUE PEARLS AND 28,000 RED PEARLS INCLUDED IN THE TOTAL.

INDONESIA EXPORT SALES: PEARLS

99,500 TONNES 94/95

OF WHICH:

BLUE	50 000 TNS
RED	29 500 TNS
OTHER	10 000 TNS
SET STONES	10 000 TNS
TOTAL	99 500 TNS

COMMENTS: INDONESIA WAS THE LARGEST WORLD SUPPLIER OF PEARLS DURING THE 1994/95 SEASON REDUCING STOCKS TO AN ESTIMATED 16,500 TONNES AT THE END OF THE SEASON ACCORDING TO THE INDONESIAN FISHERIES MINISTRY. RED PEARL STOCKS WERE REPORTED AT A FIVE-YEAR LOW OF 5,400 TONNES. FISHERIES MINISTRY CURRENTLY LOBBYING FOR EXPORT RESTRICTIONS ON UNSET RED PEARLS

Production problems

There definitely appears to be further difficulties in meeting production targets for the immediate harvest. Our in-house meteorologist suggests that Pacific storms will limit the number of pearls that can be harvest over the next week as only some 20 per cent of boats will be able to sail. The heaviest concentration of rainfall should be in the South-West harvest areas and the lightest is expected in the South-East. This will place further pressure on red pearl harvests.

EARLY OPENING CALLS!
BLUE PEARLS LEVEL
RED PEARLS LEVEL/RISING
OTHER PEARLS RISING

BLUE PEARLS: New *Jewel Reporter* expected estimates marginally less than the USDA's estimate of last Tuesday (81,000 tonnes), so should not have too much of an impact today, although it will definitely not have the bullish effect that a much lower estimate would have had and there may be a slight reaction as some traders expected the *Jewel Reporter* estimate to be below 75,000 tonnes. There was a belief in Jakarta yesterday that perhaps the Fisheries Ministry would soon announce financial support decisions for the new blue pearl harvest, which lent some support to the nearby contracts. As the Ministry could make its announcement any day, and must do so before the end of the month, the market might be reluctant to continue the current bear trend lower during the next few days. Also with the USDA Pearl Supply and Demand reports out next Friday, and with the Russian deal being the only one expected, the market should not be subject to major volatility for the time being.

RED PEARLS: The 28,000 output from Indonesia forecast by *Jewel Reporter* has been circulating in the market for some time, so the main impact on prices will be the impact of the storms on the immediate harvest and the possibility that there will be a short term supply squeeze. This pushed up New York prices in the nearby contract to new contract highs, but some analysts are still pessimistic that overseas and private supplies will come into the spot market and hold down any rapid price rises over the next week. However it seems unlikely that stockholders will wish to let their stocks enter the market now when prices are still rising, and the nearby contract probably has some way to rise yet before expiry on the 25th of this month.

7th June

Red Pearls Daily

The issue of trading notices for the red pearl contract by ABC Trading and Pearls International helped pressure the July lower in exciting, fast trading within narrow margins. The notices were issued to a large number of different houses. Market players quickly rationalized that since two of the major trade houses were effectively willing to give up pearls then the chances of a squeeze were negligible and near term supplies were—as some had suspected—more than ample. This put a sharp downward pressure on prices especially when adduced to the fact that many of the pearls issued by ABC and Pearl International would probably be retendered. The drop in the June was very swift in morning trading and although the market began to claw back its losses by late morning through profit taking from shorts it fell back again later in the day by an even greater amount. Weakness in the nearby month also fed through to the back months and pushed November especially but also March lower by four points.

RESISTANCE AND SUPPORT LEVELS IN THE MARKET
Red Pearls—Nov R2 3847 R1 3807 PIVOT 3879 S1 3839 S2 3811
9 day RSI Red Pearls—Nov 47
PROGNOSIS FOR NEXT DAY'S TRADING:

In accordance with volume spread analysis, the longs have gone from theoretically 'strong' hands to theoretically 'weak' control. This will probably keep June prices down due to quick profit taking on any rises until expiration. The psychology of the market is negative, weighed down by ideas of a big private Indonesian supply, falling Indonesian demand, poor export figures, doubts over the credit arrangements for the new Russian deal and clearly now also sufficient near term supplies. The market looks increasingly down at heel although the fact that the back months are not trading down as rapidly or as substantially as June may be of some solace to quiescent bulls. Net Indonesian export sales are again disappointing for May at 1,800 tonnes compared to 2100 in the same month last year. Indications are that June is still worse compared to June last year although probably still higher than May.

Blue Pearls Daily

November blue pearls managed a flat close, after falling on the opening, bouncing back, then staying towards the low opening levels for most of the day's trading as more blue pearls were thought to be available for delivery in that contract, especially from those that could immediately be diverted from the failure of the Singapore order last week. June, by contrast, closed up 2 points, with merchants continuing to cover their short positions and trade the June/November spread on the presumption that there may still not be as much June blue pearls available for delivery as had been thought. Volume was moderate at 12,056, in a relatively quiet market. Trading was dominated by position-rolling as June expiration approaches. The market was not yet affected by the news that Polynesia announced, that its 1995/96 harvest would be reduced by 15 per cent to 45,000 tonnes compared to the May forecast of 48,000 tonnes. Iran bought 6,000 tonnes of blue pearls of classes I, III and IV, reportedly through the Malaysian exporters, DDD Ltd.

SUPPORT AND RESISTANCE
Blue Pearls—Nov R2 2250 R1 2242 PIVOT 2233 S1 2225 S2 2216
9-Day RSI Blue Pearls—Nov 64
TOMORROW

The market appears to have steadied after its recent bear phase. However the technical picture shows a head-and-shoulders formation that could measure 45 points lower; *Jewel Reporter* does not believe this. In the last fortnight, Malaysia has lowered its 1995/96 production by 20,000 tonnes, Polynesia by 45,000, and Indonesia by 3,000 tonnes. Continuing lowered production from smaller producers, harvesting difficulties, and the beginnings of a revival in consumption inclines us to believe that the overanalysed question of Polynesian Class II blue pearl deliveries and the likelihood of refinancing on the Singapore contract, which could be announced at any stage this week, present a much more bullish fundamental picture than the technicals suggest. We continue to be long November and recommend staying so, risking a close under 2210 but no more, expecting 2230.

Some commodity markets do not have futures markets, or at least they are not very active by comparison to spot or forward trading, such as rice. Here forecasting services merge and are dominated by analysis and reporting services that can be daily, weekly or even monthly. *Agra-Europe*, *Grain and Oilseeds Report*, and *Metal Bulletin*: these are just three such organizations with their own published and on-line journals and information services. It is important to note, however, that since the late 1980s and the introduction of quite stringent legislation covering the incitement to trade and the offering of advice, journalists and analysts have become increasingly careful not to proffer trading advice in their columns.

The information acquisition process

Information on commodity prices for econometric and fundamental purposes is available from a variety of different sources. For prices, there are the UN's *Monthly Commodity Price Bulletin* and the IMF's *International Financial Statistics.* Information is also available for quantity data, for example on coffee and rubber from the FAO's *Monthly Bulletins on Agricultural Commodities,* or on copper the metal statistics available from Metallgesellschaft in Frankfurt. Official and quasi-official publications giving information on production, yields, acreage sown, trade, and forecasts of these and other statistics are vital to all forecasters. For example, in the USA, energy is covered by the Weekly Petroleum Status Report, published by the US Department of Energy every Wednesday. The American Petroleum Institute issues a complementary statistical bulletin every Tuesday. For grains and oilseeds, crop production figures are released in the USA on a monthly basis, although the exact days of release differ. Crop progress reports are issued every Monday during the growing season, between April-December. Grains stock information is released every September, as is information on pigs and hogs. Livestock information in the USA is released at the end of July and livestock slaughter and cattle feed data is published monthly. The US Bureau of Mines of the US Department of the Interior publishes its *Metal Industry Indicators* and *Mineral Industry Survey* monthly. Much of this information is timed to be released outside normal market hours so as to provide time for its digestion and not to generate panic reactions to data. Sometimes, especially in relation to USDA data about China in a whole number of different respects, this is not always possible and the data itself, for example about sown area or yield, appears to affect the price.

Amongst textiles, for example, the most readily available data are for the production of the agricultural fibres cotton and wool. Production, consumption and trade data are available for these commodities from the Food and Agriculture Organization of the United Nations (FAO), the International Wool Textile Organization (IWTO) and the ICAC and Cotlook, and the USDA. Supply data for the man-made fibres are more difficult to obtain but are available for most countries from national sources such as the Textile Economics Bureau and the International Committee for Rayon and Synthetic Fibres. Data on consumer demand, trade, prices and stock levels for fibres are often unavailable and modelling of the world textile industry is constrained by this lack of data. For example, textile product trade is identified by value and type, such as value of stocks, but the fibre proportions or weights are not included. The most readily available and perhaps most reliable data of fibre use are at the mill level where raw fibre is weighed before processing begins. At this stage, however, fibre use relates to industrial demand, which may or may not be closely related to consumer demand in the country where the manufacturing takes place—some export over half.

A large number of commodities have futures markets. Futures prices themselves are recorded by exchange staff in pits and rings or run off feeds from the electronic trading systems to systems which sell the data to companies known as *quote vendors*. These firms, such as Reuters, Knight-Ridder and Telerate, provide the information on screen in purchased packages for their clients worldwide, in practically real-time. The sorts of data available on each futures contract are:

- Sell - the lowest price being offered (*ask* in US terminology);
- Buy - the highest price bid in real time;
- Trade - the last price at which the contract traded;
- High - the highest price at which the contract traded that day;
- Low - the lowest price at which the contract traded that day;
- Volume - the number of contracts traded that day;
- Time - the time of the last trade.

Information provision on derivative and physical business has an estimated $8.5bn turnover and growing. The market is dominated by several large companies operating worldwide and they provide everything from news services and straightforward prices to personalized pages and spreadsheet integration. Every year passing sees improvements in the speed with which information on these markets is disseminated.

Information about supply, demand and stocks is not generally so readily accessible as that on prices. Moreover, the information about future supply and demand that is necessary to predict future prices is just as difficult to obtain as the prices themselves and of course arrives at the same time. Few objective analyses of world supply and demand balances for commodities exist, although F.O. Licht does so for coffee, the ICAC for cotton and the USDA for most agricultural commodities. They are, as may be imagined, huge and complicated exercises with large residual balances and error terms, usually reflected in 'stock adjustments' as the production, import and export figures do, in fact, emerge in due course.

So the majority of commodities—those with 'exclusive' trading clubs such as rice and naphtha being notable exceptions—have data on price, supply, demand and trade being regularly produced. These constitute the kernel of fundamental analysis.

Chapter 6

The history of modelling

The history of econometric and modelling analysis of commodity markets has been extensive. This applies especially to food: agricultural demand and supply was one of the first areas to have econometric techniques applied, in the 1920s. It is interesting to note that it was at a very similar time that Gann and Elliot were first developing their theories of market behaviour.

The explosion of interest in quantitative models during the 1960s brought numerous econometric and time series analysis of commodity markets, along with numerous scenario assessment models. Subsequently, however, the failure to predict the oil price shocks and other well-publicized such failures brought a tempering of enthusiasm for the quantitative methodologies of econometrics subsequently. The 1990s has seen the advent of user friendly forecasting and indeed technical analysis software, combined with inexpensive data feeds. As a result significant interest in the subject at a much wider but lower level of expertise is gradually occurring. Even then the process is proving a slow one.

Concepts of modelling and types of model

There are many different modelling approaches that have evolved and that can be applied to commodities. Each of them has different qualities, many of them directed towards policy analysis rather than forecasting. It is worth noting that, for forecasting purposes, many models have been constructed that take elements of each. Econometricians usually characterize the basic distinction, however, as being between *time series* models (often Box-Jenkins—discussed later in this chapter) *mathematical programming* and *systems dynamics* on the one hand and *regression models* and *econometrics* on the other. In the past this distinction was extremely important, and necessary for even a cursory practitioner of forecasting to understand. It is salutary to realize that, for the latest generation of econometric forecasting software, this choice of methodologies is something carried out automatically by the software on the basis of data availability and structure. The software then explains the reason for the choice to the user.

Now and ever more, detailed understanding methodologies of forecasting is becoming less important to the practitioner. On the other hand, knowing what software exists, and discovering, by fair means or foul, how good it is at its task, is becoming more important. In that sense, this section is 'old-fashioned'. It goes into more depth than most users will require in practice.

Quantitative forecasting

Prices in commodity markets have several features identified by Klein (1991) which make them at first sight attractive for quantitative study, and which can be expanded.

- The goods are well defined primary products unlike, for example, manufactured goods which may have difficult-to-draw borders;
- The markets' scope is usually global or at least regional;
- There is often a high degree of competition in the markets themselves, between origins, companies and manufacturers of end goods;
- There are frequently associated futures markets that reflect both current and future prices.

It is worth noting that traders would express scepticism about all of this as being superficial. Klein certainly exaggerates the advantages in assessing commodity prices. He claims that their units of measurement are to some extent 'meaningful and easy to handle' and oscillate. This compares to groups of commodities, or the retail prices index (RPI), which is composed of a number of different goods which require balancing and which almost inevitably just increase over time. This would eliminate problems associated with index numbers. There are several points to make on this.

- Even futures markets have extreme difficulty in deciding on the contract specifications for their markets. Whether Cuban sugar should be deliverable on the London Sugar Market was always a major point of dissension, and sufficient to make the market's price behaviour quite different. Changes to contract specifications or in government policies are sufficient to render historical data inappropriate for forecasting purposes, so even though may be much data available, demonstrating lots of variation, most of it may be useless.
- All the data must be readily available. This is not too great a problem for the commodity markets, which for centuries almost have had a vast amount of price and volume information available, at least for commodities with active futures markets such as cotton.

A good example of a primary commodity market which does not fit within Klein's convenient suppositions is rice. There are 14,000+ types of rice, with exceptionally low substitution between them. The market is heavily segmented and influenced by government policies because of the sensitivity of rice to national economies and welfare. Competition can sometimes be non-existent owing to government-to-government deals. Finally, there is only a very limited futures market, and it does not deal in the types of rice that are traded internationally. These are serious disadvantages to forecasting rice prices and the rice market, though an extreme example, demonstrates many features that are common to others. Few deny that international commodity markets are extremely complex. Even modelling experts agree that few real breakthroughs have been made: yet there have been methodological advances in the past three decades which are worth noting.

It should be clear by this point that predictions of the sort that involve explaining events which will occur at some future time are called forecasts, and the process of arriving at such explanations is called forecasting. Equally clearly, the ability to forecast time-ordered variables will be impaired without an understanding of the time structure of relationships between variables.

There are various ways of forecasting the future values of economic variables, including *intrinsic* methods, in which the future value of variables are predicted from their past values. One important statistical technique included in the intrinsic method is time-series analysis. By a time series is understood statistical data that are collected, observed or recorded at regular intervals of time, whether annual, monthly, weekly, daily or intra-daily. The frequency of observation, as long as it is regular, does not matter. This is remarkably similar in concept to technical analysis, although the two disciplines do not meet.

Econometric analysis

An econometric analysis constitutes a system of equations (or a single equation) estimated from past data, that is used to forecast economic and business variables. An econometric model is the use of functional, determining relationships between economic variables *1-(n-1)* to produce a result for variable *n*. There can be many equations linking the variables, or just one, but the whole thrust of the equation structure is causal. The structure aims to identify which variables actually determine each other and eventually the variable to be analysed. Amongst the wealth of information contained in the huge number of economic publications and data feeds are various economic indicators and commodity price series. There are series of data which tend to turn up or down before overall economic activity does. These are called leading indicators. There are also roughly coincident indicators. Finally there are series which tend to move somewhat behind overall activity, called lagging indicators. These confirm or refute the earlier directional signals. Exactly the same types of variable apply to commodity price forecasting.

Time series analysis

This is where econometric analysis starts. A time series is a sequence of data points at constant time intervals, of which price and quantity series for commodities are excellent examples. The four usually recognized parts of a time series are trend, seasonal, cycle and irregular variation. The trend component is the general upward or downward movement of the average over time. These movements may require many years of data to establish, determine or describe. The factors underlying the trend may be technological advances, productivity change, inflation and population changes. Compared to other, finished, products such as automobiles, commodities exhibit less of a trend component. This renders them less amenable to time series analysis, at least in this regard. Commodity prices, at least in the long term, are however very much subject to the other three identifiable components of a time series. These are:

- *The seasonal component*. This is a recurring fluctuation of data points above and below the trend line. Annual changes in price at harvest time and stock depletions beforehand are good examples of such seasonal fluctuations for commodities.

- *Cyclical components*. These repeat with a longer term frequency but perhaps with a different amplitude. Usually the causes of these cycles are said to be business cycles of varying length. Hence international recessions, recoveries and inflation are all relevant. Commodity prices, demand and supply are all linked to these factors and in many cases have been regarded as predictors of them.

- *Irregular components*. These are random. Shim, Siegal and Liew say that this component 'is caused by unpredictable or non-recurring events such as floods, wars, strikes, elections, environmental changes, and the passage of legislation.'[1]

[1] *Shim, Siegal and Liew, p90.*

The components of a time series can therefore be summarized as follows:

1. *Secular trend* - the smooth or regular underlying movement of a series over a fairly long period of time;

2. *Seasonal variation* - the movements in a time series which recur year after year in the same months (or quarters);

3. *Cyclical variation* - what remains in the series after the above two have been removed. This is also a way of measuring the business cycle—the recurring movements of economic activity encompassing prosperity, recession, depression, and recovery;

4. *Irregular variation* - caused by really identifiable events like elections, wars, floods, earthquakes, strikes, bank failures, etc., and also random/chance events of lesser magnitude.

Trend analysis for time series can be either linear or non-linear, amongst which common types are constant growth (proportional), modified exponential growth and logistic (S-shaped) growth. The constant rate of change—proportional—model involves determining the average historical rate of change and projecting that into the future. When prices or quantities exhibit seasonal or cyclical fluctuation, as commodity statistics usually do, classical decomposition can be used on a time series. Seasonal indices are determined using a four-quarter moving average. The data are deseasonalized; the linear least squares equation is used to identify the trend element of the forecast, and the dependent variable is then forecast for each season. These models are traditionally sited within the discipline of 'business forecasts'. There is a strong prejudice, despite the theoretical literature's backhanded advocacy of their use for short-term forecasts, against the use of time series forecasts of daily prices for trading purposes. This is despite the fact that, within a short time horizon, they may make highly effective forecasts. Obviously, the frequency of a time series determines the frequency of a forecast, although modulations can be imposed to create estimates between the actual forecasts.

The basic time series model is exclusively based on historical observations of prices or another to be predicted variable. No attempt to explain causal relationships is made. It is inexpensive to develop, store data and operate. Numerous statistical packages exist which will carry out such analysis. The simplest possible version of such a model just adds the latest absolute period-to-period change to the most recent observed level of the price level or whatever is to be forecast. Rarely can this be expected to be wholly accurate as prices only infrequently change in straight lines. Slightly increased sophistication can be found with moving average models, which employ the most recent periods in order to calculate an average. This is then used as the forecast for the following period. The choice of periods for the moving average is a measure of the relative importance to be given to recent as compared to more historical data. The concept of the moving average is simple to use, and relatively straightforward, but models based on it do require a larger amount of data, and, in the most basic version, all data in the sample are weighted equally.

In time series analysis, there is a search for observable regularities and patterns in historical series which are so persistent that they cannot be ignored. If subsequently forecasts are based on them, the forecast will inevitably just repeat history. Sometimes, as when World War I ended decades of stability or continuity, more recently when the Korean War sent wool prices shooting up, or when OPEC drove up the price of oil, this is confounded. More often that not, however, the best guide to today's price is yesterday's. Sometimes expected shocks do not materialize, or the price remains relatively stable for prolonged periods of time.

Moving averages

The next stage from using a basic time series is to work on averaging it as a way to improving the accuracy of the forecast.

Moving averages are averages that are updated as new information comes in. The forecaster uses the most recent observations, whichever number are chosen, to create an average which is used as the forecast for the subsequent period. Moving averages for commodities tend to be taken over either three months or six months. This is considerably more than the typical periods used for sales or profit forecasts, or those used for technical analysis, which are usually measured in days. Different weights can be attributed to the different historical data, either directly on the basis of the more recent, the more weight, or on a more sophisticated basis whereby appropriate data, for example seasons, are weighted accordingly. The moving average method is easy to understand and use, provided that an adequate methodologically unchanged data series is available. There are, however, major disadvantages to the use of moving averages connected with the problem of weighting the historical data. The calculation of weights to accord to each period is a complex and not easily answered question. All data in the sample, over whatever period it is considered, are weighted equally in the moving average calculation. It may be that certain types of data are more valid than others, for reasons of seasonality, or because certain data is obviously identifiable as different from the rest. This might be for example because of extraordinary weather conditions. If so, the data should be weighted differently. It is not always to discern a rational, let alone an accurate, approach to this. Seasonality means that a seasonal index is used as an intervention through moving averages. There may be other such interventions such as annual trends and business cycles even when the data is tested free from seasonal influences. For simple deseasonalizing of data, if October on average is 148 per cent of the average, then to get deseasonalized data, one should take 100/148 of October. There is, however, a better, but more complex, way of deseasonalizing data.

Step 1 is to calculate twelve-month moving totals; to calculate two-month moving totals. Then each is divided by 24 since column 3 is the sum of two twelve-month averages—thus getting the centred twelve-month moving average. Then divide the original data month by month by the corresponding values of the moving average and multiply these ratios by 100. Hence one arrives at percentages of moving average. These have to be averaged out again over a number of years to eliminate irregular fluctuations and the result is the seasonal index. Since the seasonal index for each month is supposed to be a percentage of the average month, the sum of the 12 values should equal 1200. If in practice they do not, it is necessary to multiply by a constant to make them add to 12.

Exponential smoothing

Simple moving averages can fail to reflect changes in trends, so forecasters have moved to refine the process in order to produce more accurate forecasts.

A problem with the ordinary least squares method is that the regression line fits the early data points more closely than the later ones. A method for weighting or discounting least squares circumvents this problem. As the discount factor is changed, the weights applied to older data change.

A more complex version, extremely popular in time series forecasting, is known as exponential smoothing. In this process the averages of past data are weighted. To utilize the exponential smoothing process, it is first necessary to have the initial forecast. This can be the first several actual observations or an average of them. The forecaster can adjust the smoothing coefficient to the observed data as it emerges. For practical purposes the optimal coefficient can be ascertained by using the mean squared error (MSE) principle. Most computer forecasting software contains an exponential smoothing routine which generates the least MSE and hence the optimum smoothing coefficient. When data are also subject to trend, it is possible to adduce a deterministic factor to account for this.

Exponential smoothing is therefore a basic forecasting device which evades the disadvantages of equal weighting within moving averages. This technique is well known amongst financial managers for short-term forecasting and is also used by research departments in large firms. Past data is weighted, with heavier weights for more recent information and progressively less weight to information receding into the past. It is the forecaster's equivalent of the discount rate applied to future revenue streams in cost benefit analysis. The logic behind exponential smoothing is that the future is more likely to be like the recent past than more distant events, and the potential flaws in this process are clear enough.

A formula can be expressed for exponential smoothing as follows:

$$P_{\text{(new)}} = @P_{\text{(old)}} + (1 - @)\, F_{\text{(most recent)}}$$

The higher the value of @, the higher the weight given to the more recent data.

A numerical example will bring this process into clearer focus. Suppose a price series for pearls on a monthly average as follows:

Jan	\$235
Feb	\$241
Mar	\$240
Apr	\$244
May	\$256
Jun	\$248
Jul	\$250
Aug	\$252
Sep	\$255
Oct	\$258
Nov	\$259
Dec	\$264

This price series indicates clearly enough that, during the year, pearl prices were on an upward roll, but that there were several false indications of a fall in prices. In some respects, straightforward forecasting is very useful in dealing with a series of prices such as this, which do demonstrate a long-term trend. On the other hand, any form of extrapolation forecast is bound to predict a rise in prices and this may not always be justified by events on a month-by-month basis.

Suppose the forecasting organization believes that a six-month average would be the best that could be used. Then the forecast for July would be an average of January-June = 244. The actual result for July is in fact \$6 higher than this. Can exponential smoothing come to the rescue of this ailing forecast and make it less pessimistic in its forecast for August? In part it depends on the smoothing constant. Suppose this is high at 0.5. Then the exponentially-smoothed forecast for August will be 0.5 x 250 plus 0.5 x 244 = \$247. One \$ closer. But a straight moving average of February-July would have been \$246.5 anyway. In this case, exponential smoothing brings few advantages.

The results of using different smoothing coefficients can be seen by comparing actual results over time with the forecast values in order to obtain an optimum smoothing coefficient. For example, if the forecast appears to be consistently slow in responding to increased prices, then a higher @ may be called for. The optimal @ may be established through the MSE formula. This is defined as:

n Sum t=1 (Yt - Yt-1)2/(n-o)

where *o* is the number of observations used to determine the initial forecast. This will be six in the case of a six month moving average forecast. The objective is to select the @ which minimizes the MSE, which itself is the average sum of the variations between the historical price data and the forecast values for the equivalent periods.

The objection which can be easily raised against exponentially-smoothed or otherwise moved averages, that they overlook a trend in the data, can be built into the data used for the forecast by modifying the data according to the trend. In the forecast itself this is achieved by the introduction of another weighting (smoothing) constant. The data is therefore smoothed in two separate processes—first as in the process described above, and then again according to the second smoothing coefficient. Such values having been through two mills tend to be themselves smoother than the first staged smoothed figures, making them a better indication of any trend that may be in progress. Clearly, the determination of the trend may be difficult, but looking back to previous evolutions of the price and fitting the current curve may be a satisfactory approach, at least initially, to trying to determine the long-term trend. The high tendency of commodity prices to follow substantial long-term trends puts this process high on the agenda in the formulation of time-series commodity price models.

One of the first such models was the well-known study by D.B. Suits and S. Koizumi [1]. In this model, the quantity of onions supplied in year *Yt* was related to price in year *t-1* and costs of *t-1* as:

log Yt = 0.134 + 0.0123(t-1924) + 0.324 log P(t-1) - 0.512 log C(t-1)

[1] *'The Dynamics of the Onion Market', Journal of Farm Economics, 1956, pp 475-484.*

Given the known price of onions this year and the known level of this year's production costs, the model could be used to forecast next year's supply.

To carry out an exponential smoothing forecast it is first necessary to possess an initial forecast to be smoothed. This can be the initial actual data, or an average of the data for a few periods. Suppose that pearl prices do not exhibit much seasonality (an unlikely story for any commodity) or, more likely, that the data above has already been seasonally adjusted. In this case, the result obtained from the exponential smoothing will also have to be seasonally adjusted to produce the actual forecast.

In the use of exponential smoothing for forecasting—given a constant @, the forecast for time *t* is simply a weighted average of the actual value at *t-1* and the forecasted value for *t-1,* where the actual value is weighted by @ and the forecasted value weighted by *1-@*. It can easily be shown that the forecast for time *t* is the weighted sum of the actual values prior to time *t,* where the weight attached to each value declines geometrically with the age of the observation. Exponential smoothing is often used in this way to make forecasts, particularly where there is a need for a cheap, fast and rather mechanical method to make forecasts for a large number of items. It is undoubtedly a simple method with wide applications.

The smoothed value at time *t, St,* is a weighted average of the observed value at time *t, yt,* and all the other past (historical) values in the series: *y (t-1), Y(T-2)* and *Y1*. This is not immediately obvious from the way in which the smoothed values are calculated. In practice, *S1,* the first value in the series of smoothed values, is set equal to *y1,* the first actual value in the series. Then for each new time period the new smoothed value is @ times the current observed value of *y* plus *1-@* times the previous smoothed value of *y*, where @, the smoothing constant, is a fraction between 0 and 1 which can be altered.

So *St* = *@yt* + *(1-@)St-1*

If @ is too large, too much weight is given to current values as they occur, and if too small, changes that are actually changing place will not be captured.

Exponential smoothing tends to give reasonable results when there is no randomness present in the observations and when there is no strong seasonal element present. In other words, it is not highly suitable for commodity forecasting and is not used by the professional forecasters. If they tried to suggest it to traders, the seasonal point would be made to them immediately and in no uncertain terms. Even advocates of the method admit, however, that it does not include such factors as weather, industrial or economic conditions, or the role of the prices of substitutes. All of these are especially important in commodities, because they apply both at the growing level, in terms of alternative use of productive resources (mainly land) and at the retail level (between alternative fibres for instance). Exponential smoothing models are however the most widely used forecasting models in the world. Their robustness makes them suitable for use in the absence of appropriate leading indicators, and when the data are too short or too volatile for Box-Jenkins. The method is held to be more effective in non-commodity markets, where there is no seasonality and there is randomness. And the argument that the future of commodity prices is more likely to be dependent on the recent past than the more historical periods, is demonstrably false.

It is certainly the case that models of commodity prices based on exponential smoothing methods should be approached very critically and, even if they can be demonstrated to have predicted accurately in the past, they may be highly unlikely to do so in the future as the parameters are almost certain to change. It is this which one suspects is at the root of much institutional resistance to the updating and testing of models by comparison to their construction.

Event models further extend exponential smoothing by providing adjustments for special events such as sales promotions, strikes or other unusual occurrences. The program can be adjusted for events of several different types. The models work in a similar way to seasonal index models. Each type of event, rather than every month, gets its own index, which is updated every time a similar event occurs. The difference between seasonal adjustment and event adjustment is that events can occur at irregular intervals. Multiple level exponential smoothing allows the aggregation of data into groups that can be reconciled using a top-bottom or a bottom-up approach. For commodities, this approach may be useful in amalgamating origins of a single commodity and on into groups of origins. Geographic amalgamation works on the same principle.

Census X-11 factors a time series into its major constituents, the output from which represents the trend-cycle, seasonal, trading day and irregular components. This is the procedure that the US government, for example, uses to obtain deseasonalized estimates of major macroeconomic indices. Cumulative forecasting and confidence limits are used to compute safety limits for stocks, to take another example.

The commodity application of time series models

There is little relative complexity to time series analysis by comparison to some of the more complex econometric models. Univariate time series analysis, the simplest, does not attempt any causal explanation of a time series in terms of anything other than itself. It bears an uncanny closeness to technical analysis in this regard, and makes clear the important distinction outlined in the introduction between methodologies that seek to predict through explanation, and methodologies that seek to predict through patterns. These models explain nothing, but they can produce good short-term forecasts and they need little data and are therefore cheap. More sophisticated forms can take into account cross-correlations between data series in transfer function analysis. There are numerous technical descriptions of time series analysis. For the average trader, it must be clear, even from the cursory description of time series modelling techniques given above, that a full understanding of all time series modelling options is a discipline in itself. It is not compatible with full-time active trading. What suffices for the trader and the policy-maker is:

- A knowledge of the available software;
- The ability to understand in general terms why particular forecasting procedures differ in their outcomes from one another;
- A robust insistence that it is forecasting results that matter for a forecast, not explicative power or the ability to analyse many scenarios.

Time series methods have often been applied to basic commodity variables to explain and to try to forecast basic commodity variables. In the past, time series variables have been univariate, but since the 1980s time series methods of a multivariate type can deal with several commodity prices simultaneously. Univariate models have been applied to commodity variables, to derive a representation of the generating mechanism of a commodity market variable such as price. Typically, the behaviour of a weakly stationary time series can be formulated as embodying autoregressive, (AR), moving average (MA) or a combination (ARIMA) processes. Autocorrelation with data produces the need for these autoregressive integrated moving average processes.

These models have been used as alternatives to structural models for the purpose of price forecasting. In comparison with structural, econometric models, ARMA-type models can be seen to provide more accurate forecasts on a number of occasions, an admission which it is important to wring from econometric modellers. Clearly, however, ARMA models may fail to take account of all possible sources of information, most particularly and most obviously the impact of influences on the dependent variable external to the model. Econometricians expert in commodity forecasting generally believe that a unconnected commodity prices over time can most generally be represented by a multivariate ARMA process. That is a bold assertion of which traders should take note. Such models can posit any type of causal relationship between different commodity variables. But because of the difficulties involved in identifying and estimating them, with non-linear coefficients, the models have generally been simplified for actual forecasting work.

It is a clear enough problem to understand: if the causal links are correctly depicted—and these can actually be worked out—then it is a search for ever more intricately connected and distantly correlated variables that will determine the accuracy of the forecasts of the model. If not, then the model may not predict with any accuracy.

Producing forecasts from an ARMA model is straightforward, but the computations can be long, although easily handled now on most PCs. For a stationary model, the forecasts converge to the mean of the series but, for a non-stationary model, the forecasts diverge from the mean. There can also be a deterministic time trend, which can be monthly or annual linear deterministic, quadratic or proportional.

Box-Jenkins

Box and Jenkins rightly emphasized the principle of parsimony. The model to adopt is the simplest adequate model, that which contains the fewest coefficients needed adequately to explain the behaviour of the observed data. Indeed, the great exception to the forecasting rule of greater complexity = more accuracy, is time series analysis based on the Box-Jenkins approach. Time series models used in the Box-Jenkins methodology are autoregressive (AR) and moving average (MA) models.

In particular, under Box-Jenkins, a model is identified which seeks to explain the current value of a variable in terms of its past values—called the 'autoregressive' component or AR and the 'moving average' component or MA—hence they are commonly called ARIMA (autoregressive integrated moving average) models. ARIMA models use either past values (the autoregressive model), past errors (the moving average model) or combinations of averages and errors (ARIMA). A single equation ARIMA model states how any value in a single time series is linearly related to its own past values.

The general multivariate ARIMA model is usually expressed as a dynamic simultaneous equation model (also known as a *simultaneous transfer function model*). This can be done when the time series for the relevant commodity can be isolated, and compared to some leading indicator economic trends as well as its own history as inputs, together with an ARIMA process of the error term. It is possible to test the one-way causality hypothesized in such a model and the lag structure of the variables and the error term can be specified using time series techniques. A correctly-specified ARIMA model generates minimum mean squared error forecasts among all linear univariate (single-series) models with fixed coefficients. For each time period, it is possible to produce a single-value forecast, called a *point forecast*. It is also possible to construct a confidence interval around each point forecast to generate an interval forecast. Interval forecasts are supposedly useful because they convey the possible degree of error associated with the point forecast. Too often, however, they are used as escape routes for forecasters in eluding the provision of specific forecasts to decision-makers.

An ARIMA model can, however, be used both for simulation and forecasting. Any forecast from an ARIMA model is a weighted average of past values of the series. Modellers hope that any ARIMA model they build is a useful approximation of the true underlying process, which it is not possible to observe.

The Box-Jenkins method is widely considered to be well suited to dealing with complex time series—such as commodity prices and quantities—and other forecasting needs where the underlying pattern and in particular the underlying causes (and statistical series for them) are not readily observable or believable. But there is a need for at least 72 observations, although this is rarely a problem for time series analysis for commodities where usually—but not always—long series of approximately consistent data are almost invariably available. In most cases finding several hundred observations presents no difficulty. The basic idea is to follow an iterative approach to identify a possible model from a range of alternatives. The selected model is checked against the actual data to see if it can forecast, and if not, it is replaced by another.

The Box-Jenkins approach is definitely used to forecast stock prices on a daily basis and for energy and other commodity forecasts by both trading companies and users of commodities ranging from retailers to utilities. How is this done? 'A general method of finding a suitable model is to use a backwards elimination procedure in an analogous way to its use in multiple linear regression...the modeller starts by fitting a large order state space model—for instance order 4 or 5. If any of the parameter estimates are too small to be significantly different from zero (so that the ratio of parameter estimate divided by standard error is less than, say 2 in absolute value) then the modeller sets the least significant parameter (the one with the lowest non-significant ratio) to zero and refits the model.' Only one parameter can be eliminated at once.[1]

[1] *Janacek and Swift, p 113.*

Structural time series models

These are a class of time series models in which the observations are modelled as a sum of clearly separate components. As structural models are easily placed in state space form they can be estimated using the Kalman filter and state space techniques. As with seasonal ARMA models, the order of the state can become manifold for state space estimation. This is easily done by appropriate software. It has been claimed that 'The immediately apparent advantage of structural models is that their form is suggested by the data, and that they can be decomposed into easily interpretable components. In addition, the models have few parameters, are relatively easily estimated, and component estimates for each time period can be obtained through the smoothing equations. Conversely, structural models pose considerable restrictions on the autocorrelation structure which a given time series may not conform to, and a suitable structural model may not be available.'[1] Structural models are especially useful for large and/or seasonal models where the number of parameters would become unwieldy if an ARMA model were used, and identification would become a problem. Experts therefore recommend the option of retaining software capable of structural forecasting for commodity analysis and forecasting.

Experts have concluded that: 'Such models can be particularly useful for forecasting variables such as crop yields, where theoretical explanation of variations through time is problematic. Since detailed analysis of the characteristics of data is the whole basis for the method, however, accurate data are essential'[2]. Clearly, the longer the data run, the better. Such models have yet to be fully integrated into most available commercial software, but they present no insuperable problems in this regard.

Mathematical programming models

These describe flows of a commodity between different producing and consuming regions. Prices and demands are exogenously determined. Quantities traded are based on the minimization of transport costs. The exogenous nature of the price and demand data must render even the more complex of the linear programming spatial equilibrium or transportation models of doubtful utility as far as commodity forecasting is concerned. However, more complex formulations are possible, in which the use of

[1] *Janacek and Swift, pp 194-195.*

[2] *Hallam, p5.*

quadratic programming can render prices endogenous to the model and ensure that some forecasting results can be obtained from such a model. Dynamic and recursive programming models can solve over a number of different time periods, again a necessary function for the overwhelming majority of forecasts.

Clearly, this description demonstrates what is often the case with models. The policy simulation function and the explanations of flows within a market often demands far more complexity in the construction of a model than does the demand for an accurate forecast.

Dynamic systems approaches

These generate a differential equation series based on flow representations of a given commodity market with all its feedback relationships. This approach can be used on a PC with software such as *Stella,* but it is not in widespread use. In the majority of cases, the functional relationships included in systems dynamics models are assumed, not estimated statistically from historical data, reducing their utility for forecasting purposes.

Regression models

In regression analysis, it is assumed that the output—in the case of commodity forecasting the price of the commodity or the supply or demand (*Y*)—may be linearly related to the inputs (the *X*s) by means of fixed coefficients. By linear is meant 'linear in the coefficients'. However, within this framework, it is also possible to construct relationships that are nonlinear in the variables. It is also assumed that the relationship between the output and the inputs is stochastic. The inputs do not perfectly predict the output. This imperfection is represented by an additive stochastic disturbance term that represents all variation in the output that is not associated with movements in the inputs and is responsible for errors in the model. The output *Y* is often called the 'dependent' variable, and the input *X* is called the 'independent' variable.

$$\text{In } Y = bX + a + C$$

In this equation, *b* is the average change in *Y* to be expected given a single unit change in *X,* a is the stochastic disturbance term, normally assumed to be zero about a mean and normally distributed 'white noise' level. White noise is the term usually given to any sequence of mutually independent and identically distributed random variables) with a constant variance. *C* is the estimated constant which captures the effect of all the excluded independent variables on the overall level of Y for a single Y and X or indeed a sample.

In order to obtain a good fit using regression analysis and achieve a high degree of accuracy, it is necessary to be familiar with the statistics that relate to regression. The correlation coefficient R measures the degree of correlation between Y and X. The range of values that it can have are between -1 and 1: total correlation either inverse or positive. More widely used is the coefficient $R2$, knocking out the negative values and providing a good indicator of the closeness of fit of the equation(s), the proportion of the total variation in Y that is explained by a movement in X. $R2$ is therefore a raw measure of the percent of the total sum of squares that is explained by the Xs. This, the coefficient of determination, has values of between 0 and 1. It is this coefficient which is used in the equations that generate statements like '30 per cent of the variation in grain prices is explained by weather factors'. Clearly, a low $R2$ means that there are other factors which are more important than the identified X in determining Y.

The standard error of the estimate, designated *Se*, is defined as the standard deviation of the regression. There are also prediction confidence intervals and standard errors of the regression statistic and t-statistics. The latter measure the statistical significance of the independent variable X in measuring the dependent variable Y. The t-statistic measures how many standard errors the coefficient is away from zero. This is more relevant to multiple regressions, which have more than one regression coefficient.

Finally there is the *F-statistic*, which measures the overall significance of a regression equation. Almost all software regression packages show an F-statistic.

In choosing a sample regression line, it seems reasonable to choose a line that best fits the sample data according to some statistically approximate definition of 'best'. The residuals thus become as small as possible. The aim therefore is to choose the estimates C and b so that the sum of the squared residuals is minimized. A dynamic regression model states how an output (Yt) is linearly related to current and past values of one or more inputs ($X1t$, $X2t$ etc.). It is usually assumed that observations of the various series occur at equally spaced time intervals. So, while the output may be affected by the inputs, a crucial assumption is that the inputs are not affected by the outputs. This means, in practice, single equation models.

Similarly, it is possible to introduce deterministic events into regression analysis through the use of dummy variables. These can take the value of either 1 or 0 depending on whether they represent a process in operation (such as a governmental regulation) or not. The applicability of this process to commodity forecasting—rather than policy analysis, where it could be quite useful—must of necessity be quite limited. This is because there are few occasions when a discrete process of this kind can confidently be assigned time periods. A definite previously-announced change in government policy is probably the best example. Deterministic inputs can be used in regression models, whether single or multiple, to represent identified events. They are conventionally called *interventions*. They may also be used to account for unexplained outliers (unusual observations) in a time series, e.g. pulse, one-off, step interventions, or compound interventions. Obviously a time series may be interrupted by an intervention whose existence is unknown to the analyst. The effects are often slight—even on a forecast—but they can be substantial, depending on the timing and the nature of the event. It is easily possible to produce 'what if' forecasts by including or excluding specific determined events and this is part of the lure of modelling away from forecasting itself. In practice, single equation regression models are one of the most widely used statistical forecasting tools.

So a conventional linear regression model generates a set of observations which represent the regression of the transformed dependent variables on the transformed independent variables. Linear regression therefore facilitates the application of 'band spectrum regression' in which regression is carried out in the frequency domain with certain wavelengths omitted. Band spectrum regression is particularly useful for application to commodity forecasting because it can handle seasonality, variable error and the problem of serial correlation in the error term.

Issues and problems such as time-lagged relationships and feedback, mean that using ordinary single equation regression methods when feedback is present leads to inconsistent estimates of the parameters. As the sample size grows, the repeated sampling distributions of the estimates collapse onto values that differ from the parameters by unknown amounts. The model becomes progressively distorted and cannot produce accurate forecasts.

Over the past few decades, statisticians and economists have, as a result, tended to base their forecasts less on simple trend extrapolation or single equation models and progressively more on multiple regression techniques and multi-equation models. The emphasis has shifted toward the construction and estimation of an equation or system of equations that will show the effects of a number of different independent variables on the variable or variables one wants to forecast.

This is called multiple regression analysis. It involves the use of more than one variable, so that bX measures the effect but with $X2$ constant. There is no linear relationship between any of the X variables. With more than two independent variables, the prediction equation is represented as a hyperplane, which is yet more difficult to picture.

Where a simple regression is not good enough to provide a satisfactory fit, as evidenced by a low R-squared, the need for multiple regression is evident. One type of multiple regression is to use lagged variables in addition to current ones. Another is where relationships may be non-linear. There may be a likelihood that future price increases will be less for the same supply cut, or indeed more. Or there may be S-shaped or more complex responses to independent variables depending on a variety of institutional, trading, and informational—amongst other types—of constraints. When feedback exists, it is necessary to have a multiple equation framework to specify the relationship between inputs and outputs properly. It would be equally possible to use either a vector autoregressive moving average model or a series of regression models.

The time-varying coefficient model is another development of this approach. This permits the problems of parametric variation and instabilities in relationships between commodities to be addressed by assuming that a unit change in one independent variable, *ceteris paribus*, will not have a constant expected effect on each dependent variable at all points of time. Commodity modellers have thus explored the use of stochastic coefficient estimation based on a non-stationary or a time-varying random pattern to overcome some of these instabilities.

It is worth noting that forecasts using ARIMA methods and indeed regressions may often be of the transformed (log) function and this may require retransformation; straightforwardly doing so may produce the median not the mean of the transformation. Forecasting software does this automatically.

There are a number of potential difficulties with regression analysis which present themselves so frequently that they need consideration at an early stage. These include:

- *Causation* - Some underlying theory is demanded for causation—a statistical relationship between Xs and Ys could appear to be shown without there actually being one at all.

- *Colinearity* - This is correlation among the independent variables. i.e. if two or more of the Xs are statistically identical (perfectly correlated), then the least squares method cannot be used to analyse their separate effects. Colinearity is a matter of degree, not absolutes. Equations with multicollinearity may produce spurious results. Multicollinearity can be recognized when either the t-statistics of two seemingly important independent variables are low, or the estimated coefficients on explanatory variables have the opposite sign from that which was expected. The solution to the problem is either to drop one of the highly-correlated variables from the regression. Alternatively, the structure of the equation may be changed, either by dividing both the left- and the right-hand side variables by some series that will render the fundamental economic logic, but eliminate the multicollinearity, or by estimating the equation on a first difference basis, or by combining the collinear variables into a new variable, their weighted sum.

- *Autocorrelated disturbance* - This usually suggests that an important part of the variation of the dependent variable has not been explained. It is tested for with the Durbin-Watson statistic. In general, if this statistic is between 1.5 and 2.5, there is no autocorrelation; below 1.5 suggests positive autocorrelation, and above 2.5, negative autocorrelation. The best solution to the problem is to search for other explanatory variables.

A dynamic regression model is in fact a special type of vector ARMA model. Vector ARMA models are the next important class of time series models after univariate ARIMA models and dynamic regression models. Vector ARMA models involve a set of *K* equations that show how each of a set of *K* time series is linearly related to its own past and the past of the other *K-1* series in the set. Thus, vector ARMA models are capable of wider use than either univariate ARIMA or dynamic regression models since vector ARMA models can include both multiple series and feedback effects. If any of the equations in a vector ARMA model involves no feedback effects elsewhere in the set of equations, then this equation is separately a dynamic regression model or a univariate ARIMA model. However, to put a dynamic regression model embedded in a vector ARMA model into the familiar form of dynamic regression models may require substantial algebraic rearrangements. This is especially so when there are one or more contemporaneous relationships within the dynamic regression model.

Hence the idea of a simplified model, the *vector autoregressive model* (VAR) which assumes that the polynominals in the matrix of polynomials of the error process are of degree zero. A feedback relationship among the variables is often possible, resulting in the extrapolation of existing trends rather than a 'true' forecast. Some academics believe that VAR models are very suited for commodity forecasting purposes, but even they caution that '...the estimated coefficients often have no economic interpretation attached to them..'[1] On occasion, co-integration between the commodity variables employed in these models may be observed which calls for the application of co-integration modelling Over the last two decades, i.e. since 1976, many

[1] *Granger, 1986, and Engle and Granger 1987, p. xi.*

ideas relevant to regression forecasting such as these have arisen in time series literature.

Choices

Given that they are the two main choices, why use an ARIMA model instead of a regression model? How do they fit together? Pankratz suggests several possible reasons: Firstly, to check to see whether regression is useful; a disturbance series may be autocorrelated, so the modeller may be able to apply an ARIMA forecast to the disturbance itself. There may be a need to forecast the inputs themselves. These also may be able to be forecast with an ARIMA model, which may reveal something interesting or useful about the data. This may influence the way in which the data when building a regression model is chosen. Finally, ARIMA checks for stochastic inputs are needed to perform diagnostic checks of the regression model's efficiency and to compute standard errors for the regression model forecasts.

Conclusion

What it is absolutely vital to recognize is that forecasting is only part of the reason for the construction of econometric models as opposed to time series analysis. The analysis of alternative policy implications is another, equally valid, use for them, but it must not be allowed to swamp the forecasting need which has a different set of demands as far as modelling is concerned.

All econometric forecasters concede that the markets they seek to forecast are subject to structural change. Commodity model makers are no exception. The models always show their age, with hopelessly inaccurate parameters after a few years, which perhaps explains both why long-term forecasting has become so unpopular and also why models wither on the vine. The econometrics itself may also demand the variation of parameters, as do several trading systems alter their parameters, replacing complex non-linear relationships with simpler linear ones plus outliers that must be regularly altered. Some variables may have been omitted altogether and the use of proxy variables for unexplained causes and aggregate data may have the same effect.

Forecasts can be generated from either the reduced form or the structural form of a model. In either case, academics familiar with such equations, or computer software programmed to use them, will find the necessary actual computations straightforward and routine. Future values for the exogenous variables—known, forecast or assumed—are incorporated in to the estimated model which is then solved for as many periods as the forecast is to be run. Clearly if the forecast is wrong for the first period, the erroneous results of the first period will certainly feed through into the determination of the exogenous variables for the next period. The result will be that it will increase its error in subsequent periods.

In summary, advocates believe that commodity modelling is being enhanced and extended by several new developments. These include:

- Better and increased data sources;
- Integration with other types of models;
- Incorporation of policy considerations into the commodity modelling process;
- Examination of the interrelationships between commodities and resource allocation and the quality of the environment.

As far as forecasting in particular is concerned, it must be hoped that the new ability to process non-linear relationships in n-dimensions that faster PCs have generated and the greater appreciation of policy, technological and macroeconomic considerations (provided these also are accurately forecasted) will assist in improving the accuracy of commodity forecasts.

Concepts of modelling—a theoretical model and its determinants

There are, inevitably, many commodity market modelling techniques and approaches. These include standard econometric methods, time series analysis methods, linear and non-linear programming techniques, process and engineering modelling approaches, among others, together with combinations of several of these approaches and simplifications. It is constantly claimed by econometricians that commodity market modelling often relies on interdisciplinary approaches, because it interacts with a number of fields, for example:

- Agronomy, for agricultural commodity modelling;
- Various engineering fields for energy and mineral commodity modelling, especially when process models or linear or non-linear programming models are developed.

Academics prefer not to see commodity modelling as one homogenous professional area, as commodity experts would prefer. On the contrary, they view it as one which, in practice, consists of an amalgamation of agricultural economics, energy economics, mineral economics, marine economics and, to a lesser extent, commodity futures theory and financial economics. The methodologies are varied. They include econometric methods, mathematical programming, input-output analysis and systems simulation theory and methods. Applied mathematics and statistics, computer software and algorithmics, and mathematical economics or operations research are, of course, nearly always used as basic tools in commodity market modelling. Thus the modelling techniques derive from different economic fields or subdisciplines, such as agricultural economics, energy economics, marine economics and natural resource economics. All these are related to various neighbouring fields or disciplines. In addition, institutional and historical knowledge is very often indispensable, especially when market structures, regulated price mechanisms, externalities and other non-market phenomena are being analysed in quantitative market models.

The major effort in producing an econometric forecast is in the preparatory stages:

- The assembly of data for all the exogenous variables will take time. There is never any certainty that the model maker has found all the relevant data for regression analysis. Once data has been found, correlations with the variable to be forecast are relatively easy to determine. Some data is intuitively more likely to be influential and at least highly correlated with specific commodities, such as the price of competing crops, income, interest rates and consumer demand. There still remains the possibility that other determinants have been missed. There has never been an econometric forecast without an error term of some sort.

- The model's parameters may have to be re-estimated using the latest data. The specification may have to be changed because of structural changes in the economy. This is another way of saying that shocks of one variety or another make econometric forecasting extremely difficult, hence the need for the error terms (or 'residuals') from the re-estimated equations to be examined for any systematic variation which would indicate a failure to capture all the relevant data.

- Appropriate values must be specified for the exogenous variables over the forecast period. Clearly if these are incorrect the forecast will be wrong—consistently wrong, but wrong none the less.

Forecasters have a tendency to try to get round this possibility by sloughing off responsibility through the production of a number of different 'scenarios'. If they can get away with it in discussions with senior decision-makers, they will try to fudge the underlying assumptions of each scenario. They will make the 'forecast' reduce to 'The price of oil will be $25, $20 or $15 per barrel depending on [a variety of assumptions intermixed]'. These will then carefully be numbered scenarios 1, 2 and 3. Of course, whatever the eventual outcome, provided that it does not lie outside the boundaries set by scenarios 1 and 3, the forecaster will then be able to claim victory. The decision-maker, unfortunately, does not have that luxury. It is little use pointing out that 'Responsibility for assigning probabilities to the alternative scenarios rests with the decision-maker'[1] because, in all likelihood, the decision-maker has as little idea about the future values of the exogenous variables as of the forecast variable. For example, the future price of oil will, in large measure, depend on the future price of natural gas, and of course vice versa. The head of contingency planning at the CIA has hundreds if not thousands of problems and options to contend with. How is he supposed to know any more about natural gas prices than oil prices, if forecasts for oil prices are presented to him under a variety of scenarios for future natural gas prices?

The other potential source of error in an econometric forecast is the model itself. Thorough testing and model validation by comparing historical values with ones predicted by the model should limit the extent of forecast error caused by biased parameter estimates or specification error. There can still be problems, however, caused by unforeseen structural changes which render the model obsolete. One of the best examples of this, drawn from a slightly different area, is the way that the removal of mortgage rationing by the Conservative government in the 1980s made previous econometric forecasts of property prices invalid in predicting those years. There is no escape from this problem: using an econometric model based on historic data assumes, for the most part implicitly, that the statistical relationships and their estimated parameters observed in the past will continue to apply in the future. In general, if this were the case, the future would indeed be easily predictable. Forecasting would be much more of a science. Some relationships, notably those to do with weather, biology, genetics and accounting, can be expected to hold for a considerable time into the future, although even in this case, little can be assumed. Others, and awkwardly for forecasting in general, especially the relationship between price and physical factors, are notoriously variable. Technology, political constraints, and markets as a whole change rapidly and in quantum leaps. These changes where predictable can be incorporated as changing parameters. Where not, the model will almost inevitably go adrift.

[1] *Hallam, p 169.*

Clearly, models of commodity pricing represent an intersection of demand and supply functions. The World Bank rightly believes that improvements can still be made to supply function modelling, especially in the area of metals and energy. In some respects it is certainly easier to model supply for perennial crops, as data from plantings and other crop data can be integrated with response to government initiatives and previous prices.

Agricultural markets in general have certain long term characteristics:

- *Competitiveness.* There are usually a relatively large number of competing suppliers, a homogenous product (or at least with production relatively easily switchable between suppliers) and few barriers to entry.
- *Technological change.* Farms are increasingly mechanized and electrified. There have been recent major changes owing to genetic engineering being implemented for agricultural markets—such as IRRI rice, genetically-engineered glandless cotton, and artificial insemination of cattle and other animals. There have also been reductions in the other major area of technological innovation applied to agricultural production, the use of chemicals such as fertilizers and pesticides (e.g. herbicides, fungicides and insecticides).
- *Asset rigidity.* This characteristic is, however, declining over time and may, by the end of the next century, not be applicable to agricultural production at all. Land was always regarded, since at least the 18th Century in Western Europe, as a relatively fixed resource. Additional suitable land was not easy to put into production, and the value of the land in other uses was not high. Now that urban development is much more widespread, this no longer applies: in China, for instance, silk production is being displaced to new areas as former silk areas are turned over to infrastructure and housing development. It is still the case that durable capital goods, such as buildings, equipment and machinery, are so specialized that their use for other purposes is low.

Then there are specifics underlying each agricultural market. These relate to the agronomic and biological aspects of a given commodity and include commodity growth habits, susceptibility to changes in climate, storage problems and related issues, transport issues, and nutritional values. These vary widely across agricultural markets and include such issues as storage and reproductive cycles.

For most commodities, continuous market valuation implies that the value of the commodity does not change over time. In fact, this is a simplification. For example, in the case of living or biological inventories, such as cattle, eggs and seedlings, they do change in value as they come towards maturity. Even commodities such as rice and raw textiles change in value as they move from being 'new crop' to 'old crop', between which there can be significant price differences. The cyclical nature of the inventory of many agricultural commodities is linked with the life cycle of those commodities whose reproductive cycle is directly linked with supply response. The theory of this is clear enough. Suppose oysters take about one year for the creation of a pearl. Oyster breeding can start during a defined season, say March-May, but it will be a further year before the pearls are ready to be harvested and the oysters reach the market in June-October. In this case, an identifiable lag will exist between the time that the price signal arrives in the market and the supply response. This can and should be modelled in the supply function through the introduction of a lag in supply matched in periods in the model to the biological cycle.

It is also worth noting that some agricultural products are interdependent. The best example is lamb and wool in the UK, which are co-produced. Another is that feed grains such as corn and grain sorghum are inputs into the production of meat. So an increase in feed grain price causes more beef cattle to be fed on range land rather than feedlots. This in turn lowers the demand for feed grain and cuts its prices, causing then a lowering in the area planted to feed grain. There are many other such examples: domestically in Thailand and elsewhere, for example, rice and fish are co-produced.

Asset rigidity

The extent of asset rigidity and production switches between agricultural crops has been debated. In general, what appears to be the case is that the more technically advanced the machinery, and the more expensive, the more specialized its use. Within most agricultural economies, land, warehouses, equipment and machinery are fungible to a large extent. Some capital goods have much more limited uses, such as cotton gins, useful only for cotton. Clearly, the larger the extent of capital fungibility the more elastic the supply relationship for individual commodities will be. In other words, the speed and extent to which production can switch between agricultural commodities and in and out of the agricultural sector altogether, for example between soya and rice, will be determined by what alternative use can be made of machinery (and labour).

These supply assumptions have traditionally underpinned agricultural models. They have in part been responsible for the sorts of errors noted above. The response of a modeller is perforce limited by the changes that can be brought about in the model. They are particularly acute in global and national models, where separate sector models can result in more land use than is actually available, for example. Such errors can be cut down by making arbitrary adjustments based on analysing the residuals for each estimated equation for the periods just prior to the forecast period. Clearly, a run of positive or negative results may imply a corresponding tendency towards over or under prediction of the variable being forecast. The forecast can obviously be changed by the addition or subtraction of values predicted by appropriate changes in these residuals. Econometricians call these *intercept adjustments*, and in the context of a global forecast, *balancing terms* and they may obviously either be set as constants, or they may change according to patterns. They are, in a sense, a genuflexion by econometricians in the direction of the fundamental analysts. It may be that here is the most appropriate point of intersection between the two disciplines, on which further work of integration may subsequently take place.

Subtle judgements are anyway also usually made before decision-makers are presented with the final forecast. Expert opinion will modify the raw results and adjust the model's parameters according to their impressions of the results. This is made easier by the fact that the model will almost certainly have an explicit and accessible description of the market in which the forecast is being made incorporated into the structural form of the model. This process of modification represents the dovetailing of qualitative forecasting with econometrics. It is of course a process of which decision-makers faced with demands for resources to construct econometric models 'which the forecasters then disregard in favour of their hunches' are understandably highly suspicious. In many cases, they are simply not told. In terms of the desirable sequence for the integration of all the different approaches to forecasting outlined in this book, it must however rank highly.

Requirements for a model

The requirements of an effective multi-commodity econometric model are to some extent self-evident:

- The structure of the combined model should follow the natural organization of the individual markets in terms of seasons, capital use, price fluctuations and input combinations generally as well as export markets;

- The individual markets should be separable and, just as important, modular;

- The computations must be relatively easily performed, although with the advent of increased power PCs, this requirement—important even up until the end of the 1980s—can effectively now be dropped even for relatively inexpensive commercially available models.

Recent advances

Is the discipline improving? With regard to methodologies in commodity market model building, advocates of econometric modelling claim that there have indeed been recent developments and advances. These bring together new fields of application, new methodologies and novel economic analyses based on quantitative or econometric models. It has been claimed that the 1980s saw significant advances in the global modelling of commodity markets. According to the World Bank, which played a significant role in the development of these models, the advances were in the following areas:

- i) The theoretical specification of commodity price behaviour;

- ii) The increased emphasis, in common with all other areas of economics, on the modelling of imperfect markets;

- iii) The incorporation of the interrelationships between macroeconomic and commodity market variables (one of the least successful aspects of the developments of the 1980s, as argued below) for example in the analysis of commodity trade flows, which in the light of the complexity and significance of the GATT deal is not surprising. This work has tended to reinforce the importance of modelling as a policy analysis tool for examining 'what if' scenarios—a quite different role from forecasting;

- iv) In the specification of supply response, particularly in respect of perennial crops;

- v) The realization of complementarity between time series analysis and econometrically-estimated structural models.

It is noticeable that English academics have not played a significant role in any of these developments. The World Bank, the US Applied Econometrics Association and contacts throughout Continental Europe have been drawn into the web, but British institutions appear, at least from the publication lists that are available and discussions with them, to be outside this process to a large extent. This is in marked contrast with the 1960s and before, when the experts of the Royal Academy, such as Box and Jenkins, were at the forefront of statistical development and theory.

Duncan (World Bank 1988) presents the history of commodity market modelling as an upward sweep of complexity. It is quite noticeable that he does not do so in the terms that traders and all others actually involved in the commodity markets would without doubt like to see, i.e. a graph showing the increased accuracy of forecasts over time. Duncan explains that in the early 1980s, prices were modelled as a simple linear function of stocks. Thereafter, the rational expectations hypothesis was introduced into the specification of commodity prices. The model makers are aiming for the achievement of a non-linear specification of the relationship between prices and stocks within an expectational framework, and of thereby capturing the phenomenon of rapid bull and bear markets in commodity prices. This is laudable as a theoretical aim, but what is needed is a conclusive demonstration that this does actually result in more accurate forecasts. That is missing.

Experts at the World Bank in the 1980s, such as C.L. Gilbert, made strenuous attempts to demonstrate the relationships between macroeconomic variables and primary commodity prices. It is certainly the case that the argument in favour of incorporating these variables, especially since the 1970s when both interest and exchange rates became more volatile, is strong and persuasive. One obvious example is the relationship between the large increase in the external debt of developing country producing countries and the performance of prices in the commodity markets themselves. Another is the relationships between IMF sponsored structural adjustment programmes and commodity prices. In general, the idea is that commodity prices are a leading indicator of macroeconomic prices, though this is wholly unhelpful from the point of view of commodity forecasting.

Economists do believe that commodity prices can be leading edge indicators of overall price movement. This has led to interest in commodity prices in the early 1990s when inflation has been at historically low levels throughout the Western world and signs of renewed inflation are constantly being watched for, hence the interest in the revival of primary product prices in the mid-1990s. But what the leading indicator evidence means is that macroeconomic variables are of little use in predicting commodity prices—rather the reverse.

The first task, therefore, is to survey international commodity market modelling issues and methodologies. This should focus in particular on modelling methodologies and recent advances in them, such as new methods for the analysis of imperfect competition and developments in spatial analysis with linear and non-linear programming tools. The second task is to focus on new fields of application for the above methodologies, perhaps with a view to obtaining more and integrated funding. These include agricultural commodity markets with an analysis, in terms of rational expectations, of the international coffee agreement and a World Bank international fibre model which describes the world textile industry.

As far as mineral commodity markets are concerned, a new analysis of intermaterial substitution resulting from technical progress has been developed. New ideas on regression analysis in the frequency domain have been applied to the analysis of cyclical behaviour in the copper, lead and zinc markets. Finally, examples of novel energy commodity market models have been developed. These include an analysis of linkages between crude and refined petroleum product markets, which is based on a combination of linear programming and econometric approaches, and a new model of contract behaviour on natural gas markets.

There has also been some application of the new modelling ideas and methods to commodity futures markets. The debate over whether futures markets do in fact have destabilizing properties continues. Efforts have been made, albeit in incomprehensible language in most cases, to show these models can be employed to analyse important issues related to economic decision-making planning and forecasting in these markets.

Finally, some note should be made of attempts to introduce ideas from radical economics as to methods for evaluating shadow prices, in terms of environmental and externality costs, for natural resource goods. These are ideas that are increasingly taxing econometricians.

Imperfect competition

Until the 1980s, the general assumption for commodity market models was that of perfect competition. For a set of assumptions that was further away from reality one would be hard put to do better than perfect competition, as has frequently been observed. An unlimited number of suppliers and buyers, so that no one market participant can affect the price through their actions—does that sound like any known commodity market? Certainly, since the gradual demise of the International Commodity Agreements (for example for tin and coffee) and the rise of free market policies internationally, certain commodity markets have become at least somewhat more competitive. Some have experienced a growth in the number of participating firms or exporting countries, as silk is now doing and as has happened to the metal markets for aluminium, copper and nickel. But no commodity market should be thought of as perfectly competitive. Models based on imperfect competition will always be more useful. This is especially so since the number of commodity trading firms in a number of markets has actually shrunk—although this is certainly not true of all markets.

Despite the importance of equilibria in commodity markets, there can be therefore little doubt of the importance and greater relevance of imperfect competition in trade and production models. Hughes-Hallett (1994) argues that 'As a general modelling strategy it is reasonable to suppose that market prices and quantities follow probability distributions which are determined by the structure of the market, rather than by external circumstances and the particular decision rules adopted by market agents.'[1] Even varying this assumption to produce altered parameters maintains the modelling framework within the facts of high price volatility, persistent autocorrelation in prices, strong positive skews, kurtosis and upwardly unbounded prices.

In most commodity markets, there is a high probability of a large, rather than a small, price shock, because prices spend longer below than above their mean over time. In other words, there are price 'spikes'. This pattern of price and supply behaviours arises through the asymmetries of stockholding. The demand for stocks holds up prices even in times of low demand. But the paradigm of perfect competition used in agricultural and other bulk commodity models results in spatial price equilibrium models. These demonstrate poor performance in explaining trade patterns, although at least predictably. They predict fewer bilateral trades than occur and cause a high degree of equilibrium trade level change in response to small parameter changes. The point is that with these models, starting at any feasible point, global convergence is assumed. The assumption that industry output is bounded gives a natural feasible starting point. In econometric language, this is a vector of outputs for which all marginal profits are non-positive.

Two other significant econometric restrictions are that marginal profits are concave and that the Jacobian of marginal profits has a negative diagonal. Own effects on marginal profit dominate cross effects. The effect is that in such models if everyone raises output equally the change in marginal profits will be greater from own output raise than other producers' effects. Concavity of marginal profits is the most severe restriction. Marginal profit is the sum of marginal revenue and negative marginal costs. Negative marginal costs will typically be concave, even with increasing returns. Marginal revenue however may or may not be concave. Concave demand yields concave marginal revenue. A constant elasticity of demand yields convex marginal revenue and thus possible non-concave marginal profits.

[1] *Hughes-Hallett, 1994, p5.*

All these assumptions are enough to make an economist, let alone a trader, blanch with embarrassment. The problem remains therefore of how to introduce imperfect competition. There can be little doubt that for econometrics there can be no challenge greater than that of considering equilibria under imperfect competition. How, for example, is it possible to incorporate technical characteristics into models of commodity market behaviour, e.g. how changes in the energy efficiency of a capital good will affect its costs of production? This process must contribute to introducing more realistic descriptions of institutions, technologies and markets into formal commodity models, especially in the long-term. There are some examples in the recent literature[1], but they are infrequent and dense, and hence of little use in the practice of commodity forecasting. What is necessary are easily accessible commercial imperfect competition models.

Another important function of modelling has traditionally been to assess the role of government and agencies in markets. The focus of attention in agricultural and commodity markets has always been the price at which trade takes place. In practice, the stability of prices is seldom a goal in itself. Price support schemes have been widely used as a means of raising prices, stabilizing consumers' expenditure or improving the functioning of the market. Although governments and producers often claim that the volatility of prices constitutes a prima-facie case for stabilization, price stabilization in practice usually serves as an intermediate target for a wider range of objectives. For agricultural policy, consensus policy is usually interpreted for model purposes as the survival of a minimum number of farms, arbitrarily set but defined within models as the consequence of a certain output level (usually) together with the stability of producer income levels and or consumer expenditures in the long term. A free market solution implies a much greater variability of income and expenditures than would occur by a non-separable stabilization scheme about the free market trajectory. Thus proponents of strict free-market policies must be prepared to accept greater risk to their future survival than would otherwise be necessary.

The experts say that 'Endogenizing government policy in trade analysis has taken two directions. One direction has been to assume that government policy is determined by domestic political factors and not by market power considerations. The focus of such work is on government objectives in the policy-setting process—non-economic factors are used to explain trade. A second approach to analysis with endogenous government

[1] *For example, C.D. Kolstad and L. Mathiesen, Computing Equilibria in imperfectly competitive commodity markets, ICMM, pp 51-70*

policy is to assume that such policy is motivated by economic factors; in essence, policy serves to coordinate producers and consumers so that they may exercise power in the international market.'[1] This analysis dates from the 1970s and means that international trade comes out as an oligopoly/oligopsony (i.e. with a small number of both sellers/buyers, each able to influence price through their actions).

Excluding the studies based on rational expectations, there is every indication that the question of dynamic specification in econometric models of mineral commodities, for example, is generally treated on an ad hoc basis. Yet it is precisely the case that a model's ability to explain cyclicalities of a certain nature is primarily dependent on its dynamic specification. In particular, in mineral industries where the speeds of adjustment are low and lags are lengthy, the specification of appropriate lag structures is essential for constructing realistic models. The demand equations perform well for all three 'new methodologies' for example.

Much of the analysis on commodity futures markets focuses usefully on partial equilibrium frameworks. However, linkages amongst markets implied by general equilibrium representations show that such analyses can suffer from serious limitations. In particular, studies of futures market efficiency which search for single series *martingale* or *random walk* processes cannot be expected to classify markets correctly. Linkages among markets mean that inefficiencies in one market may be transmitted to related markets. Nowhere is this more likely to be evident than in commodity futures markets. Since these markets reflect price expectations, differential information flows in the various markets will generally result in varying speeds of adjustment to causal forces. Market-specific shocks frequently can result from droughts and other weather-related phenomena. Linkages between exchange rates, interest rate markets and commodity markets are hard to track reliably. For forecasting purposes in commodities, exogenous assumptions about interest rates and other financial variables, if they are crucial to the model, render it a pliable tool of the key financial forecasts.

When prices change in response to a shock, it is often difficult to establish how much overall welfare is reduced. General equilibrium welfare measures go some way to being able to estimate this loss. Allowing for varying flexibility among exchange rates, interest rates and commodity markets and dynamic linkages among these various markets, overshooting is revealed as a common empirical phenomenon. Although interest rate, exchange rate and commodity markets are all shown by the estimated

[1] *ICMM, p.53.*

vector ARMA model to overreact to an initial shock, commodity markets (corn, cotton and wheat) do so to a much greater degree. However, the period length of this overreaction, for a major portion of the degree of disequilibrium is much shorter for the agricultural commodity markets. In the context of resource allocation decisions, the dynamic welfare measures reported suggested that the cotton and yen markets had the greatest loss as a proportion of the total consumer and producer surplus in each. For comparable elasticities of supply and demand, the total welfare losses were found to be the largest in the short-term interest and Japanese yen exchange rate markets.

Agricultural modelling

These models are many and varied, but they do have certain common characteristics. Accumulated evidence suggests that the demand for food is relatively price inelastic. People will forego other goods rather than food when food prices increase. Numerous studies have used single (sometimes simultaneous) equation econometric techniques to estimate the price elasticity of demand for food. The flip side of this is that the income elasticity of demand for food, especially in developed countries, is also low. If this sounds like econo-speak, it amounts to something very intuitively plausible: if prices fall by 20 per cent, consumption will increase by less than 20 per cent; if prices rise by 20 per cent, consumption will decrease by less than 20 per cent; if income falls by 20 per cent, consumption will fall by less than 20 per cent; if income rises by 20 per cent, consumption will rise by less than 20 per cent. The very plausible eventual conclusion of these studies is that, especially for developed countries, the overall demand level for agricultural commodities is determined by population levels.

When combined with the supply constraints and assumptions of agricultural markets and the specific features of each market, these assumptions form the basis of agricultural modelling. The combination of supply and demand factors in agricultural markets, often caused by weather factors, can and often does cause wide fluctuations in prices. Every factor is important in sector modelling in the aggregate.

Models ought to be able to be used to trace through the impact of sudden shocks causing wide fluctuations in prices. For example, if a drought causes a rise in farm gate prices in Country *A*, an increase in import demand will likely follow. This will cause a follow-on increase in prices in Country *B* supplying that export demand, and the factors of production used in agriculture will increase. These factors will be left in use when demand subsequently falls. Agricultural price cycles reflect both biology/technology and economic factors, and are therefore not of a fixed length. This entire cycle is what an agricultural model should be able to track accurately.

For each individual commodity market, the nature of the assumptions discussed above are different. For example consumers' demand for pearls may be more income sensitive than for rice. Substitutability between different commodities may be quite different in scope, and it may not work the way that looks superficially plausible. On first sight, a pearl may not have a substitute at all, whilst rice would appear to have many. But it may be that pearls can be substituted by a variety of other quite different gems. On the hand, the population of a certain country may be enormously inflexible in shifting away from a rice-based diet, and even between types of rice, and prepared to pay heavily for their insistence. Precisely this is seen in some Middle Eastern rice markets, in fact.

■ An example

One example of an econometric model might be—it has been done many times—to create a simulation study using a quarterly model of the world coffee market. There are many types of such model and the example which follows can only be taken as typical. In this model, producing and importing countries are assumed to maximize the expected utility of the present value of profits over a two-period time period. They buy and sell on the spot market, hold inventories, and hedge or speculate on the futures market. Expectations are assumed to be rational, i.e. they are equal to the conditional expectation given the model and information up to the current period. The spot and futures markets clear at each time period. Traders and analysts will immediately recognize all the simplifying assumptions here. In the real world such efficient profit maximizing is not possible owing to information constraints; expectations are rarely rational, and markets do not necessarily clear. Such a model can only be estimated for periods when the quota system of the International Coffee Agreement did not operate. The aim of particular work in the early 1980s was twofold. The first objective was to demonstrate the underlying mechanics of the market—or at least the dominant ones. The second was to analyse the impact of a substantial increase in production on prices, disappearance and inventory formation and of several policy measures aimed at reducing an imbalance between demand and supply on the coffee market by reducing production.

The model was run under the assumption that there was no ICA and that an international quota system has been agreed upon which becomes effective as soon as the spot market falls below a certain level. Attention was also paid to the impact of the distribution of initial inventories over exporting and importing countries. The working of such models demonstrated that it was possible to solve a medium-size model for an international commodity market assuming rational behaviour of the agents under uncertainty. Similar results are of importance for the discussions about price stabilization through international agreements aimed at restricting trade through a quota system.

Another example of a substantial commodity model was an attempt to model the whole of the world textile industry in the late 1980s. This was the first time that this had been attempted—previous models focused on single country or fibre. The model's authors in this case at once conceded that the complexity of the textile industry as well as limitations on data precluded modelling every stage of the industry. This cotton model consists of a cotton fibre component and a cotton textile component. The two components are separately solved but are linked through cotton manufactured into textiles. Quantities are measured in raw fibre equivalent in both models. Only a single quality of cotton and cotton textiles is considered, even though many grades of cotton are produced and traded (see Figure 6.1). Cotton prices are simultaneously determined with net trade, mill demand and the level of ending stocks. Prices are inversely related to the level of ending stocks in any one period. The ending stocks of each period become available for use in the next period.

The model adjusts to changes in economic conditions such as income or the price of a substitute crop by adjusting cotton fibre and textile prices, production, trade, consumption and stocks. A similar model is presented for the synthetic fibre sector (Figure 6.2). The total textile price is composed of the individual textile fibre prices and other demand and production cost factors. In the model, each textile fibre price enters the total textile fibre price in proportion to its share in textile production. For example, in the model, a change in the price of a non-cellulosic textile such as nylon would increase the price of total textiles and also cut the proportion of nylon in total textile production.

To use this model to project future demand use, 'The solution was derived with fibre prices exogenous and growing at historical trend rates. When the model was run, in 1990, the assumption was made that there would be three areas of demand: the western economies, developing economies *and the CPEs*'. This is a good example of a model being transcended by the sweep of major historical events and it is instructive to compare this model with the ICAC cotton models described in detail below. Clearly CPE demand, however pessimistically forecast, would have been unlikely to reflect at all accurately the collapse in demand that has been seen in these countries in the 1990s.

Mineral modelling

Mineral modelling inevitably possesses many of the same needs as agricultural modelling and is another branch of commodity modelling. For

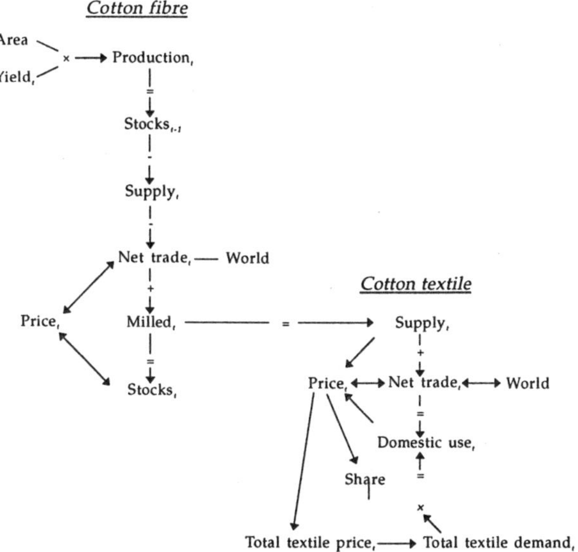

Figure 6.1 Cotton fibre flowchart

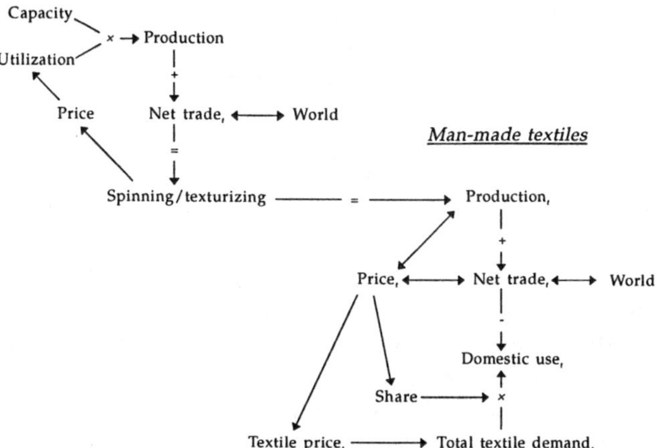

Figure 6.2 Flowchart of synthetics model

example, risk and uncertainty issues arise because of the uncertainty regarding geological deposits and that related to changes in exogenous variables such as the impact of inflationary and recessionary conditions on mineral demands. The modelling of price expectations is likewise important. So is the modelling of markets in disequilibrium, particularly since mineral markets have a complex array of stock-flow interactions. Also, government intervention is strong in many of these markets.

The mineral modellers say that they still need to explain better the intertemporal linkages or the dynamic adjustment process existing between the price signals or expectations and the responses that occur in exploration, mine development, process capacity expansion, etc. In practice, there has been little advancement in this area since the 1970s, partially because mineral investors do not appear to exhibit the same producer price response as that displayed by producers of perennial tree crops. Mineral investors appear instead to focus on market share objectives or some more complex profitability goals. Other models look at market expectations based on forward information and market dynamics. This series of observations, from those involved in mineral modelling, does seem to reflect the perhaps inevitable conviction by specialist modellers that other markets are easier to model. Agricultural modellers probably insist that mineral markets are easier to model than agricultural ones, and probably for much the same reasons.

A second need is to model the imperfect market structure that exists in mineral markets. Pure monopoly is rare and pure competition is found only occasionally. Most mineral markets have intermediate market structures whose behaviour structures are often bilateral oligopoly. In general, no extensive modelling of imperfect mineral market structures has taken place. This is a shaming admission, and reflects the complexity of so doing.

Regarding the explanation and prediction of minerals demand, modelling activity has been hampered because of the complex nature of mineral substitution patterns. Non-fuel minerals are often substitutes for each other. And mineral and non-mineral substances can often be substituted for each other in production and consumption. Substitution is therefore an important aspect of mineral modelling. If producers are cost minimizers, they will substitute one input for another when the relative price changes. How far they can do this depends on the feasible production possibilities. These will condition the impact of price on production change. Where substitution is costly, the change in factor prices may be asymmetric, for example permanent shifts away from the use of certain commodities after high price levels.

Modelling methods that are based on statistical inference from past data tend to be quite good at capturing and predicting marginal material substitution decisions which lie within the range of historical experience.

They are not so good, however, at handling substitutive decisions that occur as a result of large changes in price and availability of materials. Neither are they adept at handling markets responses that are asymmetric, for technological, institutional or consumer preference reasons. Forecasting methods based on more explicit engineering assumptions tend to be better at capturing the latter forms of substitution. However, engineering-orientated methods tend to be weaker at capturing the magnitude of substitution possibilities that derive from relative price changes, because price is typically difficult to integrate into the engineering analysis. There have been a number of examples in recent years that testify to this phenomenon, not the least being the systematic underestimation of the response of energy demand to higher prices. Engineering models suffer from the need for exogenous substitution assumptions on the basis of price, and therefore the need for an integrated model horizon, of which there are very few.

Another important mineral modelling need is to recognize that the mineral commodities used and traded within industrial requirements normally involve different stages of process and production. These can include mining, ore treatment (milling and concentration) reduction (smelting), purification (refining) and consumption by fabricators. Recycled material is an important process input for many mineral flows and many enter the supply flow at several stages. Models have been created which analyse production technologies, accounting for the important inputs (labour, energy and materials requirements) at each stage of the production process. This, in turn, demands the construction of equations representing technological and engineering production possibilities. Usually the overall production flow has been disaggregated into elementary process routes. Input-output parameters are derived from each stage of each route on the basis of engineering data. For each process, programming techniques can be used to select from among the various production options those that optimize pre-set goals. A process model can also lend itself to demand analysis by permitting a link to be made between final product demands and derived material demands. National economic activity can be used as a proxy for final product demand, but as ever, this makes the accuracy of the model for forecasting purposes depend on the accuracy of the macroeconomic forecasts utilized. But the process models are able to explain the derivation of subsequent processes for minerals.

Mineral modelling is also closely tied to inter-industry behaviour patterns. Minerals are themselves inputs to different industries which themselves create fabricated or manufactured outputs. This need has been partially met by using input-output techniques for models. These techniques have become more complex in recent years, but the objectives have remained more or less the same: to account comprehensively for the gross output of any economy by dividing it into sectors. The resulting matrices can be considered as a series of producing sector-requirements equations. These requirements are in each case dependent, according to parameters stated in the matrix, on final demand variables, and also on other intermediate industry variables further up the production chain. The effect of varying sector production and the parameters themselves can be analysed.

Mineral models also examine the strategic needs of industrial economies and their reaction to potential supply cutbacks. This is a good example of the different practical use of models and forecasts. A model which is capable of analysing in a static universe, so far as the rest of the world is concerned, the effect of a cutback in oil supplies to the West on oil prices may be quite useless for forecasting purposes. Why? Firstly, oil price levels will be set in a dynamic environment and, secondly, the model will treat oil supplies as an exogenous factor, an input, whereas the supplies themselves need to be forecast in order to forecast of oil prices. What this means is that the majority of mineral models are neither suitable for nor used for forecasting purposes.

Metals modelling

Industrial activity explains the largest portion of the cyclical variations in the consumption of these metals. This might seem intuitive for the higher frequencies but the fact that it is also valid for longer-term cycles is important. Combined with the fact that the estimated gains are larger than unity, this result shows that long-term fluctuations in total industrial activity are amplified. This is reflected in the consumption of these metals. Demand responses to their respective prices, by contrast, are limited. Own price variables are only marginally significant in the case of copper, and not significant for lead. Only for a few less common metals, such as zinc, and then only under some circumstances, can a cyclical interaction between consumption and prices be accepted with certainty. The same is true for the price of each substitute. Capacity utilization equations show a good fit for most metals. Capacity utilization has a significant association with industrial activity, as well as with prices. As for gain coefficients, when capacity utilization demonstrates significant correlation with industrial activity, the estimated gain values are greater than unity. Price gains, however, are in general smaller than unity. The implication is that cyclical variations in prices are attenuated by these equations. Time is the cause: more than 87 per cent of the variations in copper capacity were explained by a simple regression on time in one study, but only 49 per cent for lead and 33 per cent for zinc.

The dependence on industrial activity is heartening in one way: it suggests that metals at least are far from being leading indicators and that once armed with an accurate industrial forecast, a medium-term metals forecast cannot be far behind.

It appeared from that particular study that the results of detrending have been severe in that the residual variations in copper and lead capacities are very small. Quite contradictorily, it also suggests that capacity formation in the copper industry behaves in such a way as to follow a simple linear trend. Should this implication be true, then one must conclude that producers have increased their productive capacity consistently, even while facing wide fluctuations in prices, demand and short run supply. Could it be that this provides a confirmation of one popular belief that mineral investors prefer to neglect price signals and instead base their investment decisions on the desire to maintain or expand corporate market shares over time? This is certainly what happened with synthetic fibre producers in the 1970s and it strongly looks as if this cycle is being repeated in the 1990s.

Energy modelling

This sector has been consistently regarded as vital since the oil shocks of 1973-74 and has generated some important modelling needs. The importance of oil as a major energy source has created the need for models—crude oil and petroleum products are by far the most important commodities in international trade, whether by weight or monetary value.

Although the impression of declining stocks has reduced since then, it is recognized that crude oil prices are leading indicators of other prices. Oil modelling is useful in terms of such developments and also for energy economy models which, in turn, link with macroeconomic developments.

To meet the needs of explaining energy demands and supplies, standard commodity models (SCMs) have been applied because they usually employ a set of refined theoretical assumptions which underlie their equilibrium properties. Their dynamics usually rest on some lagged variable dependencies, which are more or less complex depending on the selected model details. Starting with sectoral models, the highly erratic nature of oil markets in the 1970s spawned the consideration of time series modelling techniques, for example the 'gross product worth' model of the Rotterdam spot market developed by BP. In this model, finite difference time lag equations are replaced by continuous differential equations. First order, second order and higher order finite difference equations, describing one-period, two-period and higher lag dependencies, are equivalent to, respectively, first order, second order and higher order differential equations. First order equations will, in general, generate smooth time solutions such as exponential functions.

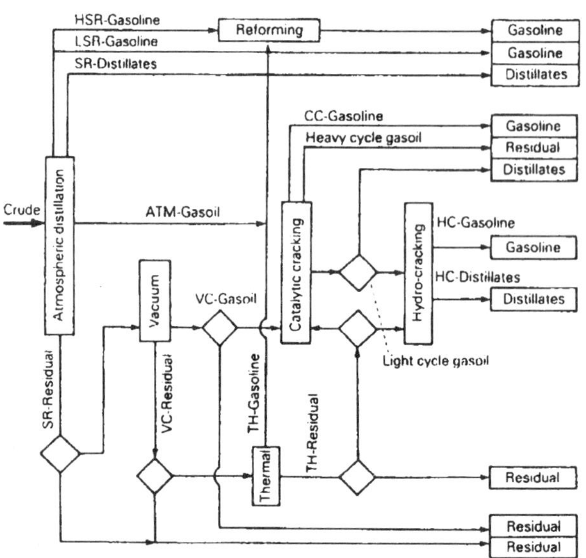

Figure 6.3 The refining of crude oil

To meet requirements for explaining energy demand and supply, it is necessary to use models that employ theoretical assumptions that generate equilibrium. Such models' dynamics rest on some lagged variable dependencies that vary in complexity. Such long-term models are usually divided into two types:

- i) Recursive simulation models, in which economic agents' behaviour results from their 'memory' of past and present events and economic variables.

- i) Intertemporal optimization models, in which oil producers maximize their discounted future rents according to theories of exhaustible resources.

Neither of these methodologies models oil supply entirely accurately, especially in explaining what happened in 1986, although recursive models can describe both the other shocks. Intertemporal optimization problems have difficulties in explaining both 1979-80 and 1986.

Why do all these models have difficulty, especially in handling 1986? Firstly, because of the need within models to provide a better than crude description of the oil market structure, for example the Stackelberg approach of allowing a price war through price cuts aimed at increasing market share. The introduction of complex market structures is one of the new directions toward which oil models, *inter alia,* are now oriented. Also, as noted by Gately and Rappoport (1988) the potential for energy savings through energy conservation policies or energy conservation management at the microeconomic level has not been adequately captured. For example, the short-term impact of energy conservation actions between 1974-79 has been overestimated, probably thus contributing to the failure of the models to represent the second oil shock of 1979-80. Conversely, the longer-term impact of energy conservation has probably been underestimated, thus contributing to difficulties in representing the reversed oil shock of 1986.

Second and higher order equations are more interesting to econometricians because they are better able to depict oscillatory and more varied, chaotic behaviour which are in fact more common in observed time series. The formulation of models embodying these properties can be seen in well-known statistical approaches such as linear and non-linear trend fitting, autoregressive integrated moving average ARIMA methods, transfer functions and vector autoregression. These methods have been used mostly for the analysis of oil prices on the Rotterdam spot market and other short-term oil price forecasts. They may, of course, be implemented by more complex models in which the time behaviour of several variables now explains the behaviour of the dependent variable, using multivariate ARIMA techniques. Short- and long-run behaviour of this variable can be further modelled using co-integration techniques.[1]. One additional feature of time series models is that they can be specified in continuous time. Another and even more important feature is that they can be specified as non-linear, although this can just as easily be done with regression models. This helps to explain very important price variations as the result of a comparatively small shock, instead of the dampened harmonic behaviour that would be the solution of a well-behaved linear differential equation system. This permits researchers to introduce non-linearities in time series models of energy markets, because most standard models have difficulties in explaining the 1973-74 and 1979-80, as well the 'reverse oil shock' of early 1986.

Of course, in the end, no mathematical system can predict such shocks, however accurately their implications can be predicted. The best hope is to construct models that provide rapid adjustment to such shocks, once they occur. Such models, however, are difficult to apply, because of difficulties

[1] *Eagle et al, 1989.*

encountered in estimating the parameters of non-linear equations and systems. Because of the recent development of oil futures markets and oil options markets, the need has arisen to extend the application of these time series methods to the analysis of oil futures market behaviour and oil option market behaviour. Of some interest in this context has been the Black-Scholes options pricing method, although this opens up the perennial problem of the continually changing forecast.

Another need which has arisen to deal with these dramatic market changes has been to explain so-called *energy gaps*. In such models, the behaviour of oil markets is explained on the basis of empirical supply and demand equations that are estimated separately for different political and economic environments. However, there is usually no underlying theoretical framework unifying them, which makes them difficult to apply in forecasting applications. In fact, these models typically have not advanced to the point where they can be represented by a formal mathematical or econometric framework which inevitably ties them together.

Any oil market model therefore also needs to include the transformation process, petroleum refining, which connects the two sides of the oil market. The demand for crude oil is a derived demand, a demand for refinery inputs. The intrinsic value of the crude oil lies entirely in the value of products which can be produced from it. Supplies of refined products are constrained both by the available supply of crude petroleum and by refining unit capacities. This means that an effective model of the petroleum market must simultaneously equilibrate the market for crude oil and for petroleum products and not leave a crude oil surplus or deficiency. This is a complex task as each of the separate oil derivatives has its own market and there is substantial storage availability too. Most quantitative work on refinery product demand also ignores the complication of refined product consumption not actually being the measured domestic disappearance of refined products from the primary sector, i.e. the amount demanded by distributors and end-users for use in storage and consumption. Secondary-tertiary stocks hidden from market analysts. The consequence is that structural econometric models of disappearance and price formation should account for hidden stock adjustments but do not appear accurately to do so.

One of the most important linked markets is natural gas. Since the beginning of the 1970s, the evolution of gas prices has been characterized by, on the one hand, a strong dependence on the price of oil and on the other hand fluctuations in the relative price of gas depending on the situation prevailing on the market as a result of the seller and buyer's bargaining powers. Two consistent pricing methods are encountered on the natural gas market: the parity method and the net-back method. According to the second approach, it is necessary to start from the average price of gas

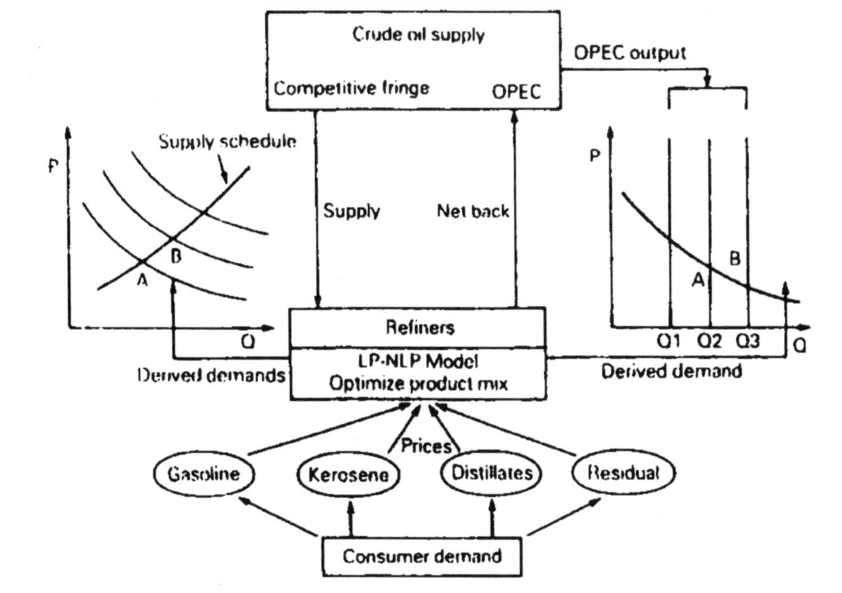

Figure 6.4 Linkages between the markets for petroleum products and crude oil

substitutes (for end-users) and then going back up the gas chain, to deduct the costs of transport, distribution, storage, eventual regassification and etc. to obtain an FOB price to exporter. Each seller on the European market has advantages in the price-bargaining process according to those who model the market: large reserves and low prices for Russia, guaranteed supplies for the Netherlands and Norway, and quite large reserves and historical relationships with Western Europe for Algeria. The capacity for natural gas to influence energy prices is low. Therefore the market remains vulnerable and dependent on oil market. In a saturated market, and owing to continued large uncertainty about the market for oil, many macroeconomic factors flow into the demand function for gas, in other words it is more sensitive to macroeconomic factors than the oil market.

It is worth noting that, in the context of the natural gas market, there has been substantial development of the economic theory of contracts and development of associated models. One, for instance, assumes a monopsonistic (single or market dominant) consumer pitted against four exporters. Contracts over the long term exist because of risk aversion, thereby creating through their multiplicity an approximate series of implicit forward delivery prices. So, for a typical natural gas market model, the price equation includes the oil price, quantities demanded, projected regulation and GDP. The need continues to exist to produce more detailed and better models of the natural gas market. Such requirements have received less attention than oil models, because the development of natural gas markets at the international level is a relatively recent development.

Similarly, the need to model the relative price competitiveness of international coal markets has not been met. At a national or domestic level, several regional coal models have been developed; they concern mainly the North American market. The development of a broad-based international coal market model to meet all the required needs would be an important research area in itself, where coal market structure, trade, transportation costs, policy variables, policy variables and environmental concerns would be the primary focus. Some important work on this has been done by Graham Weale at Wharton Econometric Forecasting Associates (WEFA) in London.

Other engineering-related models were developed during the same period of the late 1980s, mainly on the energy supply side, using linear and non-linear programming methods. Such models concentrate on the transformation of fuels and other primary products into refined fuel products and other oil products. These could be used for demand analysis, explaining demand through analysis process description. These models used techniques and representations that continue to be of interest for the engineering operation of oil refineries and other petroleum processing units, and so could be called techno-economic models. New directions in which programming models might develop in the future are essentially the same as those generally described for the other forms of commodity models. These include advanced programming methodologies such as non-linear programming, mixed integer programming and linear complementarity programming.

Still other energy models have used mpg as a proxy for design changes that affect the material composition of products. Analysts have drawn the conclusion for models that exogenous technical change is at least as important as relative prices in explaining material market shares. The interaction between macroeconomic variables and the energy sector is still not properly understood. Some linkage of different types of models has been made, for example between input-output models of the energy sector with macroeconomic models. During the 1970s, there was very considerable and indeed sustained interest in the construction of integrated world models, which became commercially available through firms like WEFA in the 1980s. Results available through these models were frankly disappointing. Exogenous sectors such as the Centrally Planned Economies (CPEs) abounded.

In the late 1980s, it was believed that a more realistic description of energy savings and energy conservation is one of the most important needs of oil modelling in particular and energy models in general, to create development of general equilibrium models oriented towards the long-term assessment of energy conservation policy. In the 1990s, and especially after the Gulf War, it was believed that a crucial aspect of the development of energy modelling is to reflect the difference that the end of the Cold War, US military dominance and the resultant dampened price cycles have made to energy markets. To use the 1970-1990 period to forecast energy prices for the next twenty years would therefore be highly dangerous.

Some recent history

The commodity market price fall in the first part of the 1980s was the largest since the Great Depression. In 1986, the commodity price index of the IMF was more than 25 per cent below its 1980 level. The situation was worse than in the 1930s when viewed in the context of movements of commodity prices relative to prices of manufactures. The sharp fall in commodity prices following the 1981 worldwide recession was expected by many economists since low price elasticities of these types of goods cause them to respond strongly to supply or demand shifts in their markets. What was unexpected was the sluggish price movements that followed the 1984 recovery in world economic activity, as well as the subsequent downturn in prices of many commodities in 1985-86. In retrospect, it is clear that abnormally large stocks, resulting from lower demand and lagged production responses to high 1979-80 prices, played a role in holding down prices of many commodities. Several specific occurrences in commodities also had significant effects on the outcomes for prices in the 1980s.

In the post-recession, 1993 onwards, commodity price formation process, the approach of Lord—whose work can be taken as representative of the state of commodity econometric theory at present—is based on separate analysis of each commodity market, rather than treating them in the aggregate. The analysis is conducted with a set of structural econometric models, not their reduced form. Lord takes actual changes in the major conditions influencing the markets as given. He then simulates the impact of these changes in each of the major determinants of market prices and estimates their impact on market prices. Lord says his approach differs in not using the reduced form of equations and the market separate approach enables him to identify separate influences on the original supply and demand relationships of commodity markets using parameter estimates from the original structural form of the system of equations in the models. The results of the analysis indicate that the initial worldwide deceleration of economic activity was the main cause of the downturn in commodity prices (no surprise there), but that the strength and duration of the downturn was caused by other factors as well, e.g. the deceleration of growth rates in 1985/86 and inventory build-ups which offset the influences from price stabilization schemes and temporary supply shortages in some commodities.

It is much less clear whether the deceleration of inflation in the industrialized countries, resulting in increased economic activity, tends to produce sharp price movements. Production often responds with a lag to price changes and the short term price elasticity of supply tends to be small. The questions to be addressed here are how much changes in economic activity in the post recession period contributed to price movements, or vice versa, and how much the early price declines contributed to later price movements. The change in the rate of economic growth was compared to the averages of past. Lord observes that 'as expected, the results show that commodity prices would have advanced in 1982, rather than dropping by an average of 15 per cent. However, the model suggests that the lagged response of production to those higher prices would also have led to lower prices in the following four years. Prices would have been somewhat lower in 1983 and they would have dropped sharply in 1984 rather than remaining unchanged. The lagged response to higher prices suggests that the downturn that actually occurred in commodity prices in 1985 could have been initiated by the economic recovery in 1983-84. Higher levels of economic activity led to expectations of continued improvements in prices and greater production. Much of this additional output may not have entered the market until 1985-86 when demand decreased as a result of another slowdown.'

Lord also tested with 1983 growth rates in all markets set at 2/3 actual which is an interesting modelling experiment, and quite typical of the diversion of resources away from forecasting. His conclusion was that lower expansion in demand for the commodities would have resulted in a smaller price rise in that year but it would have kept prices from falling as much as they did in 1985. But this would have not prevented the fall in 1985/86. Differences between commodities occur in the way shifts in demand, resulting from income changes, affect the magnitude of the price change and in the extent of the lagged response of output to price changes. For example, the short term price changes of copper and sugar are in general much larger than those of cotton and soyabeans. This is explained by their lower short term price elasticities of demand and supply. On the other hand, the lagged responses of coffee cocoa and copper production to price changes result in slow adjustments of market prices from one equilibrium state to another. Another factor contributing to the intensity of price decline after 1981 was inventory level which was high comparing actual to desired stocks, for example with respect to sugar.

Interest rates sometimes also play a key role. These were statistically significant in explaining the demand for copper stocks, but not other products. A fall in the interest rate tended to increase demand for stocks of

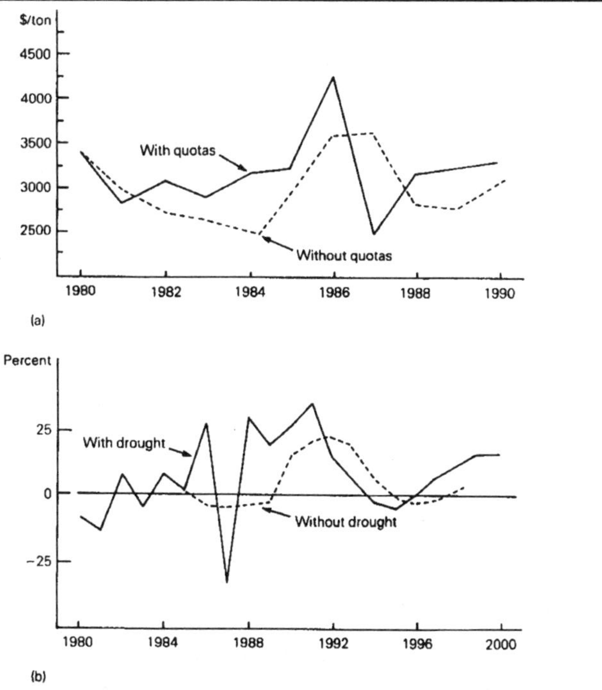

Figure 6.5 Estimated response of coffee prices (a) to reintroduction of quotas under ICA and (b) to 1986 shortfall in Brazilian production due to drought.

copper as cost of holding stocks declined. Commodity prices would have been higher had interest rates not fallen as they did. Higher prices caused by higher interest rates would have cut demand and lowered prices later, i.e. reversing the cyclical swing of 1985/86. None of this goes any way at all in helping to explain what is going to happen to commodity prices in the late 1990s after the recovery has got under way.

Price stabilization schemes

The example of the International Cocoa Agreement, typical of many, showed a failure to support prices within the established range since the financial resources of the buffer stock managers were quickly exhausted. In contrast, the International Coffee agreement, which sought to stabilize the coffee composite Indicator Price at between $1.2 and $1.4 a pound by means of export quotas, did succeed in maintaining prices. Coffee prices were kept at levels above free market prices. Several years are required for price changes to work through to supply changes—an estimated four years for robusta and seven for arabica. Higher prices in the first half of the 1980s affected the market when the International Coffee Agreement failed to be renegotiated in 1990, as what happened in 1994 showed. But the smaller amount of coffee entering the market without the quota system would have helped to raise prices in the second half of the 1980s. It is not difficult to conclude that the existence of such agreements raises prices and it is even feasible to calculate by how much. What is much more difficult, and from which econometricians shy, is how to determine the co-operation of economic and political events in the necessary conditions for the creation of such agreements, their duration and causes for their collapse. That is a real forecasting challenge which has not been taken up.

The intrusion of radical economics

There are some new ideas from radical economics which are gradually being introduced into economic modelling. Although they have a long way to go before being introduced into formal forecasting models, and may themselves be implausible, it is worth adverting to them here if only because they may influence, erroneously, formal commodity model predictions. This may be largely in the direction that the radical economists would like, confusing prediction with wish-fulfilment.

Some commodity market models have included analysis of the market environment to include 'externalities' such as commodity futures markets and related financial markets. These markets and others were seen after the events of the 1970s as acting through commodity demand through changes in industrial activity, substitute prices and factors in the economy generally, through supply such as factors of production as reflected in interest rates, the weather and exchange rates. The markets were acting through international economic conditions such as inflation, recession and changes in international economic conditions, and also through related commodity futures market activity such as speculation and hedging. Of these, monetary, exchange rate and futures market conditions have been generally thought to be the most important. From a forecasting viewpoint, the fact that futures prices influence commodity prices is entirely unhelpful. Forecasting futures prices is just as difficult as forecasting spot prices themselves. Forecasting the financial variables that impact on commodity prices is just as difficult. What this work does demonstrate is that however difficult these tasks are, forecasting commodity prices in isolation of macroeconomic, financial and futures issues is, at least from an econometric viewpoint, not likely to generate a useful answer.

That is exactly the experience, for example, of the ICAC (see later in this chapter) which, along with other such models, attempts to reduce price determination to a single reduced form price equation. Numerous theories have been tested econometrically, ranging from the role of interest rates through international liquidity to stocks and inventories to industrial production. Generally, in the examination of commodity indices 'Aggregate non-food agricultural and metal price indices were found to respond rapidly to exchange rate adjustments...Aggregate food price indices were found to lag behind these shocks, with a lag of almost two years.'[1] However, the questions of the role of commodities futures contracts as part of an international asset diversification policy, or the difference between the impact of forward markets as compared to fully-fledged futures markets, has not been thoroughly investigated.

'Ecological-economic analyses are concerned with the question of the environment-oriented implicit keys to the continuity of human societies, work and affairs. In particular, they point out the major importance of natural resource goods and services (water, wind and soil) in this respect, exploring the way that macroeconomic processes use environmental resources. They tentatively evaluate the implicit contributions within interfaced environmental and economic systems by shadow pricing those energy externalities conjointly with the inputs of human labour and economic goods and services is of immediate importance in order to avoid a misuse of these resources and to obtain a better understanding of the real basis of economic production processes.'[2]

In other words, radical theory suggests further that the entire modelling process fails to take into account real resource costs. Traders and government analysts may initially be less than interested in the hypotheses surrounding costs that do not need in practice to be paid in the market and which do not, therefore, reflect in the price of commodities. The theory suggests, however, that they should be aware when environmentally-concerned policy-makers and economists try to introduce these ideas into apparently commercial decision-making and pricing models. Environmentally concerned thinkers argue that so-called shadow pricing, for natural resource pricing for natural resource goods and services, is of paramount importance for ecological economic analysis, as well as for the commodity, financial and monetary markets and for long-run economic performance. Economic theory knows how to integrate some natural resources, those that can be considered not so differently from usual market parameters, and when related opportunity costs are present-future trade offs. These natural resources can be exchanged on organized markets. But to these thinkers there are other natural resource

[1] *'New Horizons in International Commodity Market Modelling' in ICCM, p19.*

[2] *ICCM, p. 99.*

goods and services that are never exchanged and have no market at all, although contributing to economic production of all kinds. They are environmental goods and services, e.g. sun, rail, topsoil and other environmental functions, which appear as indirect and even unrecognized energy inputs to economic processes and have been known as *energy externalities.*

Complex models ensue from attempts to integrate these externalities. Proponents justify them by claiming that misuse of these resources generally occurs which in turn may in a way imperil market equilibria. In fact, the development of a model to institute shadow prices for the unpaid goods and services owes more to institutional pressures and opportunities rather than to any economic justification. Under the *emergy* concept, embodied energy is worked into the models. At each step much of the energy is used in the transformation. A small amount is converted into a higher quality of energy i.e. a more concentrated form capable of catalytic action when fed back. The ratio of one form of energy that is required to generate another form of energy by transformation is a measure of efficiency according to the first and second law of thermodynamics under the maximum power principle i.e. a measure of energy quality in real systems where the latter tend to operate at that efficiency which produces a maximum power output. The ratio is then called *transformity.*

Embodied energy is defined by Odum as a way to measure the cumulative effect of energies in chains or webs. It is the source energy required to produce other energies. Pillet assumes that the shadow prices of environmental goods and services, per surface and period of time, are proportional in value to the GNP at that time and that the total emergy of these goods and services is proportional to the global emergy used up by the country. Traders should also be aware of the idea in ecological-economic systems whereby there is a relationship between emergy used and GNP, emergy per dollar, which is called *monergy.* The shadow price of environmental goods per hectare can be obtained by dividing their emergy by the monergy of the country.

Government programmes and private services

The estimation of structural econometric models of sectors of national agriculture has become well established in Western countries, within organizations such as the USDA, the OECD and British and US universities. Before the 1980s, such studies tended to concentrate on individual sectors in isolation, often with different periodicities and with incompatible results. Data definitions have varied and methodological approaches have been different.

One of the unintended results of these dichotomies and inconsistencies has been that the sub-discipline of econometric modelling of agricultural sectors has become increasingly divorced from trading operations. A major contribution to this has been the insistence of public policy-makers, aided and abetted both by model-makers and data-providers alike in their absolute insistence on constructing, using and forecasting only annual data—often useless for trading purposes. Even worse, policy-makers imposed a requirement that the forecasts generated by the model they commissioned in the 1980s were to be for calendar years, rather than crop years. The calendar year, as the forecasters themselves argued, 'often does not correspond to the natural harvest year involved in crop production, and it also cuts across some important institutional time periods (e.g. the milk year relevant for calculating the milk quota, the harvest year relevant for cereal intervention prices and the dates of the census).'[1]

Efforts to integrate models of the UK agricultural market have been made[2]. The UK Ministry of Agriculture, Fisheries and Food (MAFF) has been concerned to try to see constructed a unique model of all sectors of UK agriculture for policy-making purposes, suitable for policy simulations and forecasting. In some cases, this was specifically for particular publications by the government such as the output, input and net farm table of the *Annual Farm Review*. This requirement has demanded that such models have linked sectors which are consistent. The model developed at Manchester in 1987 took several different courses of action to overcome this problem, depending on the sector to be modelled. Where possible, semi-annual data was used, defined on a January-June, July-December basis, allowing calendar year values to be determined. This does open up the possibility that in the short term, semi-annual models at least could become commonplace for trading operations. For other sectors, such as cereals, where only annual data is available, annual models were used in conjunction with basic economic techniques for allocating data between two calendar years, for example year end stock equations.

The 1987 Manchester Model (see later in this chapter) used the 'directly estimated single commodity supply model' technique as described by Colman (1983). In this model, the supply response is not derived from any formal consideration of an optimization problem subject to technical constraints, but rather is derived by directly estimating reduced form equations for the supply of each product. These need not be just one equation for each sector. In the case of sectors such as livestock where there are inter-period linkages, or where supply is split into different sectors,

1 *Introduction to: An Econometric Model of the UK Agricultural Sector, M P Burton, Manchester University, 1987.*

2 *For example, Colman and Young, 1981.*

there may be several, for example splitting between output per unit and overall numbers. In some cases a group of closely-related commodities were modelled within a system of equations, using the multi-nomial logit technique, but still within a behaviourally-informal model. Restrictions were placed on the parameters of the equations. Input quantities were related directly to the supply sector utilizing the input, in order to maximize consistency between the two.

The model made the sectors interrelate through a system of price equations. Own and competing output prices were present in all supply sectors. The output prices of some sectors appear as input prices in others. These price equations were estimated using the same techniques as for supply and tended to contain output or input quantities and institutional prices. Thus a change of an exogenous variable in a particular sector will have a range of effects throughout the model by altering other prices. The amount of stability in such a system of supply equations is not imposed by restriction, but is gleaned from the accuracy of the estimated equations themselves. The model is supply side: consumer demand is reflected only in the price equations, and exports are not separately identified either. Some minor crops were modelled using ARIMA or time-trend models rather than regression.

At the time, in 1987, the model was recognized by its creators to have weaknesses in its input side. The feeding stuffs sector was modelled in quite a detailed way, but fertilizer modelling did not prove successful. As feed and fertilizer account for some 60 per cent of gross input value, a simple specification was implemented for them and time series or aggregate linked series were introduced for the remainder.

Even in an incomplete state the model included some 200 equations, and if completed it would include 400. The designers conceded that 'manipulation of such a model is cumbersome, and it is currently (1987) being used on a mainframe computer at Manchester, although software of sufficient power now exists for it to be loaded onto a PC'. The model had already by 1987 been evaluated both in respect of individual sectors and the sector as a whole, analysing historical data and looking to see the degree of fit. The designers claimed that the model was able to produce realistic results for an analysis of the impact of changes in the milk quota, for example. Yet it is certain that this model, and others like it, has not found its way into commercially-available PC software for traders and analysts of the UK markets. There are several reasons for this:

- i) Software trading programs tend to be driven by active futures markets, because the number of potential investors in such markets is so much greater than in those dominated by producers and large trading companies. In the USA, the emphasis is on the trading method rather than the market. Modelling the US agricultural sector as a whole would be a stupendous modelling task which would require a very large number of continuously updated inputs;

- ii) The UK futures market for agricultural commodities is lamentably small. Farmers distrust these techniques and do not therefore need trading software;
- iii) As with all agricultural markets, users would probably rather be able to predict the weather than any other determinant. Complex econometric models are still subject to shocks and are too slow to react to market movements on a daily, or even weekly, basis.
- iv) There is little commercial drive behind the construction of these models for MAFF purposes. The University of Manchester did not construct its model with the intention of recouping costs by selling a PC-based system with associated data feeds to farmers and traders. Nor has it tried to do so subsequently.

The USDA modelling process

According to the official position of the USDA, the organization relies more on 'expert-based', i.e. heuristic, forecasting for the 1-2 year period. These are the commodity forecasts which are done by what the professional modellers in the organization describe as 'commodity people'. USDA forecasters say with alarming dismissiveness—considering the huge importance that USDA forecasts have within global agricultural markets—that 'trend analysis within spreadsheets is probably the basis for most of it' although the official position is that there are numerous small-scale models used by commodity analysts to aid in forecasting some components, such as area or yield, of the US market.

The official USDA view is that there is a high cost, and low pay-off in the maintenance of models which account for all the factors involved in producing credible short-term forecasts. The USDA says that it maintains, and is continually developing, a set of US commodity models, a US sector model (FAPSIM) and an inventory of approximately forty 'foreign' country sector models to enhance both the rigour and the speed of USDA's global baseline (forecast) and scenario models. All of these are run by commodity and country experts rather than econometricians. The baseline is officially described (in the September 1994 release) as 'a composite of country models, domestic commodity models, and judgemental analysis. The projections are a conditional, current policy scenario with no shocks and are based on specific assumptions regarding the macroeconomy, the weather and international developments'. The process involves the development of consistent global macroeconomic and price assumptions, country projections, and the reconciliation of global supply, demand and prices. Regional analysts prepare commodity projections for (as in 1994) 44 countries (including the USA) and regions, with between 10-25 commodities for 18 major countries and 1-10 commodities for the remaining 25. The whole exercise brings in analysts from the World Agricultural Outlook Board, the Commodity Economics Division, the Agricultural Trade Analysis Division (ATAD), the Foreign Agriculture Service, the Economic Research Service. Available now is the *Country Projections and Policy Analysis* model builder, which the USDA describes as a 'user-friendly spreadsheet-based program that aids development and use of formally specified, self-documenting, country agricultural sector projections models.'

Currently, the international baseline is an annual exercise, completed by November and revised in July. The ATAD has identified areas of improvement.

- The cycle, is predictably, too expensive and slow;
- Prices are largely exogenous assumptions. This is because at present it is too cumbersome to iterate between commodity and regional analysts with new sets of prices;
- There are some inconsistencies between regions, especially technical and economic ones with regard to relative prices and cross-commodity relationships;
- There is some gap between the US and international baselines.

The emphasis now is on affordable 'linker' software that will capitalize on the sheer diversity and expertise of USDA models whilst imposing a swift and iterative homogeneity of assumptions upon them. In other words, what the USDA is seeking is a meta-language between forecasting languages. This is an ambitious goal but it will, undoubtedly, improve the system at the margins.

FAPSIM estimates many of the same agricultural economic indicators as the baseline process; once a baseline has been established, FAPSIM is routinely recalibrated to be consistent with the baseline estimates. The model includes, *inter alia*, an estimation of farm production expenses.

Critics within the USDA observe that although there have been repeated efforts to provide consistent USDA global model backup for official forecasts, and although much time and money has been spent, nothing useful for those responsible for forecasting has been created. Moreover, this lack of success has bred criticism of the modellers, and commensurate institutional advantages for the commodity and country experts. As a result, the last round of institutional changes in the major organizations which either are or have been responsible for forecasting was quite savage.

The Economic Research Service of the USDA is a good example of where 'downsizing' is at present at work. Nevertheless, the work of the baseline and the agricultural projections will continue. It continues to represent one of the most important long-term forecasting services publicly available anywhere. The time horizons, however, are too long for trading, and the issue of the numbers themselves is a more important trading event than any trading on the basis of them.

The OECD Aglink model

In the 1980s, the OECD developed its Ministerial Trade Mandate model (MTM) which was built for the purpose of assessing the impact of alternative government policies on OECD agriculture. The continuing political pressure for the ability of the secretariats to assess the impact of policies in a shorter time frame, and the institutional need for forecasting, led to the creation of AGLINK. In the fashion of so many econometric models and simulations, AGLINK combines the functions of forecasting and simulation. AGLINK integrated many national models and was a multinational effort with standardized national questionnaires.

In the mid-1990s, the AGLINK model includes specifications for the prices, supply and demand of thirteen major commodities: wheat, coarse grain, oilseeds, oilseed oil, oilseed meal, beef, pigmeat, poultrymeat, eggs, milk, butter, skim milk powder and cheese. There are six OECD countries or regions included: the EU, Australia, Canada, Japan, New Zealand and the USA. Where AGLINK clearly needs development is in the relationship between these commodities and areas and the rest of the world. The rest-of-world regions are modelled for some commodities as a single group (for example wheat and coarse grains) and in other cases in a more disaggregated way to simulate the nature of the international market concerned. The countries of the former Soviet Union are exogenous to the model—in other words it needs assumptions regarding output and exports there—but is handled separately to facilitate analysis of this vital region.

As with many other such models, the macroeconomic variables such as GNP, price changes and exchange rates are exogenous to the model. Subsidies and tariffs are specified in the model, and an attempt has been made to represent detailed policies structurally. For example, US crop programmes such as target prices, set asides, flex-acreage 'triple base' and others are incorporated. The Export Enhancement Programmes (EEPs) are modelled as a 'wedge' between domestic wheat and course grain (barley) prices. For the EU Common Agricultural Policy, the model involves a detailed specification of the crop programmes, set-aside, the compensation mechanism etc..

Similar interventions in the model exist for Canadian and Japanese farm policies. The OECD states that 'There are 1360 parameters in AGLINK, in 331 behavioural equations. With 331 regression constants, and with 160 trend parameters, the remaining 869 coefficients have been obtained..from models used by Member country governments, or from research literature..[or] estimated by the OECD Secretariat.' The forecasting cycle begins in January of each year with the distribution to member countries of a medium-term outlook questionnaire, which covers a five-year outlook period. Reponses are received by April, synthesized by the OECD Secretariat by June, and a preliminary baseline is prepared for further discussion in the commodity group meetings, which occur in September and October. The outlook is then updated with new information, and in response to the views of delegates. A revised baseline is developed and a synthesis is presented and discussed in December. The OECD Secretariat participates in an annual 'World Agricultural Outlook Meeting' involving the European Commission, World Bank, FAO, USDA, Agriculture Canada, ABARE and FAPRI. The OECD Secretariat examines and compares the world outlooks derived by a number of these organizations and uses the information in its forecasts for non-member countries.

Another example of a government-funded forecasting programme in a country with a substantial agricultural sector—in this case carried out through a nominally independent agency rather than directly by the Agriculture Ministry or Department, is ABARE in Australia. ABARE states that 'Wool industry policies are formulated within a complex market environment—raw wool is sold for processing to a diverse range of countries and may be transferred to one or more other countries for further processing before the final consumer buys a wool item. The ABARE world wool trade model represents an attempt to capture this complex environment in a comprehensive and consistent analytical framework.'

ABARE commodity forecasts are issued in a publication, *Australian Commodities.* A typical forecast for wool was this, of December 1993, beginning with the key points and concluding with the summary and projections given in Figure 6.6:

* The wool market indicator is forecast to fall marginally to average 480c/kg in 1993/94;

* Australian shorn wool production is forecast to decline by 12 per cent to 717,000 tonnes in 1993/94;

* In the medium term, prices are projected to rise in response to stronger world economic activity;

* Slight weakening in wool prices forecast for 1993-94.

The wool market indicator for the 1993/94 season is forecast to average 480c/kg clean, less than 2 per cent below the average market indicator of 488c/ kg clean in 1992/93.

The low level of economic activity in major wool importing countries continues to be a major influence on wool prices despite significantly lower forecast Australian wool production and an assumed fall in the value of the Australian dollar against the currencies of many wool importers.

Weak consumer demand for finished wool products has led to a build-up in textile stocks throughout the processing pipeline. Many countries have reduced imports of raw wool and have cut yarn and fabric production in an attempt to reduce these stocks.

Improvement in prices in second half of 1993-94

Prices fell more than expected during the first few months of the 1993-94 wool auction season as buyers withheld purchases pending the government's announcement of future marketing arrangements as a result of the Garnaut review of the Australian wool industry. The market indicator fell to a low of 411c/kg clean at the start of September and averaged 429c/ kg for the quarter. Prices are expected to continue to improve from this low base during the second half of the season, with the greatest recovery being seen in the finer micron wools and the carding types.

Prices to improve further over the medium term

Beyond 1993-94 the downward trend of the past several years is expected to be reversed, with wool prices projected to improve in 1994-95. An assumed return to stronger economic growth in 1994-95, particularly in Japan and Western Europe, is expected to result in increased consumer incomes and therefore some strengthening in consumer spending on wool products. However, rebuilding textile production to meet increasing demand for wool textiles and clothing entails first using pipeline stocks of yarns and fabrics. Imports of raw wool and wool tops by major users are expected to rise as stocks fall.

World growth is assumed to average close to 4 per cent from around 1995. Economic growth in OECD countries is assumed to strengthen further as many of these countries recover from recession. Growth in Asia is expected to remain relatively strong. Although economic growth in China is not expected to be as high as in recent years, growth is expected to remain strong relative to other countries. Consequently, the wool indicator price is projected to rise through most of the projection period, largely as a result of improving wool demand.

Production falling in 1993/94

Australian shorn wool production is forecast by the Wool Production Forecasting Committee to fall by 12 per cent to 717,000 tonnes in 1993-94. This would be the lowest level of production since 1983-84. The decline reflects the continued low prices received by growers over the past three years. Forecast increases in both lamb slaughterings and adult turnoff, in the form of increased live sheep exports, are expected to result in a fall of around 9 per cent in sheep numbers—from 140m in 1992-93 to around 128m in 1993-94. The number of sheep and lambs is forecast to fall by 11 per cent to 159m in 1993-94.

In Queensland continued dry conditions in the second half of 1993 are expected to further contribute to a decline in the number of sheep shorn in 1993-94. In South Australia reduced pasture availability combined with significant fly strike losses are also expected to lead to a reduction in the number of sheep shorn in that state.

Regional changes in wool receipts

[Between 1998-89 and 1881-92 wool and mutton prices halved and lamb prices fell by 13 per cent.]

Marked regional differences in the declines of the percentages of receipts from wool/sheep can be attributed to declining wool production and movements into alternative enterprises such as wheat and cattle. While some areas show little change in the percentage of output due to limitations in the ability to change enterprise mix (notably the pastoral areas of Queensland and the high rainfall areas of New South Wales), the actual receipts will have declined due to falling wool prices and production.

Continued decline in production until price turnaround

Shorn wool production is expected to decline by a further 10 per cent to around 645,000 tonnes in 1994-95. Production is then projected to increase to around 740,000 tonnes in 1988-89 as a result of improving wool prices. A turnaround in the downward trend in sheep numbers is not likely to occur until there is a significant turnaround in the real price of wool. Given that the real price of wool is expected to improve in 1994-95, it is forecast that sheep numbers will bottom out in 1995-96 and increase in the following years.

In the medium term, a steady increase in wool cut per head is also expected to be an important factor leading to rising wool production. Flock reductions in the early 1990s led to an increase in the proportion of females within the flock and a consequent fall in the average wool cut per head. As sheep numbers increase and the proportion of females within the flock declines the average wool cut is likely to increase.

Minimal stock sales in second half of 1993-94

Sales from the stockpile of around 30,000 tonnes are assumed for 1993-94, 43 per cent more than the 21,000 tonnes, or 121 672 bales, sold during 1992-93. Sales from the stockpile have been greater in the first half of 1993-94 relative to the same period in the previous year. However, sales are assumed to slow during the second half of the season.

Stock sales fixed in medium term

As a result of the recent changes to Australian wool marketing arrangements, the stockpile is to be reduced according to a fixed quantity selling schedule commencing in July 1994 through to June 1997. By July 1997, the residual stocks in the stockpile are expected to be 310,000 tonnes or 1.76m bales.

Exports to decline in 1993-94

Lower supplies and limited stock sales into a weak market in 1993-94 are forecast to result in total wool exports of 805,000 tonnes, a fall of around 59,000 tonnes or 7 per cent from 1992-93 exports of 864,000 tonnes. Lower export volumes and marginally lower prices are likely to result in a total value of wool exports of $2.68bn in 1993-94, a fall of 20 per cent from $3.36bn in 1992-93.

The economies of Japan and Western Europe contracted further during 1992-93 but are expected to turn around in 1994. In expectation of strengthening consumer demand and given the lead time between greasy wool purchases and sales of garments to consumers, exports will increase their demand for wool once the pipeline clears. Whereas in 1992-93 China became Australia's major single wool export destination, exports to China are expected to ease during 1993-94. Lack of foreign currency availability is expected to continue to hamper Chinese purchasing. However, China is still expected to be a significant importer of Australian wool in 1993-94.

Gradual improvement in exports over the medium term

Australian wool exports are expected to resume modest growth in 1994-95 after the downward trend experienced over the past two years, rising by 3 per cent to 823,000 tonnes. Projected improvements in economic activity in user countries will result in this uptrend trend in exports gathering momentum over the medium term.

		1991 -92	1992 -93[p]	1993 -94[f]	1994 -95[f]	1995 -96[z]	1996 -97[z]	1997 -98[z]	1998 -99[z]
Sheep numbers[a]	million	151	140	128	124	123	124	129	135
Sheep numbers[b]	million	148	137	125	122	120	122	126	133
Sheep numbers shorn	million	181	179	159	145	148	152	158	161
Cuts per head	kg	4.42	4.55	4.50	4.45	4.52	4.54	4.59	4.60
Wool production[c]	kt	875	869	770	695	720	740	775	790
- *shorn*	kt	801	815	717	645	670	690	725	740
AWRC closing stocks[d]	'000 bales	4069	3947	3778	3233	2483	1733	938	170
	kt	716	695	665	569	437	305	165	30
Market indicator									
- *nominal*	c/kg clean	557	488	480	545	625	660	675	700
- *real*[e]	c/kg clean	581	504	480	528	585	596	590	590
Exports[g]	kt	945	864	805	823	865	875	910	920
Export value									
- *nominal*	$m	3829	3361	2681	2962	3573	3856	4126	4309
-*real*[e]	$m	3994	3471	2681	2867	3342	3484	3604	3633

[a]*Sheep and lambs at 31 March on enterprises with an estimated value of agricultural operations (EVAO) of $5000 or more.* [b]*Sheep and lambs at 31 March on enterprises with an EVAO of $22,500 or more.* [c]*Includes shorn wool, wool on sheepskins, fellmongered and slipe wool.* [d]*Stocks held by Australian Wool Realisation Commission until December 1993, and Wool International thereafter.* [e]*In 1993-94 dollars.* [g]*Balance of payments basis.* [p]*Preliminary. fABARE forecast.* [z]*ABARE projection.*

Figure 6.6 Summary and projections of key wool statistics

Source: Australian Bureau of Statistics; Australian Wool Corporation; ABARE.

It is also worth noting that there are a large number of private firms and consultants that specialize in forecasting. Some organizations which sell forecasting services take very specific attitudes to the forecasting process. A very good example is DB Research, which is held in high esteem by textile companies in the UK and abroad. DB Research concentrates on textile forecasting, and in particular of final demand and mill consumption of various fibres. DB Research postulates that fibre demand at any level cannot be forecast without first establishing the underlying consumer demand for finished textile products, what DB calls 'final demand', which it is not possible to establish at the level of all individual fibres. At best, the firm argues, this can be done for wool, cotton and man-made fibres, but it might also be possible to separate staple and filament fibres at the final demand stage. DB further argues that it is simply wrong to assume that the apparent consumption figures for consumer demand contain only random errors and therefore to use standard regression analysis to detect a trend. DB's approach is based on the idea that apparent consumption figures actually reflect genuine movements of products within the textile system, often representing pipeline stock movements and thereby creating a business cycle. DB Research states that: 'Changes in Pipeline Stock in a given year equal Apparent Consumption LESS Real Consumption (Note changes can be negative). Previous year Pipeline Stocks plus or minus changes in current year Pipeline Stocks equal cumulative Pipeline Stocks, and these can clearly never fall below zero (in which case the Real Consumption line may be changed appropriately)'.

The next stage in this approach is to forecast downstream trade movements using exchange rate predictions, which DB Research suggests in the long term follow purchasing power parity trends and to see what might happen to the pipeline in the future. This enables a forecast of individual fibre demand, i.e. mill consumption estimates to be made. The importance within such an approach of consistent global data, and a global integration of supplying and consuming regions, is clear.

Examples of the available software

Numerous computer software programs for forecasting purposes exist. They are generally either stand-alone forecasting packages or general purpose statistical packages, many of them adapted to PCs from old-fashioned mainframe use. What is vital to realize is that although most of these programs could be used for forecasting commodities, most of them currently are not.

One of the best known of the commercially available software forecasting packages is *Micro TSP* from Quantitative Micro Software, now on Version 7 and available both for the PC and the Macintosh. *EViews* is a basically similar package with improved more user-friendly command syntax and user interface. The program includes a wide variety of forecasting methodologies with potential applications to commodity forecasting. Firstly, there are single equation estimation techniques, which include ordinary least squares (multiple regression), two-stage least squares, nonlinear least squares, probit and logit. Weighted estimation is an option for most of these. The linear specifications may include polynomial lag structures on any number of independent variables. *TSP* allows the estimation of autoregressive and moving average models with Box-Jenkins techniques, with the inclusion of seasonal autoregression and moving average specification. *TSP* offers a procedure known as ARMAX which combines an ARMA model and a regression model with estimation by full generalized least squares.

Box-Jenkins models are cheap and are usually included as options in commercially-available forecasting software and non-specialist statistical packages. Such statistical packages as *Minitab, Systat, MicroTSP* and *Sibyl/Runner* all contain Box-Jenkins routines whilst there is also specialist PC software such as *ARIMA* and *Micro-BJ*. Almost all computer forecasting software of the next generation will include Box-Jenkins forecasting options. Experts from mathematical disciplines have suggested: 'When you use statistical software to fit a time series model it is not always clear how the model is estimated. For ARMA model estimation, software manuals usually describe some variant of least squares or cite Box-Jenkins methods. For instance, *Minitab* uses least squares, *Systat* cites Box-Jenkins whereas *STAMP* (Structured Time Series Analyser, Modeller and Predictor), uses exact maximum likelihood. To the uninitiated there appear to be several competing estimation methods. It is crucial to remember, however, that these are all variants or approximations to maximum likelihood'.[1] As noted, however, this is already changing with more intelligent 'self-justifying' software which explains its choice between forecasting methods to the user. Their contention, rather without evidence, that similar results are likely whichever procedure is used, should also be challenged, but can only be so with exhaustive comparative assessment of forecasting software.

Forecasting packages on PCs also almost invariably have exponential smoothing routines built into them. Using exponential smoothing in combination with a seasonal price adjustment factor may achieve meaningful results at the level of individual commodities, at least when taken in conjunction with a good measure of conjecture and qualitative forecasting. There are several exponential smoothing methods available with *TSP*, for example: single exponential, double exponential, Holt-Winters with additive seasonal, Holt-Winters multiplicative seasonal and no seasonal. The user can specify the smoothing parameters or alternatively allow *TSP* to do so. Two-stage estimates can be made for all

[1] *Janacek and Swift, p103.*

these equations. Linear and non-linear equation systems can be estimated by seemingly unrelated regression, three-stage least squares. Commercially-available forecasting software of the iterative selection type, such as *Forecast Pro*, usually includes a variety of exponential smoothing models. *Forecast Pro* has nine different such models to incorporate a wide range of data characteristics: simple one-parameter smoothing, Holt two parameter smoothing, Winters three parameter smoothing (multiplicative and additive), trendless seasonal models and damped trend versions of Holt and Winters, suitable for longer horizon forecasting.

A battery of tests is available for equation estimates in *TSP v.7*. 'These include Wald tests of linear and non-linear coefficient restrictions in equations and systems, likelihood ratio and F-tests for omitted variables, Lagrange multiplier tests for serial correlation and ARCH, White heteroscedasticity tests, Ramsey RESET tests, and Chow forecast and break point tests.' (*TSP* sales literature). The software, which is stand-alone as with most of its generation, will compute a forecast with one command after having estimated the forecasting equation.

Another excellent example of the new generation of integrated software incorporating many of the econometric principles outlined in this book is the *SmartForecast v.3* from *Smart Software*. This is currently used primarily for demand forecasting and planning, for example in the healthcare industry. The first version was launched in 1984 and it has now reached version 3.

Using forecasts such as *SmartForecast* is extremely quick and straightforward by comparison to constructing a regression model oneself. Smart Systems recommend that it is sensible to review and clean the data first, checking for outliers and considering possible data transformations. *SmartForecast*'s 'timeplot' command can do this and the software can even, using the 'decompose' command, replace outliers with more typical data. Some data can be simplified for forecasting purposes by transformation and the 'define' command does this, for example through taking a square root. Smart Systems say that although 'automatic' is usually the best solution, some custom handling may be necessary. Timeplots can of course be viewed to examine whether they need amendment.

There is an automatic facility for the projection of sales, product demand and inventory levels. Data can be forecast at any degree of periodicity from daily, weekly, monthly, quarterly and annual. Data with a different level of periodicity can also be forecast. Either one big file, with an almost unlimited amount of data, or up to 200 'multi-files' containing up to 1,200 items with up to 520 time periods for each item can be forecast. Each forecast session produces a forecast audit/summary report that enumerates the forecasting method uses and provides statistics on the average absolute forecasting error and the average absolute percentage error.

The option 'automatic' has an expert system which selects the most appropriate forecasting method and provide the needed statistical baseline. 'Automatic' determines an appropriate forecasting method for each item, organizes the method's parameter's (weights), generate, report and store the method's forecasts for further analysis or implementation. 'For each data series, *SmartForecast* conducts a tournament among five forecasting methods. Two of these are based on moving averages (simple and linear moving average) and the other three upon the related technique of exponential smoothing (single, double and Winters' exponential smoothing).' In such an approach, weighted averages of the data are computed in a way that gives more emphasis to events in the recent than the distant past. Trend values are established from inter-period change, and the ratios of data to trend are used to determine seasonality, which, because of the fact that Winters' exponential smoothing acknowledges seasonality in the data, means that it will inevitably be chosen for data exhibiting strong seasonality. 'The program tries each of the methods with four different sets of internally generated parameter values for a total of 20 possible forecasting formulae. The formula that most accurately forecasts more recent values of the data series from earlier ones is declared the winner with a ranking of the other forecasting methods, showing how much less accurate each of these was by comparison to the winner. This selection procedure is called a sliding simulation'.[1]

There is also a 'regression' capability built into the software which also deseasonalizes data. 'Correlate' looks to see whether some data functions as a leading indicator and therefore whether they should be integrated into the 'regression' program for use in the forecast. The interactive mode for forecasting allows the forecaster to fit trend curves, try S-curves for new product forecasts, and make 'eyeball' extrapolations from graphical representation of data. Most of the options do not require any particular econometric skill, which is important in considering the potential application of such forecasts to commodities companies and traders, but there are some, such as the ARIMA option, which do require statistical expertise. *SmartForecast* therefore represents a clever integration in one software package of time series, single and multiple regression, all made possible by the increased power and speed of 32-bit software in 386/486, and especially Pentium, chips by comparison with their predecessors.

The software works with the latest releases of *Lotus 1-2-3* and *Excel* and can be expected to continue to do so. ASCII and DIF files with the data to

[1] *See S Makridakis Sliding simulation: A new approach to time series forecasting, Management Science No 36, 1990, pp505-512*

be forecast and/or correlated are compatible. *SmartForecast* is compatible with *Microsoft Windows 3.x* and therefore gives access to *Windows* tools like *Paintbrush, Clipboard,* etc. Commercial forecasts such as *SmartForecast* place a high importance on the integration of their output directly into high quality presentational material, in marked contrast to forecast outputs from first generation forecasting tools such as *SPSSX*. There is a multi-user version for local area networks such as Novell and Banyan.

The similar package of *Forecast Pro,* is available from Business Forecast Systems/Palisade Corporation. This works in the same way: a built-in expert system examines the data and in this case, suggests either exponential smoothing, Box-Jenkins or regression as a forecasting method—whichever method suits the data best. The program, like *SmartForecast,* determines the characteristics of the data and the power of potential explanatory variables or leading indicators. The basic *Forecast Pro* takes 640k of memory and 1Mb of disc space. A more advanced, XE model of the package adds 'event' models, multiple-level forecasting, Census X-11, cumulative forecasting and expanded batch forecasting (up from 50 data files to 100 time series, and able to forecast up to 100 series in batch mode or at multiple levels of aggregation). These later versions take 2Mb of memory themselves, and 1Mb of disc space.

Like *SmartForecast, Forecast Pro* has a dynamic regression model capability. Up to 50 independent variables can be integrated, including lagged and/or transformed variables. Autoregressive error models of the generalized Cochrane-Orcutt type can be built. The software displays how it is constructing model dynamics and how the independent variables are to be specified.

However the makers say that '*Forecast Pro* is primarily a time series package. The premise of time series analysis is that detectable trends and patterns exist in historical data and can be extrapolated into the future. While this is the case for many types of data, especially business/sales data, commodity forecasting does not always lend itself well to this kind of analysis. Whilst occasionally there may be these kind of patterns, seasonality for example, usually the commodity market is driven by so many other factors that regression is frequently the only potential forecasting tool. Our program does include a regression model, but the primary focus of the package is on time series methods. ...use *Forecast Pro* as one of many tools, primarily to test for these historical patterns'.

Structural models

These do not yet seem to be incorporated into the commercially-available multi-method forecast software, although this can only be a matter of time. Specific *STAMP* software can be obtained from the LSE for these models if required. The LSE states that, 'The program enables the user to set up a structural time series model in terms of components of interest. Once the model has been specified it can be estimated, and the fit assessed by examining residuals and diagnostics. The series may then be broken down into its components. Finally, the forecasts of future values of the components, and of the series as a whole, may be made...The models can be extended by adding observable explanatory variables to the right-hand side of the equation above. Intervention variables, which are dummy variables representing particular events or policy changes, can also be included. Regression can therefore be carried out as a special case. However, *STAMP* was not written primarily as a regression program and, because of space constraints, the number of explanatory variables it can handle is limited.' It may be expected that future versions of *STAMP* will eliminate this constraint. But the programme is stated to handle series 'from annual to weekly' rather than daily prices. What is noticeable is that the program requires only 512Kb of RAM.

StatPlan IV is a stand-alone programme for expert statisticians. The forecasting methods include multiple regression, stepwise multiple regression, polynomial regression, bivariate curve fitting, autocorrelation analysis, trend and cycle analysis, and exponential smoothing.

Geneva Statistical Forecasting, another stand-alone program, can batch-process forecasts for thousands of data series, a useful feature for those interested in forecasts for commodity indices or those concerned to trade spreads or distribute risk between markets. The software automatically tries out up to nine forecasting methods, including six linear and non-linear regressions and three exponential smoothing techniques, before selecting the best fit to the historical data. This program, along with many others, incorporates reforecasting file saves. Files are retrieved and the additional data added and a reforecast carried out—although it must be worth, given the limited amount of time involved in the iterative procedure, allowing the program to check whether the new data have not changed the best applicable forecasting routine.

Tomorrow, another standalone forecasting software package, uses an optimized combination of linear regression and a wide range of exponential smoothing methods and is exceptionally user-friendly to existing data records.

The use of spreadsheets

Spreadsheets such as *Lotus 1-2-3* and *Excel* have become essential tools for forecasting. First of all they have basic regression forecasting techniques built into them, and secondly they represent an excellent way of recording forecasts and variables and showing the effect of changes in assumptions on forecast outcomes.

Spreadsheet programs, such as even the venerable *Lotus 1-2-3,* have a regression routine, which is incorporated into the second generation forecasting programs. With *Lotus 1-2-3* it is first necessary to determine the intercept (constant) and the *X* coefficients, then use the *X* coefficients and the constant obtained to forecast the next level for the *Y* variable. The more advanced forecasting programs do this automatically and indeed this is precisely what the regression forecasting routines on these programmes are designed to do. Moreover, *1-2-3* does not calculate many statistics such as Durbin-Watson and R-bar squared or F-statistic. Regression packages such as *SPSS, SAS,* and *STATPACK*—to name but three—do so as of course do the specialized forecasting software packages.

Palisade/BFS also market the simpler *Forecalc,* which is an add-in to *Lotus 1-2-3,* and *Symphony* spreadsheets. *Forecalc* uses the same expert system approach as its larger sisters, but takes only 512k of memory; there are nine forecasting techniques and the software includes both automatic and manual modes. It also eliminates the need to export or re-enter data. In automatic mode the user need only highlight the data to be forecast, and the program tests several exponential smoothing models and selects the one that fits the data best. Forecast results can be shifted to spreadsheets with upper and lower confidence limits. All the different parametered exponential smoothing methods are included, and the manual mode allows the user to select a preferred method. Application of the program to commodity forecasting must be limited because of the use of only exponential smoothing methods.

General-purpose statistical software systems

Probably the best known of these are Systat, SAS Application System, *Statgraphics, SPSS* (probably the best known and certainly one of the longest running), *PC-90, Minitab* (immensely popular), *STATPACK, RATS* and *BMD.* These packages are used by professional commodity forecasters in major institutions when time series forecasts or regressions are required. Many statisticians and forecasters have been working with these, in many cases quite user-unfriendly, statistical packages for many years and see no reason to change. They also have no need of the expert system guidance of the forecasting packages as well as requiring the flexibility that the full statistical packages can bring. However, for a trader or an analyst in the commercial sector, the forecasting packages must now represent an increasingly attractive option. They mean that it is no longer necessary actually to be a statistician to develop, maintain and issue forecasts to the same standards as statisticians a decade ago. This is an important change to which the commodities business as a whole has not yet become acclimatized.

The application of the software

In the mid-1990s, it seems impossible to find a commercial trading operation trading commodities for profit that relies on such a software package, although many have one or more installed. The picture remains very much as one manufacturer described their situation before the introduction of advanced PC-based forecasting software: 'Things were rather chaotic. We had identified our product variability, but we lacked reliable statistical methods for generating a valid production plan. Too often, we were in a reactive mode.' It is very interesting that Business Forecast Systems, the makers of *Forecast Pro,* specifically suggest that the system was not intended to be applied to commodity forecasting. BFS states: 'While *Forecast Pro* has many applications and can be used with a variety of time series, commodity market forecasting is not one of our intended applications. *Forecast Pro* is designed for the average business person, one without an extensive knowledge of statistics. Commodity forecasting can be rather tricky and requires an in-depth knowledge of statistics.'[1] *TSP* is advertised as providing 'the tools most frequently used in econometric and forecasting work'. 'Areas of application include financial analysis, economic research, sales forecasting, utility load forecasting, cost analysis, macroeconomic forecasting, interest rate forecasting, and scientific data analysis and evaluation.'[2] It is noticeable that forecasting commodities and prices in general does not feature on this list. These evaluations are probably typical of forecasting software manufacturers, and it reflects an unhappiness both with commodities as a difficult subject area and with the use of such software to forecast any fast moving market, rather than one where reliable monthly or annual data are available.

In manufacturing, the position could not be more different. Forecasting software plays an important role in the establishment of production plans, analysing for example the historical demand patterns of existing, phase-out products and thereby estimating the expected patterns of new, phase-in production. Numerous firms use *SmartForecast,* including several which have commodities as their major inputs, for example Cadbury Confectionery Ltd., Dole Packaged Foods, Dupont Agricultural Products,

[1] *K.C. Heming, Marketing Director of BFS, letter to the author, 25 July 1994.*

[2] *Sales literature, TSP.*

Goodyear Tyre and Rubber, Hoffmann-la Roche Ltd, Kraft General Foods and Tropicana. Users of *Forecast Pro* include Alcoa, R.J. Reynolds Tobacco, and Tropicana. There is evidence from these two short lists alone that major manufacturing firms do not rely on just one forecasting package, but use more than one and compare the results—eminently sensibly.

Why the lack of application to commodities?

That econometric forecasting software has not yet properly reached the commodity trading world is clear. Traders do not arrive at hotels, plug into the Internet, update their statistics, adjust their model parameters, and run off a quick forecast before dinner and the negotiation of a deal. No, econometric forecasting comes bottom of the list of priorities as far as forecasting techniques are concerned, and if traders are asked about which type of forecasting technique they would like to know more, they almost invariably reply technical analysis or one specific branch of it, not econometric modelling. Econometric forecasting software is distrusted and regarded as the province of academics and government.

If pushed as to why, traders will reply that:

- In their belief, the results of such software is too slow in generating results;
- The results are too long term;
- The results depend too much on assumptions which are precisely what the trader needs to forecast;
- The prices generated tend to be annual, or at best monthly, when positions can vary very substantially on a daily basis;
- There is no evidence that such forecasts are successful.

Larger trading companies do of course run models, and prominent amongst them are companies such as Merrill Lynch in the USA. They do so in conjunction always with a variety of other systems of analysis, usually including technical analysis and consultation with experts, principally but not exclusively their in-house analysts. Large-scale commodity forecasting is the purview of government and quasi-government organizations whose forecasts rapidly become public knowledge.

The ICAC cotton models

It has been argued that the world cotton market is a more transparent market than other commodities, as distortions have been maintained in a relatively stable way over time. The ICAC therefore hypothesized that changes in international cotton prices can be better understood by means of inverted demand and supply equations than for other commodities such as rice or antimony, or even one with an active futures market such as sugar or gold. However, by 1992, the ICAC's view was that unexpected events had altered price formation with the consequence that expectations about future prices appeared to play an increasingly important role.

To forecast the Cotlook A Index, the model uses exogenous production, mill consumption, trade and stocks data generated by the Secretariat of the ICAC and futures prices from the New York Cotton Exchange. 'Forecasts of the Cotlook A Index for 1993/94 and 1994/95 depend on projections developed by the Secretariat of world stocks and consumption, net trade by China Mainland and barter trade, and on the behaviour of futures prices in 1991, 1992 and 1993'[1]

The initial ICAC cotton price model was developed in 1987/88 as a simple inverted single equation relating prices to world supply and demand conditions. The model differentiated between prices originating in China (mainland), the world's biggest cotton consumer and producer, which has been integrated into the world cotton market since the 1970s, on the one hand, and those from the rest of the world on the other. The model used China's net cotton trade impact on world stocks-to-use ratio and the stocks-to-use ratio in the rest of the world. Mainland China has changed its trade position several times since the mid-1970s, oscillating from being self-sufficient in raw cotton to being a net importer. The model suggested that a decrease of about 53,000 tonnes in China's net trade adds about 1 cent to the price of cotton.

The results were published in *Cotton*, a bi-monthly magazine in which the ICAC reviewed the world cotton situation and presented estimates of average cotton prices for the next two seasons. This initial version of the model was used to predict with some accuracy the direction and level of season average international cotton prices (as measured by the Cotlook A Index) from 1988/89 to 1990/91 with an average difference of less than 6 cents from the actual price. Despite the relative success of the model during this period, the ICAC continued research efforts to compare other available models, but found the alternatives to have less predictive power. These results were summarized in *Cotton* in the March/April 1990 edition which compared five other models of cotton prices to that selected by the ICAC. The 1990 modelling efforts attempted to introduce the effects of the location of stocks, perceptions in the market due to the past behaviour of the stocks-to-use ratio, and price changes of competing crops. These elements

1 *'Incorporating Expectations into a Model of the Cotlook A Index' p20, in Cotton: Review of the World Situation, July-August 1993, ICAC, Washington DC.*

have traditionally been thought to play an important role in the price formation mechanism of the cotton market, but their inclusion brought no noticeable improvement in the econometric explanation of cotton price changes.

The organization's caution about its model's universal predictive power was, however, quite justified. In 1991/92, the cotton market, along with other commodity markets, was fundamentally altered by several important factors, the most significant amongst which was the disintegration of the former USSR. The existing ICAC model served as a basis for predicting the decline of cotton prices in that season, but was able to predict only 10 cents of the 20-cent decline that was actually experienced. The ICAC Secretariat studied the reasons for this unexpected steep fall in cotton prices over the following year. Statistical tests suggested that the actual specification of the model at that stage used relevant—highly correlated—information, but that some additional information which was obviously critical to the formation of prices in the 1991/92 season was obviously absent.

The ICAC was able to explain the reasons for the steep fall well enough in retrospect. Firstly, prices were compensating for being too high the previous season, failing to take account of the fall in consumption that was an inevitable concomitant of the fall of the USSR and its allies. Secondly, there was an increase in barter trade with the newly independent Central Asian Republics. The organization decided that it needed to incorporate information generally used by the market in judging the likely course of future prices and that the fresh results should be incorporated into and tested against the ICAC price model. As a result, a new version of the ICAC Cotton Price Model which included variables accounting for market expectations and barter trade was introduced in June 1993.

The price model now provides a simple quantitative basis for the evaluation of conventional supply and demand factors in commodity markets. It is a particular version of an inverted supply and demand model. The schedule is assumed thus:

$S = s$ (quantity offered, price)
$D = d$ (quantity demanded, price)

So, in equilibrium:

$S=D$ and the *change in stocks = consumption-production*
Change in stocks/consumption = 1—production/consumption.

This demonstrates that the fundamental relationship between supply and demand in a market can be represented by a simple stocks-to-use ratio. This does imply that the cotton market represents a market in perfect competition, such that the price depends on available supply. By inverting the side of the price variable in these equations to isolate price, we can write:

price = f (stocks/consumption)

If the world market can be differentiated between Mainland China and the rest of the world, the equation for the rest of the world becomes

Change in stocks rw/ consumption rw = 1 - (production rw + (M rw - X rw)) /consumption rw

where,
rw signifies the rest of the world without mainland China, *M rw* are imports of *rw* from China and *X rw* exports of *rw* to mainland China.
In this hypothesized bilateral trading world:

(M rw - X rw) = X ch - M ch = net trade by mainland China

(an identity in the model, not a proof of anything at all) then the change in stocks can be rewritten as:

(Change in stocks rw—net trade by mainland China/consumption rw = 1 - production rw / consumption rw

The ratio on the left-hand side of this equation measures the supply and demand situation in the rest of the world. In addition, the ratio net trade by mainland China/ consumption rw measures mainland China's impact in the market in the rest of the world.

Using these equations, the ICAC model can be expressed as:

price = f (X1, X2)

where,
X1 represents net exports by mainland China as a share of rest of the world consumption, and *X2* represents rest of the world ending stocks less net exports by mainland China as a share of rest of the world consumption.

The new model reflects historical events better than its predecessor (see the graphs in Figures 6.7 and 6.8 and the associated table in Figure 6.9). Several tests have been applied by the ICAC to the model: a Recursive Residual test and a CUSOM test suggested parameter stability in all but the 1991/92 season. The ICAC now wanted to know what had caused the problem in the 1991/92 season. They surmised that the factors which had

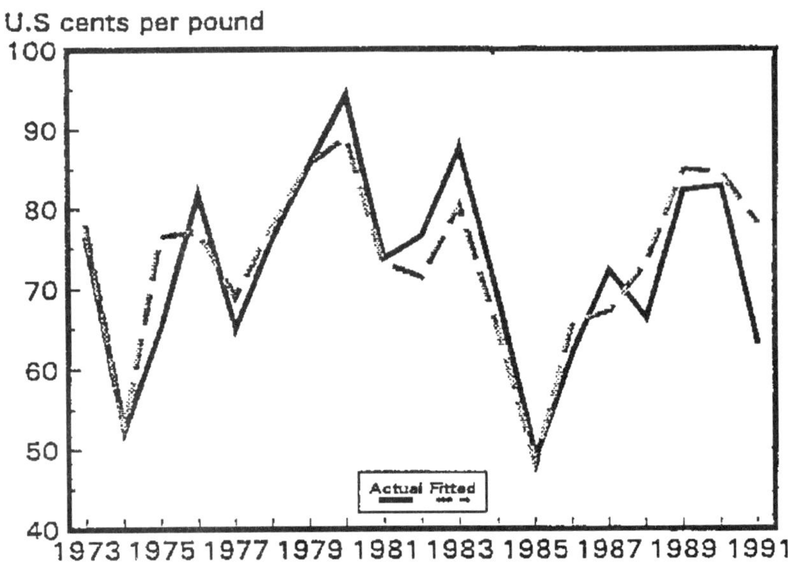

Figure 6.7 Actual and fitted values of Cotlook A Index: ICAC Model
Source: Carlos Valderrama

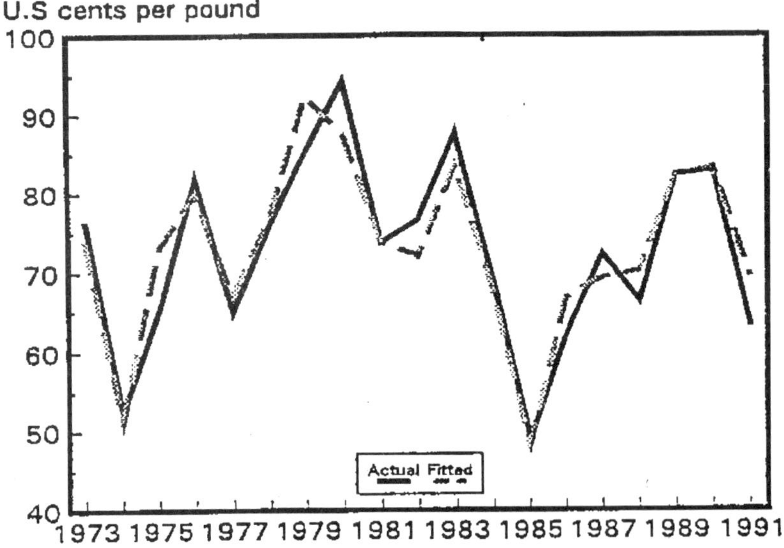

Figure 6.8 Actual and fitted values of Cotlook A Index: Alternative Model
Source: Carlos Valderrama

Dependent variable: Cotlook A Index

Period	Constant	X1	X2	NovFeb (-1)	NovFeb (-2)	Balance (-1)	R2	Standard Error	Durbin-Watson
ICAC MODEL									
1973-1988	127.04	-2.72	-1.20				0.83	5.39	2.15
	(12.72)	(-7.06)	(-5.80)						
1973-1990	123.62	-2.67	-1.13				0.84	5.11	2.09
	(15.17)	(-7.46)	(-6.57)						
1973-1991	120.12	-2.62	-1.07				0.76	6.14	1.68
ALTERNATIVE MODEL									
1973-1991	105.20	-2.75	-0.67	-1.84	-1.80	-5.59	0.89	4.60	2.42
	(12.69)	(-7.81)	(-3.51)	(-2.73)	(-3.19)	(-1.90)			

Figure 6.9 Regression results

made that season different might reoccur, and that they could look for additional information that would refine the model still further. A BDS test suggested that there was a pattern in the forecast error. This, in turn, led to the derivation of a hypothetical variable which in turn cut the forecast error significantly. However, for forecasting purposes, a hypothetical variable is not of any use. The ICAC noticed that the variable would be likely to have a cycle that repeats itself every three to four seasons. Since the ICAC was already fairly certain that it was expectations about future prices that had caused the price fall, their task now reduced to finding a proxy variable for expectations. The introduction of a variable or set of variables that can account for price expectations is possible through using a particular hypothesis about the formation of expectations or by including information used by the market. An adaptive expectations hypothesis and a partial adjustment combination did not improve the model.

A set of variables thought to contain relevant information widely used by agents in the cotton market was therefore devised. These variables capture:

- The price differential of the futures market between February (when planting decisions are being formed in the Northern hemisphere) and November (the closest month before the expiration of a December futures contract);

- The size of world production in relation to consumption;
- The amount of cotton barter transactions in relation to all export transactions by bartering countries.

Several specifications were designed that included this additional information. Agents in the market were assumed to form their expectations about future prices based on the performance of the futures market in the two previous seasons, whether current production is above consumption and the current amount of barter trade. An expectations factor was therefore constructed. This was approximated most closely by the logarithm of the difference between the November and February quotations of the December futures contract on the NYCE. This was found closely to resemble the pattern necessary to improve the NYCE model. However, such a variable cannot be forecast independently and therefore is not of any use. It is, however, very interesting that at this point the ICAC would certainly come close to a technical analysis viewpoint as at least a potential contributor to their model.
What the ICAC did was to re-specify their price model as being:

price = f (X1, X2, expectations factor)

Assuming that agents in the market form their expectations about future prices based on past performance and whether production is above consumption, an expectations fact was constructed such that:

Expectations factor = NovFeb (-1) + NovFeb (-2) + Balance (t) + Barter (t)

where,
NovFeb is the logarithm of the absolute difference between the November and February quotations of the December futures contract, *Balance* is a variable that changes the intercept of the equation when world production is above consumption, and *Barter* is the percentage of world trade between the former USSR and the rest of the world in relation to total former USSR exports. Although the model produces better performance, the variable 'Balance' seems unstable, the ICAC note, for different sample sizes.

Due to a low Durbin-Watson statistic, the model was corrected for autocorrelation. The corrected model lowers the standard error of the forecasts and those generated with the corrected model converge with actual values, decreasing the standard error of the fitted equation. The model has now become more sensitive to changes in mainland China and in the rest of the world, from 2.7 to 3.2 and 1.1 to 1.6 respectively. The model indicates that an increase of 10 percentage points in barter trade from Central Asia causes a fall of 3.7 cents in the Cotlook A Index. When world production is above consumption, the constant term of the model is altered by 10 cents and the Cotlook A Index becomes accordingly less sensitive to the other variables in the model. A 10 per cent decrease in futures prices between February and November of the previous season causes a 2 cent fall in the index compared to a 4 cent decrease two seasons before.

The overall econometric exercise suggests unsurprisingly that expectations play a role in the formation of prices, and the ICAC is now engaged in trying to evaluate other possible sets of variables that represent price expectations.

The ICAC textile and cotton demand model is a set of equations that forecasts apparent consumption of cotton and all other textile fibres. The model rests on basic principles of consumption economics, making textile and cotton consumption dependent upon income, population and prices. However, the ICAC also uses what it calls an 'innovative' approach to prices with the inclusion of the ICAC Textile Fibre Price Index variables. In addition, the model uses a set of weighted income and price variables that account for recession and non-recession environments in short-term forecasting. The model uses GDP data from the World Bank, the IMF and other international agencies, population data from the United Nations and fibre prices from Cotlook Ltd. and the US National Cotton Council. The ratio of cotton prices to those of non-cotton textiles are assumed in the model to continue the trend of the last fifteen years, and increases in the all textile fibre index are assumed to be in line with inflation. Generally, the model is highly susceptible to changes in the exogenous GDP and population forecasts as well as to long-term alterations in the balance between cotton and other fibre prices.

The results of the model are used by the ICAC to adjust the mill consumption element in supply and utilization accounts by country, which are the basis of the ICAC supply/use projections. These use yield and area equations to forecast base production and determine final production, trade, mill consumption and stocks with most current information from each country.

In 1993-94, the integrated world cotton market model based on the ICAC textile and cotton demand model was further developed by the introduction of fresh production equations, and was produced jointly by the ICAC and the Food and Agriculture Organization (FAO) of the United Nations, which is based in Rome. Currently this model forecasts the main elements of the cotton and textile market in the long term. The ICAC/FAO full world cotton market model is a global partial equilibrium model which uses a set of supply and utilization accounts in which all elements are converted into cotton lint equivalents. The components of production within the model and the end use of cotton determine the equilibrium price and the level at which cotton production is equal to consumption. Two additional components have been developed:

- Mill cotton consumption is modelled to provide for the specific influences determining output at the intermediate level of industrial processing. Projected trade in raw cotton is derived from estimates of production and mill consumption (assumed equal to total textile production). Net trade in cotton textiles is derived from mill consumption and end-use consumption.

- To establish the market share of cotton and adjust end use cotton consumption, the model includes estimates of the end use of other textile fibres and their end-use consumption. The textile market is hypothesized to be composed as cotton and wool as natural fibres, and cellulosic and synthetic as chemical fibres. Silk, as yet, plays no part in the ICAC model.

There are an impressive array of countries included in the model: forty countries, accounting for over 90 per cent of world production and 75 per cent of world consumption, are explicitly included.

The core model is for the production and end-use demand for cotton. Harvested area and yield are modelled as separate elements. Cotton area has been considered to be a function of:

- Cotton prices. This is a potential problem of circularity with the model, given the determination of those prices;
- Prices of farm products which the ICAC considers to be competitors;
- Previous year's area;
- In some cases, a trend factor.

The ICAC considers that crops which compete with cotton are different between countries but are usually cereals, rice, sugar cane and oilseeds. Typically, these are determined as follows:

$$AHt = bo + b1\ AH(t\text{-}1) + b2\ PP\ (t) + b3PP\ (t\text{-}1) + b4PCt + b5PC\ (t\text{-}1) + et$$

where,
AH is the area of cotton harvested, *PP* is the producer price of cotton, *PC* is the producer price of the competing products, *t* is this year etc., and *b*s are coefficients of determination. All variables in the model are expressed in natural logarithms, so the coefficients can be considered to be elasticities of price with respect to each variable.

Yields are modelled as a function of input prices, the producer price of cotton, a trend factor again, and lagged yields as a representation of capacity constraints, which may include the availability of inputs such as fertilizer at an affordable price and irrigation limits. The ICAC found that no input price variables were statistically important explanatory variables. At the estimation stage, dummy variables were included to account for unpredictable exogenous events in the past, especially the important matter of weather events, and to provide a *de-evented* (as with deseasonalized) version of the other parameters. No dummy variables were included in the forecasts themselves—in other words, the forecasts yield represents trends based on current known factors rather than incorporating major unexpected events. In this they encapsulate the major problem of forecasting worldwide. One eminent business expert once remarked that 'the one thing you can guarantee about a forecast is that it will be wrong' but of course forecast trends in yields are very important even if major events can throw them off course in particular years. Typically then, the ICAC model determines yields as follows:

$$Yt = b6 + b7\,PP\,(t\text{-}1) + b8T + b9Dn + b10\,Y\,(t\text{-}1) + et$$

In this equation, *Y* refers to yields, *PP* to the producer price of cotton, *t* represents the current year, *Dn* is a dummy and *T* a trend variable. The ICAC notes that seed cotton is produced from area *x* yield—but its world model is in cotton lint. Therefore a given set of country-specific ginning ratios is applied to projected seed cotton production, which are assumed to remain unchanged over the projection period. All models of this kind involve some simplifications, and this is one. The ICAC in these projections is to forecast future production trends, not to predict cyclical highs and lows. It would not be difficult, one presumes, to run the model with gradually increasing ginning ratios, or even to complicate matters further by forecasting the ginning ratios themselves, perhaps on a simple time series basis.

The ICAC assumes that the demand for cotton consumer goods is determined by income, population, cotton prices and the prices of competing products. This is a logical assumption confirmed by statistical tests. In the vast majority of equations, the model exhibited statistically significant correlation coefficients and good fits to the historical data, so the ICAC concludes that the model explains consumer behaviour adequately.

These equations are therefore specified in the world cotton model as:

$$CTCt = b11 + b12GDP\,(t) + b13CRP\,(t\text{-}1) + b14CTC\,(t\text{-}1) + et$$

In this equation, *CTC* refers to per capita final consumption of cotton, *GDP* is gross domestic product and *CRP* is the ratio of the Cotlook A Index to an index of non-cotton fibre prices. This is because cotton competes with other fibres in the same market. The price variable should therefore reflect the relationship between cotton and non-cotton prices rather than that of textiles and other goods competing for a fixed amount of income. The current year is shown as *t*. All variables are again expressed in natural logarithms. Clearly, the *per capita* factor can be switched to determine overall cotton consumption by putting it as a function of GDP.

For market clearance and international-to-domestic price linkage in the world model, the equilibrium price of cotton as represented by the Cotlook A Index is determined endogenously in the model. The ICAC assumes that producers respond to producer prices of cotton and consumers to the 'A' index so they were obliged for the purposes of the model to construct and model the connection between the two. A price transmission equation was therefore estimated for every country modelled. These price transmission coefficients reflect the various reasons which are the cause of the non-correlations between the 'A' Index and the domestic producer price. These are either arbitrary, e.g. producer price policies and trade barriers, or absolute, e.g. geographic location for a country. Clearly, in a country with no trade barriers, it can be presumed that any change in the 'A' Index will translate quickly and totally into a change in the domestic producer price. Similarly, a country isolated from the world market will be less sensitive to changes in world prices. The 'A' Index can be seen as a benchmark around which specific countries' prices oscillate—not just as a quality benchmark around which prices are structured. The ICAC believes that if domestic producer prices are above the index they will tend to move down, and vice versa. The two arguments are complementary, anyway, as different countries tend to have very different quality types of cotton. The ICAC has produced models which analyse the concept of the available supply of exportables. In these models, the available supply of exportables impacts on prices, and the additional supply of exportables determines fluctuations around the benchmark price level.

Using the price transmission equation in the model, with coefficients estimated from past data and applied to the future, implies an assumption that any changes in agricultural policies and other factors influencing the transmission of world prices to producers will not leave the structure of production unchanged within the forecast period. The model linking the two prices is formally specified as follows:

$$PP\ it = b15 + b16PP\ (it\text{-}1) + b17\ AIndex\ (t) + b18\ AIndex\ (t\text{-}1) + et$$

In this equation, *PPit* is the producer price in country *i, AIndex* is the Cotlook A Index of cotton prices and *t* is current year. All variables are expressed in natural logarithms. The model employs a market clearing mechanism to ensure that world supply and demand reach equilibrium. This is an iterative procedure where the required changes in the equilibrium price are provided by a simplified Newton algorithm, repeated for every year until the end of the forecast period.

The world model contains a number of other features. A model of mill consumption has been developed to estimate the consumption of raw cotton in individual countries, and so to allow estimates to be made of trade flows in raw cotton and in cotton textiles. The ICAC believes that demand for cotton can, in a simplified fashion, be considered as a two-stage process. In the first instance, there is demand for raw cotton or mill consumption; secondly, there is demand for final cotton goods or the end-use of cotton. Cotton fibre is primarily used as a raw material for the textile industry and converted in many complex operations into a variety of intermediate 'gray goods', that in turn make up cotton goods. Textile manufacturers, it is suggested, usually have a variety of different fibres from which to choose for their products. This must, however, be diminishing in relevance as products become more specific and product related. The ICAC says that the decision to use a particular fibre or mixture of fibres is usually based on the desired properties of the end-product, relative fibre prices and consumer preferences. One suspects that a trend factor needs to be built in for each product line and this summated as product fibre use becomes increasingly differentiated. In the ICAC model, to account for these influences, mill cotton consumption is assumed to be driven by the growth of demand for cotton products. This includes the domestic market for all countries and regions modelled and the export market for a number of textile-exporting countries, the relative prices of cotton and other fibres, and a number of other economic factors built into the lagged dependent variable of the respective equations. The growth of demand for cotton products is captured in the model through GDP per capita.

Prices for other fibres are indicated through the index compiled by the ICAC which incorporates the prices of polyester, rayon and wool, weighted by demand for each. Currently, the International Wool Secretariat is conversely interested in the idea of cotton prices as a leading indicator for wool prices, although one might have imagined that this debate would have been settled by now. Finally, in recognition of the importance that exports have in the textile sectors of many countries, especially the fast-growing countries of South-East Asia, GDP per capita in the respective export market was successfully implemented in many equations.

Mill consumption in the model is therefore estimated as:

$$MCt = b19 + b20\ GDPD\ (t) + b21\ GDPE\ (t) + b22\ CRP\ (t\text{-}1) + b23\ MC\ (t\text{-}1) + et$$

In this equation, *MC* is mill consumption, *GDPD* is GDP in the country, *GDPE* equates to gross domestic product in the export industry, *CRP* to the ratio of the 'A' Index to the index of non-cotton fibres, and *t* is again the current year. All variables are in natural logarithms, with the coefficients representing elasticities. To retain consistency between the overall level of mill consumption and end-use projections, the results of the mill consumption levels were adjusted on a pro-rata basis for all the countries. There can be no possible objection to this process in this case, and it is a familiar one from econometric modelling. What it really means is that the equations do not sum completely and there are missing explanatory variables or smaller countries which, if added, would make them do so. It is yet another example of the type of compromise which is typical of this type of econometric model.

The world model also incorporates equations for the end use of all textile and non-cotton textile fibres. For many countries, the shares of the textile market between cotton and non-cotton represented by separate equations do reproduce the historical trends. For some countries, however, overestimation of one of the fibres resulted in unlikely market shares. In all such cases, the all textile fibre equation was used to determine market share. Final consumption of both cotton and non-cotton were compared and adjusted as required to fit the final consumption of all textile fibres. This was assumed to be a function of income, population and textile prices. It seems unlikely that these would be in any way linear functions given the diminishing marginal utility of textiles with respect to income, so the use of linear functions would tend to overestimate demand towards the end of the forecast period. The equation representing this is:

$$ATCt = b24 + b25\ GDP\ (t\text{-}1) + b26\ TPI\ (t\text{-}1) + b27\ ATC\ (t\text{-}1) + et$$

In this equation, *ATC* refers to final consumption of all textile fibres, *GDP* to gross domestic product per capita, *TPI* to a demand-weighted index of all textile fibres deflated by the IMF world consumer price index, *t* is the current year; all variables are in natural logarithms. By comparison, end-use non-cotton textile fibre consumption has been modelled along lines similar to that of cotton end-use consumption, and the non-cotton consumption equations produced equally satisfactory statistical results. Non-cotton textile demand is formally specified in the model as:

$$NTCt = b\ 28 + b29\ GDP\ (t\text{-}1) + b30\ RPN\ (t\text{-}1) + b31\ NTC\ (t\text{-}1) + et$$

Here, *NTC* refers to per capita consumption of non-cotton textile fibres, *GDP* again to gross domestic product, *RPN* the ratio of the non-cotton fibres index to the 'A' Index and *t* to the year; the equation again is expressed in natural logarithms.

Current research in respect of international cotton price differentials and relative scarcity of supply by the ICAC is developing price linkage equations by country that will permit the creation of short-term stock and price projections.

The Manchester Model

In the 1987 Manchester Model, commissioned by the UK Ministry of Agriculture, the price equations form a flow diagram, starting with wheat prices. The constructors of the model analysed wheat prices, for example, determining that their major determinants at that time were policy prices, i.e. the intervention and effective threshold prices. They followed their own previous work in this field in believing that the influence of each would vary depending on the half of the harvest year. Thus in the first half, when stocks are high, the intervention price is more likely to be supporting the price, whilst in the second half the threshold price will be more influential. To reflect this, a compound variable was constructed which was equal to the intervention price in the first half of the harvest year—the second half of the calendar year—and a weighted average of the two policy prices in the second period. The designers experimented with using the size of on farm stocks as a proportion of harvested output so that, as the size of the stocks increased, greater weight was given to the intervention price. However, the proportion of the output harvested is still that on farm at December was found to be fairly constant at around 50 per cent, and so fixed weights were also tried, giving a 50:50 weight to each policy price in the second period. Since this gave almost equivalent results and was simpler to include in the model, this was adopted.

The dependent variable used is the wheat price index for the UK, deflated by the composite policy price. The undeflated price, with the (undeflated) policy price on the right-hand side of the equation, was also tried by the designers of the model, but the adopted specification gave a better Durbin-Watson statistic. The explanatory prices used are the import price of wheat, deflated by the threshold price. This has the expected positive effect, as does the number of birds recorded for the table at the beginning of each period, which is used as a demand shifter. Wheat production itself has the expected negative impact on price, although not to a great extent because of support policy, so that production tends to determine where price sits within the support bands.

What is entirely noteworthy about this series of determinants is that there is just one single leading indicator amongst them. Without advance information as to the two policy prices, and without information on the current import price of wheat, the only relevant determinant which would be available at the start of a season is the bird on table number. Secondly, this equation seems unlikely to produce more than an average price for the entire season. It is not designed for constant iteration on a daily basis to look ahead short distances. It is an excellent example of the difference between constructing econometric identities in current time periods to explain the functioning of systems, which can be useful in their own right as models which can be employed to analyse the implications of policy changes, and forecasting models which work in real-time on data that is available now.

It is instructive to examine the subsequent history of the Manchester model, especially in the light of Vernon Roeningen's comments below[1] The University of Manchester took the view that the model was constructed for the benefit of MAFF, and transferred it to them. MAFF do not believe, as they have confirmed, in long-term modelling activity, so there seems little rationality in this step at first sight. The university did carry out some further work, based on equations up to 1987 and with a data set extended to 1992. However, the model's principal author, M.P. Burton, has stated that the model has not been exploited commercially or kept up-to-date 'mainly because it is so time consuming to maintain the model in an up-to-date version...For policy and forecasting purposes it would need a substantial degree of continuing effort to maintain the model, and there is no history, at Manchester, of devoting resources to this kind of commercial work.'[2] Burton also makes the perfectly valid point that he would end up doing little else than running the model and he prefers to diversify his own work portfolio. This story of agricultural modelling in the UK rather typifies the entire modelling story in the majority of cases. On-going developmental work, such as that of the ICAC, is the exception to the rather dismal rule of a great deal of effort going in to constructing models which become institutionally redundant rather than technically obsolete. It is a clear case of inefficiency which greater communication and openness between model-builders could expect to break down.

[1] *pp165-6*

[2] *M P Burton, letter to the author, 19 August 94*

Chapter 7

The use of futures markets as forecasts

Many commodity markets have corresponding futures markets, especially energy, metals and some softs. Information is thereby available for these commodities that is not available for other markets, for example retail markets, or for commodities sold by auction, such as tea. Futures prices show what traders and those involved in the market currently believe prices will be at a series of future dates and they have committed financial resources to their beliefs. As a result, futures prices are a continuous market of opinions about the future, and these are useful as an input of expectations. These may be used as inputs for demand and supply estimation, but they may also be useful for testing theories about the way expectations are formed. Klein, for example, believes that futures prices are highly valuable and potentially informative bodies of data for the economic testing of expectations theory and possibly for improving forecasts of parts of the economy. His view is shared by numerous economists who are delighted by the surfeit of data that futures markets generate.

There are some objections that others have raised to this optimism:

- Futures price change all the time, at least in liquid markets. Clearly the most accurate state of expectations is not an average of futures prices over time—defining the period over which futures prices should be averaged will never itself be easy—but the immediate present state of expectations. The result of using this, of course, is that the forecasting model would change its results all the time that the futures market was itself changing its prices. Whilst a forecasting model that sometimes changes is clearly necessary, there must clearly be some independence of constant fluctuations, or else the model cannot be used for any planning purposes at all. Its output will have changed before anything can be done on the basis of it.

- Futures prices reflect expectations on the part of some, but not all, of those with vested interests in market direction, as well as speculators, whilst what is perhaps required is either a totally disinterested view of all non-participants, or better, a complete consensus of all market participants. Neither of these are possible.

- Futures market specifications frequently change, invalidating historical data.

Because of the development of oil futures markets and oil options markets, complete with their associated Black-Scholes and other related options pricing methodologies, econometrics has been forced to apply time series methods to futures pricing.

But it cannot be stressed too much that as of the mid-1990s, futures pricing and time series modelling have not yet conjoined. They are separate and different skills, meeting different economic needs and producing results that are consumed by different audiences.

Futures market prices are radically different as forecasting methods to the other types of forecasts discussed in this book. For a start, the forecasting aspect of futures is incidental to their main purpose. Certainly, accurate price discovery through forward prices has always been regarded as an important function of futures markets. Futures prices are allegedly critical to market participants, as in many cases they are claimed at least to be used for forecasting purposes. However, futures prices are publicly available rather than (usually) privately constructed—although models like the ICAC are an exception to this—and they are also free. They are specific to a certain quality of the commodity which may not be the one desired to be forecast or indeed traded, hence the existence of what is called basis risk. The futures prices refer to specific months in the future, almost invariably with a time horizon no longer than two years at the most. This renders them relatively useless for long-term forecasting except in conjunction with other forecasting methods. Moreover they are—perhaps most importantly of all—constantly changing. All forecasts change on the input of new data, of course, so futures prices are no exception to that rule, but there is clear necessity to carry out some averaging process of futures prices in order to generate any form of forecast on which to operate.

Some attempts have been made in the past to establish whether futures markets embody all the relevant information contained in previous prices (known as *weak form tests*). Since they did inevitably change and approach the spot price at expiry in what appears to be a confused way, it is also important to discover how they fail to reflect it. In a forecasting sense, therefore, a wholly-efficient futures market based on complete information available presumably at zero cost provides the most accurate possible representation of future spot prices. But, undoubtedly, a better approach is to compare the accuracy of futures prices with other forecasting methods (see Chapter 9). In practice, risk aversion, irrational market behaviour, imperfect capital markets and transactions costs are several of the contributory factors towards the inaccuracy of futures markets as forecasting tools.

Leuthold and Garcia[1] claim that 'many market participants use these prices for production, processing, pricing and marketing decisions.' They draw on earlier academic work to support this contention, mainly in the USA and not very extensive. Several facts militate against this contention. For example, in 1993, when Agra-Europe, one of Europe's leading agricultural analysis companies, offered to provide a futures analysis service to its clients, there was no response to the offer. Another example is the fact that the London Commodity Exchange has had extreme difficulties in promoting its agricultural contracts—although this seemed to be lessening in 1994/95. Therefore it seems unlikely that, in the UK at least, agricultural futures prices, certainly, are taken very seriously as forecasts of future spot prices—at least to the alarming extent suggested by Leuthold and Garcia. There seems to be a complete absence of any empirical work on the subject of the relative use of different forecasting methods by practitioners, especially traders (let alone farmers), for institutional reasons. The use of futures for forecasting purposes seems especially unlikely for futures market traders who, after all, need to trade the futures market and would be highly unlikely to do so if they believed that at all times they could never improve on the forecast of the future spot market that the futures market contained.

[1] *Goss, 1992, p52*

Chapter 8

Technological forecasting

Long-term forecasting

The forecasting methods described in this book—including futures markets—have all been short- and medium-term forecasting in Keynesian economic terms. Long-term forecasting, for commodities as much as for anything else, involves changes in one or more available technologies, but it also includes major changes in long-term weather cycles and resource levels. A good example in commodities was the development of synthetic rubber and the impact this had on natural rubber demand, trade and prices. Another example was the impact of refrigeration on lamb prices internationally. Similarly, in the future, the technical development of synthetic fibres will have a major impact on demand, market share and prices of cotton and other competing natural fibres as it has already done in respect of the size of the jute market and the price of jute. It is not just a question of synthetic competitors, either: new rice varieties could easily affect the international rice trade, as they have in the past, new greenhouse technologies could affect tomato production, and new engines could require different fuels. Changes in weather patterns, previously thought practically stable in overall terms, and cyclical if difficult to predict, could change production ratios between different locations for many commodities. Finally there may be new discoveries of oil in countries with a different input into oil price determination than those at present. All of these are relevant to long-term commodity forecasting.

But if short- and medium-term commodity forecasting is difficult, long-term forecasting is virtually impossible. Almost all the laudable efforts that have been made this century (let alone last century) to sketch out detailed futures have been proved wrong. Interestingly, from a private study of these alternative futures, it seems clear that there is a dominant theme in differentiating those that have proved to be at least along the right lines and those that have been quite out of touch, and that is, perhaps surprisingly, political orientation. However unpalatable it may be to concede, very right-wing technological forecasts from the early 1960s of the year 2000 (from such organizations as the Hudson Institute and the RAND Corporation) have turned out far closer to reality than the more liberal and radical notions that have been wishfully entertained subsequently, such as Alvin Toffler's *Future Shock* and others of the same genre. There is no necessary reason to presume that this criterion will be as effective in evaluating long-term forecasts in the future as it has proved in the past.

Moreover, for commodity forecasting purposes, the inaccuracy of long-term (technological) forecasting and the wholly inadequate range of means at its disposal such as trend extrapolation, consultations between experts, diffusion analysis and input-output models must render this type of work virtually useless for trading purposes. Its horizon is far too long for any profit-maximizing strategy to be designed—and too long to be practical even for policy-making purposes. On this point, most forecasters seem unwilling to agree, recommending the investment of more resources in the area. Fortunately, for most trading and manufacturing companies such long-term horizons are irrelevant.

Chapter 9

Forecasting methods

Those both tangentially and closely associated with economic forecasting may be summarized as follows:

1. *Qualitative approach*—based on judgement and opinion and experience:
   - expert opinion
   - Delphi technique
   - sampling of producers'/traders' opinions
   - surveys of production
   - PERT derived techniques for sampling expert opinion

2. *Quantitative approaches*

   i) Forecasts based on historical price/volume data—time series approach:
   - naive methods—straight extrapolation
   - moving averages
   - exponential smoothing
   - trend analysis
   - decomposition of time series
   - Box-Jenkins
   - structural models
   - mathematical programming

   ii) Associative (causal) forecasts:
   - simple regression
   - multiple regression
   - econometric modelling

3. *Indirect methods*
   - market surveys/ crop surveys
   - input/output analysis
   - economic and weather indicators

Quantitative methods work well provided that there are no systemic shocks which invalidate previous assumptions and correlations. It is no use using a model to predict pearl prices based on a demand from the Soviet Union which peaks in the autumn—when the Annual Plan always used to call for pearl imports—now that the Soviet Union is no longer around. At such a juncture the importance of experienced human judgement in the markets is indispensable. Change can be identified more quickly, and human beings are surprisingly good at judging the quantitative impact of qualitative change. Mathematically, it is something the brain is well adjusted to; the remarkable thing is that there are so few road accidents involving pedestrians, not that there are so many.

How does this relate to the choice of forecasting systems for trading? Most systems used in commodity trading are autoregressive, for example moving averages, breakout systems (such as point and figure) and swing techniques too. Studies in random price movement are not intended to discredit long-term trends. The effects of seasonality and inflation exist in markets—hence moving averages and other trading techniques. If a series of commodity prices is decomposed by extracting the seasonal trend, the long-term inflationary bias and the industrial cycle, what remains is a short term fluctuation that is expected to be random.

'Most mechanical trading systems are trend-following systems. All trend-following systems have one thing in common; that is, they are usually very profitable when the market is in a good trending mode and usually unprofitable in non-trending, sideways market.'[1] Yet, 'Very profitable investment strategies are available to the investor who is aware of the non-random price changes to be expected in the barrier area. The problem from the investor's point of view is to determine the existence of a reflecting barrier and to determine the price boundaries of the region. Transfer function models are capable of modelling an intervention variable that indicates the movement into a barrier region.'[2]

What are the advantages and disadvantages of different forecasting methods? Clearly in many cases no one forecast is in practice used. A mixed forecast is the alternative, in which the evidence provided by technical, fundamental, qualitative and econometric forecasting is all weighted. In the simplest version of this process, each forecast would be equally weighted: but the weights may be altered depending on how accurate each forecast has been. There seems to be a dearth of theoretical literature on this score, perhaps accounted for by the fact that the theoretical literature is not produced by those who need forecasts in

[1] *J Welles Wilder in Kaufman, p69.*

[2] *Testa and Hargrove in Kaufman, 1978.*

practice. Equally clearly, mixed forecasting may often lead to a better result than relying on one single forecast, especially over a long period.

It is an empirical matter to decide which forecast performs best and an intuitive one as to which forecast has best captured the parameters under which the independent variable will be created in the future.

QUALITATIVE (JUDGEMENTAL) METHODS

Technique	**Delphi Method**	**Expert Opinions**
Description	A panel of experts is interrogated by a sequence of questionnaires in which the responses to one questionnaire are used to produce the next questionnaire. Any set of information available to some experts and not to others is thus passed on to the others, enabling all the experts to have access to all the information for forecasting	Based on the assumption that several experts can arrive at a better forecast than can one person. There is no secrecy, and communication is encouraged. Forecasts are sometimes influenced by social factors and may not reflect a true consensus.
Accuracy:		
Short-term (0-3mo)	Fair to very good	Poor to fair
Medium-term (3mo-2yr)	Fair to very good	Poor to fair
Long-term (2yr and over)	Fair to very good	Poor
Identification of turning point	Fair to good	Poor to fair
Typical application	Long-range forecasts; technological forecasting.	Long-range forecasts; technological forecasting.
Data required	A co-ordinator issues the sequence of questionnaires, editing and consolidating the responses.	Information from a panel of experts is presented openly in group meetings to arrive at a consensus forecast. Minimum is two sets of reports over time.
Cost of forecasting with a computer	Expensive	Minimal
Time required to develop an application and make forecasts	1 month	Two weeks

Cont.

(cont.)

Technique	PERT-Derived	Consumer Surveys
Description	Based on three estimates provided by experts: pessimistic, most likely, and optimistic.	Based on market surveys regarding specific consumer purchases.
Accuracy:		
Short-term (0-3mo)	Fair	Fair to good
Medium-term (3mo-2yr)	Poor	Poor
Long-term (2yr and over)	Poor	Poor
Identification of turning point	Poor to fair	Poor
Typical application	Same as expert opinions.	Short-term forecasts.
Data required	Same as expert opinions.	Telephone contacts, personal interviews or questionnaires.
Cost of forecasting with a computer	Minimal	Expensive
Time required to develop an application and make forecasts	Two weeks	More than a month

INDIRECT METHODS

Technique	Input-Output Mode	Leading Indicator
Description	A method of analysis concerned with the inter-industry or inter-departmental flow of goods or services in the economy or a commodity and its markets. It shows what flow of inputs must occur to obtain outputs.	Time series of an economic activity whose movement in a given direction precedes the movement of some other time series in the same direction.
Accuracy:		
Short-term (0-3mo)	Not applicable	Poor to good
Medium-term (3mo-2yr)	Good to very good	Poor to good
Long-term (2yr and over)	Good to very good	Very poor
Identification of turning point	Fair	Good
Typical application	Forecasts of demand, supply and stocks	Forecasts of price by commodity

Cont.

(cont.)

Data application	Ten or fifteen years' history. Considerable amounts of information on flows within a trade for each year for which input-output analysis is desired.	Five to ten years' history for each commodity.
Cost of forecasting with a computer	Expensive	Varies with application
Time require to develop an application and make forecasts	More than a month	One month

QUANTITATIVE FORECASTING

Technique	Regression Analysis	Econometric Model	Markov Analysis
Description	Functionally relates to other economic, competitive, or internal variables and estimates an equation using the least-squares technique.	A system of interdependent regression equations. The parameters of the regression equations are usually estimated simultaneously.	Models based on learned behaviour.
Accuracy			
Short-term (0-3mo)	Good to very good	Good to very good	Excellent
Medium-term (3mo-2yr)	Good to very good	Very good to excellent	Poor
Long-term (2yr and over)	Poor	Good	Poor
Identification of turning point	Good	Excellent	Good
Typical application	Forecasts of price by commodity.	Forecasts of price by commodity.	Forecasts of price by commodity.
Data required	At least 30 observations are recommended for acceptable results.	The same as for regression.	Data required for transaction probabilities.
Cost of forecasting with a computer	Varies with application	Expensive	Expensive
Time required to develop an application and make forecasts	Depends on ability to identify relationships	More than a month	More than a month

Cont.

(cont.)

TIME SERIES FORECASTING

Technique	Moving Average	Exponential Smoothing	Trend Analysis
Description	Averages are updated as the latest information is received; weighted average of a number of consecutive points in the series.	Similar to moving average, except that more recent data points are given more weight. Effective when there is random demand and no seasonal fluctuation in the data series.	Fits a trend line to time-series data. There are two variations: the linear and non-linear methods.
Accuracy			
Short-term (0-3mo)	Poor to good	Fair to very good	Very good
Medium-term (3mo-2yr)	Poor	Poor to good	Good
Long-term (2yr and over)	Very poor	Very poor	Good
Identification of turning point	Poor	Poor	Poor
Typical application	Forecasting low transaction volume.	Limited applications to commodities.	Long-term forecasting.
Data required	A minimum of two years of price history if seasonals are present. Otherwise fewer data (Of course, the more history the better.) The moving average must be specific.	The same as for moving average.	Varies with the technique used. However, a good rule of thumb is to use a minimum of five years' annual data to start. Thereafter, the complete history.
Cost of forecasting with a computer	Very minimal	Minimal	Varies with application
Time required to develop an application and make forecasts	One day	One day	One day

Cont.

(cont.)

TIME SERIES METHODS

Technique	Classical Decomposition	Box-Jenkins
Description	Decomposes a time series into seasonals, trend cycles, and irregular elements. Primarily used for detailed time-series analysis (including estimating seasonals).	Iterative procedure that produces an autoregressive, integrated moving average model, adjusts for seasonal and trend factors, estimates appropriate weighting parameters, tests the model, and repeats the cycle as appropriate.
Accuracy		
Short-term (0-3mo)	Very good to excellent	Very good to excellent
Medium-term (3mo-2yr)	Good	Poor to good
Long-term (2yr and over)	Very poor	Very poor
Identification of turning point	Very good	Fair
Typical application	Tracking and warning, forecasts of price and transaction data.	Supply, demand, stock and price forecasting.
Data required	A minimum of three years' history to start. Thereafter, the complete history.	Usually as for ARMA models.
Cost of forecasting with a computer	Minimal	Expensive
Time required to develop an application and make forecasts	One day	Two days

Figure 9.1 The advantages and disadvantages of different forecasting methods
Source: Heavily adapted form Strategic Business Forecasting, pp 159-164.

Different applications by firms, government, etc.

The viewpoint of the academics actually constructing econometric models is typified by Hallam's contention that 'Paradoxically, it is often where circumstances are known to be changing that the predictions of econometric models are particularly considered: in examining the likely effects of planned policy changes, for example.'[1] There is, in fact, no paradox here at all. Econometric models should be able to handle changed circumstances: and forecasts should predict them. No one thinks it 'paradoxical' that first aid boxes are only opened in emergencies, or that parachutes should only open when rip-cords are pulled.

The policy-makers themselves say that 'MAFF economists are frequently required to forecast developments on commodity markets so as to assess policy options and proposals as they affect UK and EC agriculture.'[2] MAFF's view is that although from time to time models have been commissioned, mainly from universities, for forecasting purposes which contain an element of commodity forecasting—the 1987 Manchester University model was especially noted by MAFF—'On the basis of past experience, we are not convinced that the cost of building and maintaining a comprehensive model of the UK or EC agricultural sector can be justified. MAFF's limited modelling needs can usually be met, either by using existing models developed by others, or by constructing simpler individual commodity models.'(ibid.) The UK MAFF argues that it does not have the resources to develop the large-scale general equilibrium models which are necessary to assess policy developments in an international context.

Against this, MAFF does not appear to have analysed the relative costs between a one-off expense of establishing a detailed global model (with its commercial potential) by comparison to many, possibly contradictory, one-off projects handed out to other organizations. So, although MAFF says that '*SORITEC* appears to be an effective statistical package'[3], their usage is confined to very simple simulations. By contrast, MAFF argues, the Eurostat SPEL model has not been of great value because it is unable to take into account adequately the complexities of the different CAP regimes. The USDA SWOPSIM and OECD AGLINK models, MAFF says, have been more useful in the context of understanding international trade relationships and MAFF does deploy results and parameter estimates from these models. The World Bank and the OECD Development Centre in 1992 developed an agricultural trade liberalization model, RUNS, which builds on the original work of Tyers and Anderson—but then scenario analysis, however complex, is not forecasting.

MAFF therefore constructed, for example, a model of the banana market using exogenous elasticity estimates to assess the impact of the Single

[1] *Hallam, p 170*

[2] *Nick Haigh, Economics (International) Division, MAFF, letter to the author, 6 April 1994.*

[3] *Letter to the author 16 September 1994.*

European Market on EC banana policy. What has happened to this model subsequently is not related. MAFF economists have access to, and use, a number of other agricultural models developed in Europe and the USA. Amongst these are:

- The OECD AGLINK model which runs on *SORITEC* software and produces forecasts of production and consumption of major agricultural products for a wide range of countries;
- The Eurostat SPEL model, which is a sectoral production and income model of EC agriculture;
- The USDA SWOPSIM model.

Use is also made of ABARE, World Bank models, the EIU 'World Commodity Forecasts' and subscription is taken to a wide range of market information bulletins from sources such as the International Wheat Council, ED&F Man (Sugar) and F.O. Licht (Coffee). So, for example, when the UK government had a particular need to determine policy with respect to international commodity agreements, the *SORITEC* package was used to forecast world prices under different assumptions about the operation of price stabilization and support schemes. In 1994, the UK MAFF commissioned a study to evaluate existing econometric models of UK farming and to report on appropriate future developments. This may have been the beginning of an overdue systematization of UK agricultural modelling and, if so, it was very much to be welcomed.

USDA baseline projections (see Chapter 6) are used in USDA budgeting and periodic analysis of policy scenarios, such as the implementation of GATT, NAFTA or a Farm Bill, building forecasts and scenarios from a modelling base. The official position is that the baseline projections are used in the USDA to support on-going activities such as the impact of foreign developments on US agriculture, budget reviews, farm programme administration and management, and assessing issues related to world food security. This makes a nonsense of refusing to describe them as forecasts, as the USDA continue to do.

Vernon Roningen, the creator of *SWOPSIM*, accurately and sharply characterized as *modelcide* what is frequently being applied to models within government and quasi-government institutions. Those involved in the industry understand very well intuitively what Roningen means by this idea and his belief that universities and private organizations are exempt from the rule may be over-optimistic. To spell it out: modelling is essentially a dynamic process. The original creation of the model is but one initial stage; its constant refinement, as with the ICAC model, can bring benefits far out of proportion to the further investment required in terms of the accuracy of the model. But the requirements for forecast data are static, specific, occasional and budget-controlled. There may be an urgent need for a forecast of the international rice trade, or UK egg production, this year: next year there may be none. The model is commissioned, designed, built and used: then it is left to rot, with the team disbanded. There are literally dozens, perhaps hundreds of models, in this condition all over the United States, Japan, and Europe. There is not even a catalogue of their existence, let alone of their accuracy.

A high-placed government modeller says: 'In modelling, many hear the call and promise to do things but few actually deliver the goods at a price an organization is willing to pay (e.g. most model building is by amateurs fresh from doing dissertations). Besides, there is a basic political problem in that modeller success threatens the livelihood of a lot of people whose jobs are justified by their monopoly on 'back of the envelope' intuitive forecasting. Most government managers have no modelling experience and can not really effectively judge who can do the job and who can't. And modelling is a tough time-consuming job and the modeller doesn't have time to deal with the internal politics of model acceptance'.

These are harsh words, but they embody a great deal that is true.

The performance of forecasting

Forecasters on the whole are reluctant to discuss how accurate they have been in the past, despite the huge costs that erroneous forecasts when acted upon can generate. They prefer to stress the difficulties involved in their task, the professional skills and experience that they have brought to this difficult task, and frequently the novel, significant or better (than rival systems) qualities of their particular forecasting approach or system. Forecasters of all types are often usually strong on:

- Historical data;
- Analysis of the past;
- The regrettable, but immensely institutionally popular, process of creating 'scenarios'—which are usually very specific in their assumptions—as opposed to definite forecasts which are often not;
- Graphical/report presentation of their scenarios/forecasts.

This applies especially to those professional forecasters selling into the commercial sector. Forecasting software manufacturers concentrate in their sales literature on who has bought the software and what 'features' it has, not on how accurate it has proved to be in service. Almost, but not all, forecasters, are weak on the empirical results of using their forecasts over time. 'Editors of the *Journal of Political Economy* and the *Journal of Money,*

Credit and Banking have often complained that failed attempts to fit data have not been reported.'[1]

But in fact the *only* real utility of a forecast is how effective it is in predicting the future, not how effective it has been in the past. This can only be a guide to its future performance and which may be as erroneous in judging the future as the forecasts themselves. What makes the omissions so disturbing is that the performance of a forecast can be checked against its own record, usually relatively easy to obtain by comparison to publicly-available data on commodity prices, and also by comparison to other forecasts—which may be more difficult to obtain in the absence of a central organization reviewing commodity forecasts. Part of the problem is that the superficially easy question of assessing the performance of a forecast turns out on closer examination to be far from easy. A wide range of statistical measures exists whereby the forecast's accuracy can be checked. The most well-known measures for establishing forecast errors are mean absolute deviation, mean squared error (probably the best known) the root mean squared error, the mean absolute percentage error (which is calculated from the absolute error of each period divided by the actual value for that period, and averaging the two percentage errors) and the Theil U-statistic (often included in computer statistical packages) which compares the predicted and observed change. All of these are different in their evaluations of forecasts only at the margins, and in the majority of evaluations establish the same hierarchy of accuracy between forecasts. Other somewhat differently-aimed accuracy tests consider the number of turning point errors, based on the total number of reversals of trends which is often applied to all market forecasts including commodity forecasts, as knowledge of the direction of prices is often virtually as useful than knowledge of the exact evolution of prices.

Clearly, it is important to monitor forecasts for their accuracy, and there are two obvious tools for this purpose.

- i) *Tracking signals.* These are based on the ratio of cumulative forecast error to the corresponding value of the mean absolute deviation which can itself be updated continuously using exponential smoothing. These values are compared to predetermined, but often arbitrary, limits based on experience, judgement and need.

[1] *Boland, p144.*

- ii) *Control charts.* These can be used to set upper and lower limits for individual forecasts rather than cumulative errors. The limits are multiples of the estimated standard deviation of forecast, which is the square root of the mean squared error. Frequently control limits are set at 2 or 3 standard deviations.

Although price forecasts are typically evaluated on the basis of the types of statistical criteria discussed above, it may be that these methods are not ideal for the purposes to which the forecasts are put. Gerlow, Irwin and Liu (1993) basing their work on much earlier (1979) work by Brandt—indicating the relative lack of commitment to the task of working out the commercial effectiveness of forecasting—suggest that price forecasts could alternatively be analysed using economic criteria. The four criteria suggested are:

- i) *Zero mean returns.* By examining mean percentage rates of return against an assumed efficient market (zero rate of return) the effect of forecasting errors is incorporated into the evaluation process, although the assumed risk-neutrality of the decision-maker may be a problem.

- ii) *Zero risk-adjusted mean returns.* In this case, the problem is that there is as yet no generally-accepted consensus regarding the proper definition of the market return in applications of the capital asset pricing model to commodity markets.

- iii) *The Merton test of market timing ability,* which is a combination of the accuracy of price direction change in both directions (models may, of course, predict the timing of increases better than falls and vice versa) irrespective of the magnitude of change.

- iv) *The Cumby-Modest test of market timing ability.*

The authors rightly stress that further research will be necessary to determine the reasons for the divergence between statistical and economic evaluation of commodity price models and the range of models over which these conclusions apply. The conclusion they draw, that econometric models may have much greater economic use than statistical appreciations suggest, may be limited to the hog market models that they analysed.

The study of the effectiveness of econometric forecasting models, along with all other types of forecasting, has become clouded by several issues apart from this superfluity of potentially conflicting methods of assessment:

- Models are used for policy analysis, usually *before* they have been properly tested against developing real events. Their function as explanatory models is therefore able to be discussed quite independently of their accuracy as forecasting models—a situation which very much suits the legions of academics who produce such models in universities, the World Bank and elsewhere.

- Models with excellent historical fits do not necessarily predict the future accurately, especially in commodity markets subject to structural change. Model makers tend to present their conclusions, funded to a certain point, and then go on to make something else. The model ages, withers, and is then confined to history.

- There are few incentives on model-makers to run their models over a long period of time and publish the results of their models in terms of their accuracy as forecasts. No central organization monitors the accuracy of forecasts and few organizations even publish the accuracy of their own forecasts.

Consumers of these forecasts, whether in the private or the public sector, have yet to become anywhere near as discerning as for example, automobile or computer buyers, who are provided with magazines which analyse the construction, function, quality and competitors of specific products and present these analyses for potential buyers. With forecasting, there is a superfluity of intensely academic debate over methodology, the overwhelming majority of which—both in econometric/fundamental analysis and in technical analysis—passes straight over the potential user's head—and vastly too little serious comparative analysis, presented in an easily comprehensible form, of the accuracy of different types of forecast. One suspects this may be because the complexity of the technique bears more relation to the interest of the forecaster in the model that has been built rather than the accuracy of the result over the selected period—which is what the user must keep permanently in sight when analysing and choosing, let alone believing, forecasts.

There are, in fact, few commodity models which are constantly updated and where the results are continually announced and any associated forecasting errors and problems are elucidated publicly. The ICAC cotton price model is an exception to this general rule and would represent, were a similar model available commercially for other commodities, a good potential investment for a company looking for a reliable commodity price model. It is, however, much to be regretted that a central organization does not compile published commodity forecasts making the comparison of their output feasible along the lines above in the same way that Consensus

Forecasts does for macroeconomic forecasts. Part of the reason this is not generally done is that unlike in macroeconomics there are numerous different indicators as well as hundreds of different commodities. The problem is not insuperable, however. Where there is an active futures market, such as in cotton or coffee, or even where there is an established spot price, such as in wool or to a lesser extent rice with the Bangkok market price (however inaccurate it is) then the possibility exists of collecting a series of forecasts of that indicator.

Extended discussions on methodology, and disputes between the different types of technique, are far more prevalent than empirical investigations into the track records of models. It could be strongly argued that these should, however, be precisely the starting point for the effectiveness of models and any other form of forecasting. Hallam states comprehensively, and with disarming honesty, the important fact that: 'econometric models are not the only, and certainly not necessarily the best, means of generating forecasts of economic variables'. In fact, in the few comparative studies which have been made, econometric forecasting models have not emerged as uniformly superior in terms of accuracy to the alternatives such as Box-Jenkins time series models, futures market quotations, or pure expert judgement.

Neither does there appear to be strong general support for the common belief that the relative accuracy of econometric forecasts improves with the length of forecast horizon. As might be expected, the performance of econometric models differs from one commodity to another, and may be superior the more volatile the behaviour of the forecast variable. It is difficult to draw general conclusions from this evidence concerning the value of econometric models in forecasting. The results themselves are not compelling in favour of any particular methodology.'[1]

Some organizations such as the EIU and ABARE are reasonably open with the accuracy of their forecasts, and this is much to be welcomed. Companies publishing their results do not tend to be software manufacturers who, as noted, publicize the technical merits of their software, not its performance in specific cases. To be fair, their successes are their clients' successes and not public knowledge. The USDA and ICAC are exceptionally open, and this is very much to be welcomed. The accuracy of the ICAC's price forecasts over the period 1989-93 was published in the ICAC publication *World Textile Demand* in October 1993 (see Figure 9.2). As expected, although the one-year forecasts were very accurate, two- and

[1] *Hallam, p171.*

three-year forecasts fluctuated, with the GDP forecasts used by the model being taken mainly from World Bank figures, which are themselves frequently wrong. The revised model now also predicted with a good degree of accuracy average prices in 1992/93. In 1994, cotton price increases also tended to validate the model forecast.

The accuracy of the world textile fibre consumption model developed by the ICAC is shown in Figure 9.3. A very considerable improvement to this fit can be created by the introduction of a dummy variable which reflects

Forecast Date	Same-year Forecast	Most Current estimate	Difference
	1000 Metric Tons		Percent
Fall/92	38665.5	38646.3	0.0
Fall/91*	38932.0	37857.0	2.8
Fall/90**	38740.8	37889.3	2.2
Fall/89	38293.4	38168.2	0.3

* *In 1992, wool consumption data were revised down from 327,000 tons, equivalent to 0.9% of textile consumption.*

** *In 1992, wool consumption were revised down 434,000 tons, equivalent to 1.1% of textile consumption*

Figure 9.2 Comparison of most current estimates of world textile consumption with ICAC textile demand forecasts.

severe falls in textile consumption under conditions of recession, but this makes the forecast even more sensitive to the accuracy of general economic cycle prediction and brings the problem full-circle back to the fact that what makes cotton run, like every other commodity, is money, and what is going to happen to money is the most difficult thing in the world to predict.

The World Agriculture Outlook Board produced, in September 1994, an analysis of the differences between the USDA September projections and reality over the extended period of 13 years (see Figure 9.4).

The most important criterion for the assessment of the accuracy of the forecast is the percentage variation. On this basis, the USDA appears to be best at forecasting the global rice market in terms of production, and least satisfactory in respect of oats and cotton—although, in any event, error of the order of 4 per cent over the long term is highly respectable. But, for US production, the errors are closely bunched and the only 1.2 per cent error for wheat production and similar results for eggs, millet and broilers are truly remarkable. Forecasting exports is more difficult and the error figures reflect this—in the case of oats being 100 per cent out—suggesting some fundamental problem with the model, or radical market change. And

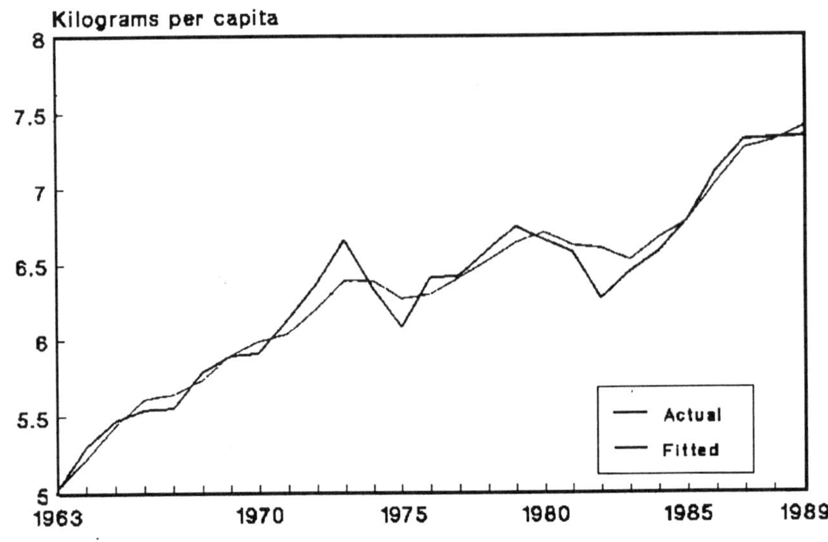

Figure 9.3 **World textile fibre consumption as explained by Model 1**

although mill use forecasts seem relatively accurate, stocks are predicted the least well, which suggests that forecasting errors for production and exports move in the same direction and are therefore cumulative in their effect on stocks. Interestingly, on closer examination, other patterns emerge: for example, that a greatly increased accuracy of prediction is achieved for world rice production and exports than for either the USA or the rest of the world separately, as the errors have consistently been in opposite directions.

With respect to energy forecasts, in the past such assessments as have been made are far from sympathetic. 'Among some eight prominent models reviewed by the EMF (1982) and by Gately (1986), only two were able to explain the significant price collapse from 1986 to 1990 when they were used for projections according to an optimistic scenario. Furthermore, minimum prices reached during the price collapse were largely overestimated by these two successful projections, with the IEES-OMS model predicting a minimum price of oil of $16 in 1981 and the model of Gately predicting a minimum price of $27 (1981) against an actual minimum of $7 to $10 in 1986.'[1] This is frankly a dismal performance. It is inconceivable that any trader would be enthusiastic about conducting trades on the basis of this evidence.

Commodity & region	Difference between proj. and final estimate, 1981/82-93/94[1] Avg. Percent	Avg	Difference		Below final	Above final
		Million metric tons			Number of years[2]	
WHEAT						
Production						
World	2.2	11.3	-30.7	8.9	7	6
US	1.2	0.8	-1.4	2.5	6	7
Foreign	2.5	11.2	-30.9	7.8	7	6
Exports						
World	3.6	4.0	-9.7	6.2	9	4
US	10.7	3.7	-10.0	7.2	5	8
Foreign	4.3	3.2	-9.7	2.7	9	4
Domestic use						
World	1.7	8.4	-23.4	10.0	8	5
US	7.3	2.2	-3.7	3.6	7	6
Foreign	1.5	7.0	-21.0	8.2	10	3
Ending stocks						
World	7.6	9.4	-26.0	14.3	9	4
US	15.3	4.1	-9.1	12.4	7	6
Foreign	8.3	7.7	-25.4	5.9	8	5
COARSE GRAINS[3]						
Production						
World	1.5	12.1	-39.4	20.9	10	3
US	3.9	8.0	-19.9	26.0	9	4
Foreign	1.5	8.7	-19.5	9.1	8	5
Exports						
World	6.7	6.8	-11.5	16.5	7	6
US	14.1	7.4	-14.5	14.5	5	8
Foreign	11.0	5.6	-10.2	9.6	7	6
Domestic use						
World	1.2	9.2	-29.1	19.8	4	9
US	3.8	6.5	-13.4	13.2	8	5
Foreign	1.5	8.9	-20.2	17.5	6	7
Ending stocks						
World	10.4	14.4	-43.2	26.7	9	4
US	17.4	11.5	-32.2	27.4	7	6
Foreign	12.5	7.9	-16.8	7.7	10	3
RICE, milled						
Production						
World	2.2	7.1	-24.1	3.4	11	2
US	4.8	0.2	-0.5	0.4	8	5
Foreign	2.3	7.1	-24.4	3.6	11	2
Exports						
World	6.7	0.9	-2.6	0.8	8	5
US	8.2	0.2	-0.4	0.9	5	7
Foreign	7.7	0.9	-2.1	0.7	9	4
Domestic use						
World	1.9	6.1	-22.7	3.2	10	3
US	6.3	0.1	-0.3	0.4	7	6
Foreign	2.0	6.1	-23.1	3.2	10	3
Ending stocks						
World	12.8	3.8	-7.5	5.2	10	3
US	17.9	0.2	-0.9	0.3	8	5
Foreign	14.0	3.8	-7.3	6.1	10	3

For notes, see end of figure.

(cont.)

Commodity & region	Difference between proj. and final estimate, 1981/82-93/94[1] Avg. Percent	Avg Million metric tons	Difference		Below final Number of years[2]	Above final
SOYBEANS						
Production						
World	2.9	2.8	-6.8	4.7	7	6
US	4.6	2.4	-4.6	4.6	7	6
Foreign	5.2	2.5	-5.0	4.6	6	7
Exports						
World	5.6	1.5	-3.5	2.5	8	6
US	10.0	1.9	-3.6	5.5	7	6
Foreign	16.0	1.0	-3.8	1.9	5	8
Domestic use						
World	2.7	2.7	-6.0	3.1	6	7
US	3.3	1.1	-3.2	1.5	9	4
Foreign	3.7	2.5	-4.6	3.7	7	6
Ending stocks						
World	16.0	2.8	-6.6	6.8	7	6
US	26.9	2.1	-3.5	4.8	5	8
Foreign	16.7	1.7	-4.3	2.4	7	6
COTTON		Million 480-pound bales				
Production						
World	4.3	3.4	-10.9	9.5	7	6
US	4.5	0.6	-1.9	1.7	6	6
Foreign	4.7	3.2	-11.2	9.8	6	7
Exports						
World	4.6	1.1	-3.3	0.9	7	6
US	17.4	0.8	-1.6	2.0	6	7
Foreign	6.8	1.2	-3.3	1.9	7	6
Mill use						
World	2.6	2.0	-6.6	3.2	5	8
US	6.8	0.5	-1.1	0.9	9	2
Foreign	2.5	1.8	-5.9	4.0	5	7
Ending stocks						
World	15.3	5.1	-12.7	12.5	7	6
US	29.8	1.3	-2.3	2.5	5	8
Foreign	15.0	4.4	-13.2	10.9	6	7
CORN		Million bushels				
Production	4.2	290	-709	885	8	5
Exports	14.3	254	-425	483	4	9
Domestic use	4.4	249	-508	430	8	5
Ending stocks	21.0	419	-1321	934	7	6
SORGHUM						
Production	4.6	33	-69	81	7	6
Exports	22.6	55	-115	97	6	7
Domestic use	8.7	44	-114	78	7	6
Ending stocks	29.1	67	-155	155	4	9
BARLEY						
Production	2.8	13	-29	36	7	6
Exports	39.6	26	-82	38	6	6
Domestic use	6.2	26	-47	70	8	4
Ending stocks	12.1	27	-61	70	6	7

For notes, see end of figure.

(cont.)

Commodity & region	Avg. Percent	Avg	Difference		Below final	Above final
	Difference between proj. and final estimate, 1981/82-93/94[1]					
	Percent	Million bushels			Number of years[2]	
OATS						
Production	4.9	15	-19	44	4	8
Exports	100.7	2	-5	8	3	7
Domestic use	3.6	16	-39	27	5	8
Ending stocks	14.4	22	-40	47	9	4
SOYBEAN MEAL			Thousand short tons			
Production	3.5	925	-2388	1342	9	4
Exports	10.1	619	-1400	741	5	8
Domestic use	3.7	756	-1550	1075	10	3
Ending stocks	39.5	94	-179	368	5	7
SOYBEAN OIL			Million pounds			
Production	3.6	460	-954	791	8	5
Exports	18.5	243	-650	575	7	6
Domestic use	2.5	281	-985	300	10	3
Ending stocks	31.4	438	-975	1143	6	7
ANIMAL PRODUCTS[4]			Million pounds			
Beef	4.0	948	-333	2438	7	4
Pork	2.4	371	-400	1242	6	5
Broilers	1.6	287	-101	622	9	2
Turkeys	2.7	101	-123	235	10	1
			Million dozen			
Eggs	1.6	91	-111	140	9	2
			Billion pounds			
Milk	1.3	1.8	-1.0	4.6	6	5

[1]*Final estimate for 1981/82-92/93 is defined as the first November estimate following the marketing year and for 1993/94 as last month's estimate.* [2]*May not total 13 for crops and 11 for animal products if projection was the same as final estimate.* [3]*Includes corn, sorghum, barley, oats, rye, millet and mixed grain.* [4]*Calendar years 1983 through 1993 for meat and eggs; October-September years 1982/83 through 1992/93 for milk. Final for animal products is defined latest annual production estimate published by NASS.*

Figure 9.4 Reliability of September predictions

Using world wheat production as an example, changes between the September projection and the final estimaate have averaged 11.3m tons (2.2%) ranging from -30.7 to 8.9m tons. The September projection has been below the estimate 7 times and above 6 times

Source: USDA WAOB

Some limited information also exists on the use of futures prices themselves as forecasts. Just and Rausser (1981) demonstrated that the ability of live cattle futures prices to forecast subsequent spot prices improved, very unsurprisingly, as the contract approached maturity, and that these short-term forecasts outperformed commercially-available forecasting services which would have used a variety of econometrically- and technically-based methods. The same result pertained for the hog market one quarter forward; however, they found just the opposite for the hog market four quarters forward. Leuthold and Hartmann (1976, 1981) compared the forecasting accuracy of the live hog futures market on a monthly basis, and both the live hog and the cattle futures markets on a quarterly basis, with separate appropriate econometric models in each case. Goss (1992) modelled the results of several different types of models compared to futures prices in terms of their mean squared error. He concluded that: 'For cattle, through the first year of forecasts (182) the composite model was the most accurate for the one-month horizon, while the econometric model performed the best for the two-month to six-month horizon. By the end of the fourth forecast year (1985), the composite model was the most accurate for the one-month to five-month horizons, while the econometric model was marginally superior for the six-month horizon. For hogs, the econometric model begins in 1983 as the most accurate forecaster of the three models for all horizons. By the end of the fourth year (1986), however, the time series model is the most accurate for the one month horizon.'[1] Goss notes that, unsurprisingly, for time horizons of between two to six months, the composite model eventually becomes the best performer during the forecast period in each case. All these authors, on balance, concluded that although in some periods the futures market was a more accurate predictor, the econometric software outperformed in the longer term. This would at first suggest that traders could benefit by simply following the advice of a decent econometric model which would, on balance, produce more profitable than losing trades, but of course as has been frequently pointed out this does not necessarily mean that these models' results could be directly translated into profits.

Leuthold and Garcia[2] actually carried out a simulation of buying and selling an imaginary portfolio on the basis of the recommendations implied by the econometric software, without producing profits when trading costs and the cost of buying and maintaining the models are taken into account.

[1] *Leuthold and Garcia in Goss, p64-65.*

[2] *In Goss, 1992.*

This work is extremely important, especially since buried in the caveats and his recognition in respect of other similar work carried out with colleagues in studying the US oats market that 'The model is a superior predictor to the futures price, although the difference between the two is not significant.'[1] which allowed Goss to make the important statement that: 'the models are capable of generating substantial profits over the three year simulation period'[2].

It is welcome after this inadequate vista that with respect to trading software a very different picture prevails. The Futures Truth Co., based in North Carolina, has acquired a dominant and deserved position in the US market. It is recommended by software manufacturers and others alike, for the exhaustive testing of trading programmes against real market conditions in order to establish the extent to which they meet their objective of profit-making. So important has it already become that at least one trading software manufacturer has tried unsuccessfully to prevent it from publishing results. Others have formally requested Futures Truth not to evaluate their systems. In a zero-sum game like futures trading, it is not surprising to find that trading programmes are far from guaranteed money-makers. Futures Truth rank trading systems by commodity, as well as evaluating their performance across a selected range of commodities. There are several financials included in the list, but the commodities included are pork bellies, sugar, soybeans, gold, live cattle, coffee and cotton.

The company points out that: 'A large number of the systems that we track are designed to trade a large portfolio. Due to lack of resources we are unable to track more than six or seven commodities. The performance that we show on the portfolio that we track does not necessarily mean that this same performance would be reflected when trading a different or larger portfolio. We have heard of people trading the same systems that we track, but with different portfolios, realizing different returns than what we show. We encourage contacting the system vendor and asking what has been the total maximum drawdown and return for the *entire portfolio*. Taking a different range of commodities—and many systems are said by their designers to be applicable to a full range—could well produce different results.' Only therefore a long-term average of the Futures Truth results can be regarded as at all significant. The format of their results and the performance of trading systems for the commodities tracked can be seen for

[1] *Goss et al in Goss, p 161.*

[2] *Leuthold and Garcia in Goss, p70.*

	MPT Rank	System Name	Sys #	%Chng Min. Req Cap.
		SOYBEANS SYSTEMS		
1	12	Parabolic Stop	65	173.0
2	13	Universal	133	170.5
3	23	Kylie	193	144.3
4	89	Pattern Probability	165	2.2
5	119	Swing Index System	84	-43.5
6	152	Dual Cross System	125	-121.7
7	177	Miracle Trading Method	31	-245.9
		LIVE CATTLE SYTEMS		
1	11	Grand Cayman System	177	182.7
2	19	T-Rex	185	161.7
3	123	Reverse Trend Entry	123	-49.4
4	158	Murlantic Cattle Method	34	-128.1
5	173	Black or White	124	-198.0
		COTTON SYSTEMS		
1	14	Benchmark	182	169.1
2	17	Grand Cayman System	177	164.2
3	32	Black or White	124	107.2
4	75	Reaction Trend System	83	15.2
		GOLD SYSTEMS		
1	1	Volatility Movement	85	441.4
2	3	Dr. Jenkins System	62	283.3
3	24	Watch and Wait	126	138.3
4	44	DAX #2 Gold Daytrade	101b	74.1
5	160	DAX #3 Gold Daytrade	101c	-138.3
6	165	DAX #4 Gold Daytrade	101a	-149.4
		SUGAR SYSTEMS		
1	25	1-2-3 System	106	135.7
2	30	DCS II	111	116.1
3	83	Grand Cayman System	177	10.7
4	92	Directional Movement	82	-1.2
		COFFEE SYSTEMS		
1	8	Ultimate III	173	215.2
2	18	Ultimate II	135	163.8
3	26	Ultimate IV	190	122.6
4	27	Squeeze	174	121.9
5	47	Universal	133	71.9
6	58	DCS II	111	51.3
7	61	Benchmark	182	50.6
8	88	Watch and Wait	126	2.7
9	91	Scooter	105	0.0
10	109	Pattern Probability	165	-22.8
11	132	1-2-3 System	106	-64.3
12	139	Daytrade Pro	192	-83.0
13	157	Kylie	193	-127.8
14	163	Grand Master Thrust	178	-146.4
15	186	Trend Balance Point	78	-483.9
		PORK BELLY SYSTEMS		
1	42	DCS II	111	77.5
2	65	Watch and Wait	126	42.1
3	180	Dual Cross System	125	-273.2
4	185	Miracle Trading Method	31	-352.0

Figure 9.5 Futures Truth evaluation of software systems, February/March 1994

Source: Futures Truth

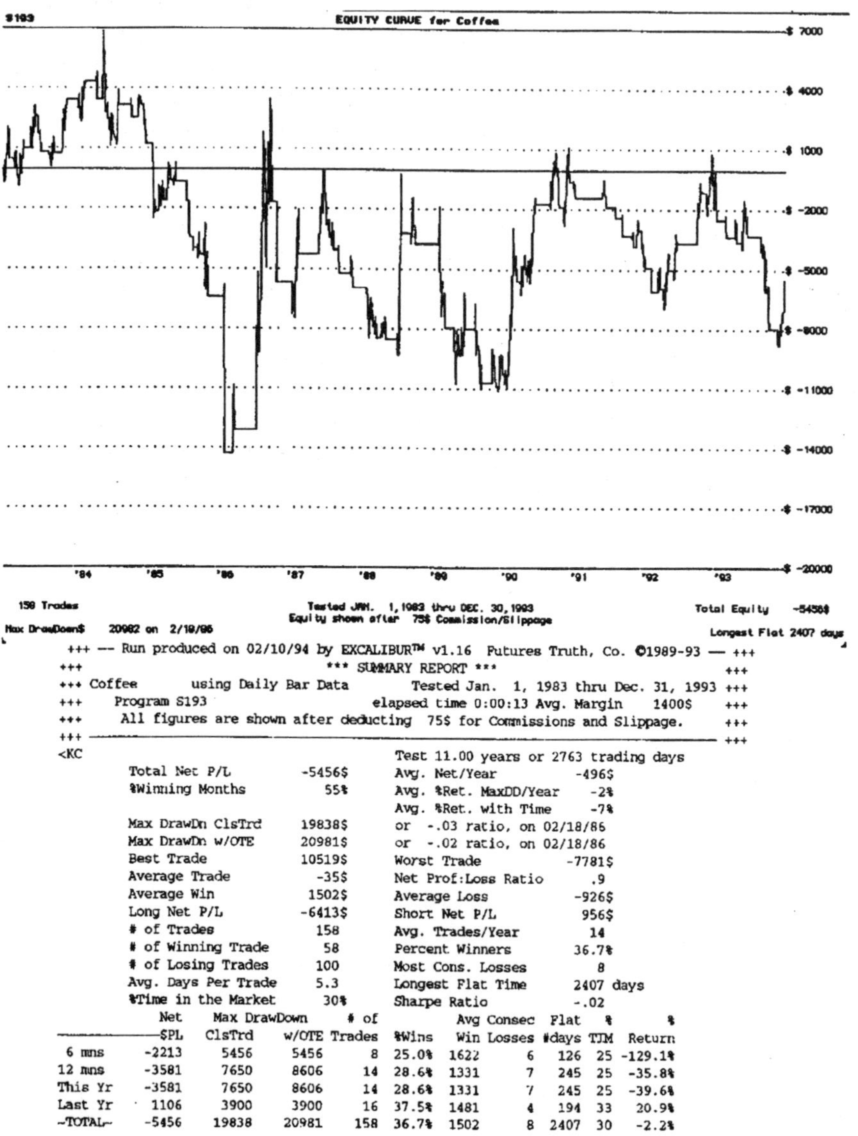


```
+++ -- Run produced on 02/10/94 by EXCALIBUR™ v1.16  Futures Truth, Co. ©1989-93 — +++
+++                          *** SUMMARY REPORT ***                              +++
+++ Coffee       using Daily Bar Data         Tested Jan.  1, 1983 thru Dec. 31, 1993 +++
+++    Program S193                         elapsed time 0:00:13 Avg. Margin    1400$   +++
+++    All figures are shown after deducting  75$ for Commissions and Slippage.        +++
+++ ---------------------------------------------------------------------------- +++
<KC                                          Test 11.00 years or 2763 trading days
         Total Net P/L             -5456$    Avg. Net/Year             -496$
         %Winning Months              55%    Avg. %Ret. MaxDD/Year       -2%
                                             Avg. %Ret. with Time        -7%
         Max DrawDn ClsTrd         19838$    or  -.03 ratio, on 02/18/86
         Max DrawDn w/OTE          20981$    or  -.02 ratio, on 02/18/86
         Best Trade                10519$    Worst Trade              -7781$
         Average Trade               -35$    Net Prof:Loss Ratio         .9
         Average Win                1502$    Average Loss              -926$
         Long Net P/L              -6413$    Short Net P/L              956$
         # of Trades                 158     Avg. Trades/Year           14
         # of Winning Trade           58     Percent Winners          36.7%
         # of Losing Trades          100     Most Cons. Losses           8
         Avg. Days Per Trade         5.3     Longest Flat Time       2407 days
         %Time in the Market         30%     Sharpe Ratio              -.02
```

	Net $PL	Max DrawDown ClsTrd	Max DrawDown w/OTE	# of Trades	%Wins	Avg Win	Consec Losses	Flat #days	% TJM	% Return
6 mns	-2213	5456	5456	8	25.0%	1622	6	126	25	-129.1%
12 mns	-3581	7650	8606	14	28.6%	1331	7	245	25	-35.8%
This Yr	-3581	7650	8606	14	28.6%	1331	7	245	25	-39.6%
Last Yr	1106	3900	3900	16	37.5%	1481	4	194	33	20.9%
~TOTAL~	-5456	19838	20981	158	36.7%	1502	8	2407	30	-2.2%

Figure 9.6 Futures Truth: A detailed report on *Kylie*

Source: Futures Truth

February/March 1994 in Figure 9.5 with a specific example of the performance of one tested system illustrated in Figure 9.6. Over time, these rankings can and will of course change, so Figure 9.5 should be seen only as an indication of format rather than an actual guide. Systems are withdrawn from the market and others enter, too, which is another reason for changes in the figures. But Futures Truth maintains a complete database of available software, together with names and addresses, and the company's products are an invaluable benefit to the potential user of trading software.

Subscription to Futures Truth is not expensive; the Master Performance table is published every two months, the subscription cost was $150 in mid-1994 and detailed reports on specific trading systems currently cost $50 at the same time.

It would be highly desirable were this company, or another, to evaluate commercially-available forecasting systems similarly, with a range of forecasting problems presented such as cotton prices, US GDP and so on, and similarly present the accuracy of each forecast and the methods that the system adopted to reach it. Futures Truth have been asked to do so and are considering the idea.

Chapter 10

The current role of forecasting in commodity markets

In reality, commodity forecasting is largely neglected and separated, even in many trading firms. This is especially true of small firms, where there is no present awareness of the ease with which off-the-shelf computer software programs can be used to generate forecasts for their commodity. Traders and managers often argue that quantitative forecasting is useless because it is resource-intensive—which, by comparison to even a decade ago, it no longer is—and because it does not provide a guaranteed answer. As a result, companies which depend on commodity prices, either as traders or manufacturers, find it impossible to develop a hedging strategy with any precision, despite the obvious fact that the failure to forecast commodity price evolution accurately can have a disastrous effect on their earnings and profits.

Much the same picture emerges from government. Allen, as long ago as 1977, interviewed government economists and 'Virtually everyone Allen interviewed noted that there was seldom sufficient time to employ the sophisticated modelling techniques employed in graduate school and still meet the demands placed on practising government economists'.[1] This suggests that pure theorists seek total explanation and apply philosophical criteria of falsifiability to the models they build. Stochastic models such as regression models with unexplained variability, which can only ever hope to be approximate answers, inevitably come in for criticism by these so-called pure theorists. Against this is posited instrumentalism, 'Where conventionalism asserts that theories are neither true nor false but only better or worse, instrumentalism asserts that if the theory or model works its truth status does not matter.'[2] But at least in commodity forecasting, it must be seriously doubted as to whether any of these so-called pure

[1] *Boland, p 13 (Boland 1989, and much previous work).*
[2] *Boland p88.*

theorists actually exist. The fact is that even approximation models are very complex and there are institutional pressures against testing results.

Forecasting forecasting

After having discussed forecasting methods very largely in quantitative terms in this book, it may come as something of a disappointment for the reader to learn that there will be neither technical analysis nor an econometric model of forecasting in this chapter. The reason is obvious: there are as yet no detailed statistics on forecasting. We might be able to use the sales figures of leading forecasting companies and products as proxies for the growth in the industry overall. If we did, we should see an industry that is growing in most countries and most respects at a rate slightly faster than that of GDP, as well as diversifying and entering progressively more industries. Soft and other commodities forecasting remains in its infancy, however, by comparison to that of metals and especially energy. This gap is bound to narrow.

The distinction between the different methods of forecasting are bound to diminish. Already, to some extent, the different quantitative methods are being seen as complementary rather than in competition. In particular, throughout the forecasting world, work has been carried out which suggests that time series analysis of economic variables may be necessary before carrying out econometric modelling using equations. The strict boundaries between technical and fundamental forecasting will mean much less when they are combined as part of an iterative process searching for accuracy on a PC-based multi-method forecasting software system. Smart Systems would not find it difficult to integrate the IRC methodology into their *SmartForecast* software, for example, and such examples abound.

The future for forecasting, then, can already be seen and its characteristics clearly identified. As usual, the USA is ahead of the rest of the world in this regard, but even there many of these improvements have yet to come about.

- *Forecasting will become increasingly a PC-based activity* like the construction of graphs or the keeping of historical records, rather than either a mainframe, a paper or an entirely cerebral exercise. Its scale, resource level and scope will become much more human, its mystique will begin to disappear, and the level of employee given responsibility for it will, owing to its automation, begin a slow decline.
  There is absolutely no reason why some of the 'new generation' of commercial forecasting software tools could not be applied to commodities, although it seems certain that the refinement of these programs for specific application to commodities forecasting is

possible. The president of one leading US forecasting company said that he 'assumed that commodity forecasting involves the processing of a large number of items and large amounts of data during each forecasting session'. The two worlds do not—yet—talk to one another, but the Internet may change all that. The distance can, and will, diminish as a new generation of computer-literate traders, accustomed to trading at least partially on PC-based trading systems such as SYCOM, APT and GLOBEX engage the services of a variety of different forecasting systems to improve their trading performance. All these systems will be based on their Pentium and subsequent better and faster PCs and all will be able to be run simultaneously and integrated with custom-built software into an overall highly individual result based on typical forecast combination structures. In some cases this will feed through into trading directly, with the trader functioning only as an authorizer, responsibility-taker, and software programmer. An excellent example of the new generation of integrated software incorporating many of the econometric principles outlined in this book is the *SmartForecasts v3* from Smart Software, and no doubt version 4 and later will follow on. This is part—just part—of the shape of the future.

- *Specialist forecasting firms will increasingly dominate the market*, providing either standard or customized forecasting software applicable to a variety of markets. The accuracy of a forecast will start to depend on how expensive it was to buy, rather than just the luck of the draw. That is not to suggest that forecasts will become more inaccurate; on the contrary, depending on the ratio of the number of economic 'shocks' over the next thirty years compared to the last, it may well become much more accurate. It is highly likely that claims will continue to be made by econometricians and technical analysts alike that the past few years, or months, are in some way uniquely difficult to have forecasted. They are, they will say, subject to a series of special events which cannot possibly be expected to reoccur. Each successive period in economics has its own uniqueness: inflation in the 1970s, for example, unemployment and fast growth in the 1980s, uncertainty in the 1990s. Commodities likewise, both as a group, in their categories and as individual markets, have their phases. The whole point is surely that the future will inevitably bring a series of unusual and quite different events, whether in respect of new agricultural technology, combinations of weather systems, new political alignments and policy combinations, or even wars, famines and diseases of plants and man. A good forecast is one that anticipates both the scale and the magnitude, as well as the directional implications, not just of a continuation of yesterday's trends, but also of tomorrow's. It is a difficult task and, if in the end forecasts are reflections of yesterday's view of today rather than a clear view of tomorrow, then that is understandable and unlikely to change radically.

- *Use and understanding will diverge.* Understanding of how ever more complex and arcane forecasting methods work will become—were it possible—the preserve of an even smaller clique of academics and software designers. They will no longer be professional forecasters themselves and will be concentrated ever more not in corporations, but in the design and implementation teams of the PC forecasting software companies themselves. Meanwhile, the use of their products, forecasting software, will become much more widespread. An analogy with the automobile is appropriate. Comparing 1920 with now, many more people drive and own cars but a much smaller percentage of owners and drivers understand how they work and can maintain them. This is the face of commodity forecasting of the future, in which a sharp division exists between the understanding of the forecasting techniques outlined in this book—which will remain unknown but will become unnecessary for the trader—and an understanding of the available commercial forecasting models and their characteristics and integration possibilities. This latter will become ever more desirable for a trader.

- *Forecasting data will become much more freely available,* especially at the macroeconomic level for individual commodities and for areas not absolutely critical to profit-making. A parallel with macroeconomic forecasting in the period since 1960 can easily be seen. At that time, such forecasts were expensive and individual. Now, they are handed out free in publicity literature from stockbrokers. Much the same must apply to commodity forecasts. Indeed, the process is already underway, with some property forecasts, for example, now being published by chartered surveyors for property and with market prospectuses being regularly issued by commodities brokers and specific forecasts regularly issued by the USDA. The next stage will be for the relative accuracy of different forecasts to be professionally compared on a subscription basis by such organizations as Consensus Forecasts and their equivalents worldwide. At present, Consensus state that: 'We have never conducted a survey or systematic analysis of the different types of forecasting systems used by individual contributors, which range from judgemental analysis supplemented by spreadsheets containing simple accounting identities to fully specified global econometric models.'[1] But this can be expected to change—or, as has happened in other fields, consumer magazines such as the PC journals will start to carry reviews of the accuracy of different systems, and these articles will find their way back of course to the software purchasers and manufacturers. Consensus is, however, always studying the possibility of expanding its coverage to include sectoral, including commodity, forecasts, and other companies such as Futures Truth could enter the field. The market for the comparative evaluation of forecasts is so clear that it will inevitably draw economics companies and analysts.

- *Costs are bound to fall in real terms* as the market becomes better understood and more competitive. Smart Systems' *Smart Forecasts* basic version already comes in at a mere $595. This compares to a full portfolio simulation and forecast from IPD, the UK property portfolio analysts, index makers and forecasters, of £8500. The gap between the two can surely be expected to fall as further PC forecasting models come onto the market and become better known.

This, then, is the future of forecasting: an altogether more businesslike and commercial future. Forecasts will stand and fall by their much-discussed accuracy and in which software and professional companies compete for contracts in the same way that, for example, back office systems now do. It is an exciting future, and one which those who have a good track record in forecasting must welcome.

What real use does forecasting have?

What traders actually say on this subject varies enormously. Most believe that a synthesis of different views, not least intuition, is the right way to forecast commodity markets and indeed any other market; '..in my opinion a single indicator should not be used by itself to generate buy and sell signals, but rather a combination of indicators to build up a picture that gives you confidence to trade your system.'[2] Inevitably, perhaps more to do with the psychology of those who become traders rather than any objective analysis—there is, after all, precious little of it—econometric software comes low down on the list. Technical analysis is not always understood or highly

1 *Michael Sykes, Editor, Consensus Forecasts, letter to the author, 15 March 1994.*
2 *R. Hexton.*

regarded. Of the three, fundamental analysis probably enjoys the highest reputation, and all traders pay close attention to the fundamentals in their commodity.

Shim, Siegal and Liew (1994) claim that there are six basic steps in the forecasting process, and they are obvious steps in commodity forecasting as much as in any other area of business or government. First, determine the requirements of the forecast. Why is it being carried out and who is prepared to pay what for the results? Who carries the responsibility for inaccurate forecasts and how much accuracy and detail is actually required? What decisions rest on the forecast? Linked to this process is what these authors call the second stage of the process, the determination of a time horizon for the forecast. There are two different types of definition of the distinction between short-, medium- and long-term forecasts. One, the economists' definition, looks to unalterable resource levels as the short term, changes in inputs as the medium term, and change in technology as the long term. The other, colloquial, usage of the term is usually up to one year, 1-5 years and over five years. It should be clear from this book which usage is frequently used by econometric model builders and which is more useful to traders. The third stage is that the forecasting technique to develop a model or otherwise must be selected.

The data are then assembled, tested and the forecast developed in stage four, with stage five being the identification of necessary assumptions (one would be inclined to put that before the construction of the model, in line with Boland's observations about falsifiability). Finally in stage six—very frequently neglected—are the monitoring of the forecast, the improvement of the model or its replacement by a better one or a different technique altogether, and the integration in the long term of the forecast process with decision-making.

Choosing between forecasting methods

The choice in practice is largely determined by the institutional framework of the company or the individual. A given company may have experienced commodity traders and may operate in a market, such as rice, where the market is opaque and a forecast needs to be little more complicated that up or down. Under these circumstances, sophisticated econometric forecasts would neither be appropriate nor culturally acceptable. On the other hand, a major non-trading institution such as the ICAC, catering to a sophisticated market which has complex futures markets and an enormous appetite for accurate futures price prediction, has a sophisticated price and volume model which represents an important part of its activity.

It is noticeable that commodity forecasting is to be distinguished from product forecasting in that there is a constant need for it rather than a cycle through the lifetime of the product.

Certainly companies involved in commodities should pay careful attention to the selection of forecasting methods. It is remarkable how little serious forecasting there is in the commodities business. That which exists is almost entirely based on scepticism about econometric methods. This is despite the fact that large potential rewards and equally high potential losses, highly-geared instruments and a constant search for safe methods of securing returns involving the right commodity to buy and sell, and the right time to do both, is the essence of the commodities business.

The selection of an appropriate forecasting method is not a simple matter in itself. Some methods are quite simple and cheap—the least expensive being to rely directly on a single person's intuition. Other techniques are expensive, complex and require a considerable amount of time to administer, whether they are in house or bought in. Different types of forecasts are suitable for different time horizons—some for short terms and others for longer.

Several criteria are important in the selection of a forecasting technique for commodities:

- Perhaps the most important is to compare the cost of developing, updating with fresh data and also from an administrative point of view in running whatever technique is selected by comparison to the potential losses. It is no accident that it is in the commodity markets in which there are high levels of gearing—and thus in which small price changes can cause much larger changes in profit—that accurate and complex models are frequently encountered.

- Secondly, the relationships involved—their degree of complexity and the difficulty there is in obtaining information about the variables involved. There may be high costs in obtaining the necessary data or in verifying their accuracy. A professional trading software executive also observed sagely that 'Trading and forecasting are two separate things. If a person has the most accurate information possible about future trend changes in any given market, that doesn't mean he will make money. His ability to make money using this information is a function of his trading skill.'[1] The relationship between the forecast

[1] *Eddie Kwong, Kasanjian Research, letter to the author, 25 August 1994*

and the trading operation, clearly, is crucial for the profitable use of forecasts. Transactions costs are crucial in the translation of forecasts to profitable trading.

- Thirdly, and closely-related to this issue, is the question of short-run or long-run purposes. The time horizon involved in the forecasting process of the company concerned is central to the choice of forecasting method—the shorter term the forecast, the less likely that more sophisticated methods will be necessary. From the forecaster's point of view, the question of the degree of accuracy of the forecast and the confidence levels that senior decision-makers will require is the most important aspect to the selection of forecasting method. If just general direction and trends are required, then different methodology will be required compared to a need for precise figures.

- Linked to this is the question of a minimum tolerance level of errors. Forecasting has importance and should have a place even when it can be demonstrated that it is not possible to produce entirely accurate results, which in commodity forecasting it rarely is. The extent and direction of a trend may be, in practical terms, as valuable trading information as the exact extent of price change. Decision-makers themselves, however, may rightly be highly suspicious that the choice of forecasting methodology has anything much to do with the accuracy of the eventual results or the number of errors that ensue.

By comparison, choosing the best regression equation to fit the available data is very much a second order consideration which can safely be left to the forecasters themselves. Siegal, Slim and Liew (1994) advise that the first objective should be to remove equations that do not make sense. Given the complexity of these equations, such a task must definitely be left to the forecasters who understand their equations. It does seem as if there is little institutional pressure to discard sensible equations. Even here, some suspicion must surround economists' unwillingness to use simple time series models or to employ apparently causally unrelated series as independent variables, and to question the process whereby independent variables are selected.

Econometricians do seem to have a habit of selecting only those series for which data is readily accessible. There is a marked reluctance to be responsible for creating data through sampling, questionnaire responses or field work. They much prefer to work with other peoples' data, for the accuracy of which they do not admit responsibility.

Secondly, they suggest, equations with low t-statistics should be eliminated. 'These equations should be re-estimated or dropped in favour of equations in which all independent variables are significant. This test will eliminate equations where multicollinearity is a problem.'[1]

Next there is the question of a low *R2* result. Normally, amongst forecasters, the level of *R2* is used as an approximate guide to selecting the optimum equation. The lower the *R2* the more likely it is that a key variable is missing, that other combinations of these variables might be more desirable or that, in any event, the equation has the wrong functional form. It is generally also believed that the best Durbin-Watson statistic, closest to 2.0, is a good next step for selection.

All these issues are resolved automatically by most forecasting software, which is why it is now stated that: '...the stand-alone packages currently available provide the most accurate forecasts and are the easiest to use. In addition, they make several forecasting models available and can automatically select the best one for a particular data set.'[2]

The best method for selecting an equation for forecasting must be its accuracy in predicting future values. This can be done retrospectively in terms of using regressions (or ARIMA techniques) with the last term missing and then the last two, etc., weighting the accuracy results according to some in turn smoothed method—there are many choices, but the forecasting literature is remarkably thin on practical examples of this selection process as are the brochures for the forecasting software. The problem is exacerbated as fresh results come in, because the parameters may need to be changed. Ultimately, fresh forecasts will be constructed with the advent of every new *Y*, for unless the *Y* exactly corresponds to the predicted result, it will by definition alter the slope of the regression line and the intercept and therefore necessitate a recalculation of the parameters. There is no necessary reason why this process would accelerate in the absence of random shocks. They, themselves, could amount to white noise—but decision-makers should always ask what the forecast values of equations have been for as long as it is possible to generate them. This would entail stripping out as many existing data points as feasible and then evaluating the forecast in this light. It is important to realize that the equation may not forecast earlier data points as well as, armed with this data, it then forecasts later ones. This is precisely because it embeds a later shape to the impact of the independent variables upon the dependent ones. Fortunately, the forecasting software that is available charts the best

1 *Shim, Seigal and Liew, p82.*

2 *Shim, Seigal and Liew, p177.*

possible course through this particular maze and that is itself a major argument in its favour.

The real trouble in forecasting and planning for the future is that there are altogether too many variables which need to be taken into account. Some of these are at least quantifiable and essentially predictable, but some are clearly not. In analysing the future spot price of cotton, for example, it may be possible to determine supply over the next few months. But future national demand and changes in government policies which might affect the availability and price of cotton, changes in export opportunities, and possible revisions of export and import laws, as well as future tax decisions, may all affect the supply/demand balance and hence price. Waiting is no use either, since there is no possibility of waiting until all, or sometimes even any, of the basic questions are settled finally.

By that time, the time horizon of the forecast itself will have been reached. There is no forecast more useless for policy purposes than an out-of-date one. The projection of past experience to the uncertain future is always to some extent speculative and hazardous but, on occasions, decisions simply have to be made on the basis of the available incomplete knowledge; otherwise, nothing gets done. Generally speaking, experts agree that realistic forecasts, which contribute both to individual success and the stability of the economy, are the results of applying sound business experience and judgement to relevant and timely statistical analyses.

Except for a few irreversible decisions, however, few are irrevocably committed to a forecast, to survive or perish with it once it has been made. For instance, a large trading company trading a number of different commodities may have to make changes in its price forecasts across the board in response to the conclusion of a World Trade Organization agreement, for example, and other things such as USDA programs which could not be foreseen at the time the forecasts were made. Actually, forecasts are tentative things—special kinds of hypotheses—which can and most certainly should be modified or revised in response to changing conditions. Which forecasts are revised, when and how, depends as much on the cost of forecasting and trading need as anything else. When forecasts are revised in the light of new information, all those concerned must take whatever steps are necessary to translate revised production, trading, or other goals into action. Intelligent forecasting and planning demand one's continued attention to changing conditions.

That said, it is equally important that the organization maintains a constant watch, using one or more of the methods described above, on the accuracy of the forecasts it produces, That point is rarely insisted upon in the literature. A clear system must be established tying together resources to be injected into the forecasting process—especially in later stages when forecasts may prove inaccurate, managers' tempers may fray, and direction may be difficult to re-establish, or when inertia and inaccuracy have become institutionalized.

In conclusion, it cannot be stressed too much that, for every consumer of forecasts, a checking system is as essential as the management integration system in order to monitor how effective forecasting systems have been. If forecasts appear to work, then they still need monitoring, because circumstances may change radically and invalidate the hypotheses on which they are based. If they do not, then there is no point in repeating the exercise on the same basis for another round. It will be necessary to deconstruct the forecast, to find out what went wrong and whether another system would have worked better, and then to try again.

Glossary

This glossary provides a combination of a futures and a forecasting glossary. It is adapted from Shim, Siegal and Liew, *Strategic Business Forecasting* and Roche, *Commodity-Linked Derivatives.*

A

accuracy
The criterion for evaluating the performance of a forecast. Can be measured using mean squared error (MSE) or mean absolute percentage error (MAPE).

actuals
The physical, or cash, commodity, as distinct from the derivative.

American-style option
One which can be exercised into its underlying instrument at any time up until expiry.

arbitrage
The purchase or sale of an instrument and the simultaneous taking of an equal and opposite position in a related instrument when the pricing relationship is out of line. This takes advantage of profitable opportunities arising from misplaced anomalies. This is usually risk-free ('closed') although sometimes higher risk arbitrage is undertaken.

ARIMA
Acronym for Auto Regressive Integrated Moving Average, a broad class of time series models in which AR (autoregressive) terms and past error values from forecasting (MA) terms are combined.

assignment
Notice to an option writer that an option has been exercised by an option holder. An assignment notice is generally issued by the clearing house for exchange-traded options.

at-the-money
The strike/exercise price closest to the current price of the underlying instrument. A call or put option that is 'at-the-money' has no intrinsic value (q.v.) and will not be worthwhile to exercise.

autocorrelation
The degree to which a time series variable, lagged one or more observations, correlates with itself. There are two sub-definitions, firstly serial correlation of independent variables in a regression, identified by the Durbin-Watson statistic and, secondly, the pattern to identify seasonality in a time series, to identify appropriate time series models and to determine the presence of stationarity in data.

automatic exercise
A procedure for exchange-listed options whereby the clearing house automatically exercises in-the-money (q.v.) options at expiration.

autoregressive (AR)
A type of regression where the dependent variable is related to its own previous values with varying time lags.

B

backwardation
When the nearby month of a futures contract is trading at a premium to later months.

basis
The difference between the price of a futures contract and the futures equivalent price of the underlying instrument. Normally quoted as cash price minus futures price (i.e. a positive number indicates a futures discount and vice versa).

basis point
See **tick**.

bear
One who believes prices will fall. A bearish market is one where sentiment is pessimistic about prices.

bear spread
Being short the nearby month and long the later month, whether in a forward market, futures, options or cash. The position will be profitable if the spread strengthens, i.e. if the nearby falls relative to the other month. A bull spread is the opposite.

bid price
The price at which a trader or market maker is prepared to buy.

Black-Scholes
Commonly used formula for pricing options.

Box-Jenkins
The general iterative approach suggested by these authors for applying ARIMA models to time series forecasting.

Box-Pierce Q Statistic
A test on the autocorrelations of the residuals of the ARIMA model.

break-even point
The futures price at which a given option strategy is neither in profit nor loss. For call options, it is the strike price plus the premium; for put options is it is the strike price less the premium.

broker
A person or organization acting on behalf of another in a market, such as a futures broker or a chartered surveyor. Brokers' fees are called brokerage and are usually charged either on a fixed rate or percentage basis.

bull
One who expects prices to rise. A bullish market is dominated by the sentiment that prices will rise.

buyer
The purchaser of either a call or a put option. The buyer may also be called the option holder. Option buyers receive the right, but not the obligation, to enter a futures market position.

C

call
An option contract which gives the buyer of an option the right, but not the obligation, to buy a specific quantity of shares at a fixed price on or before some specific date. The seller of the option has the obligation to sell the specific quantity of shares/futures at a fixed price on or before a specific future date should he be exercised against.

call option
An option that gives the buyer the right (but not the obligation) to buy a specific quantity of the underlying instrument at a fixed price, on or before a specified date. The writer (seller) of the option has the obligation to deliver the underlying instrument if the option is exercised by the buyer.

cash commodity
The physical commodity itself sold on the spot, or cash, market as opposed to any derivative market. Hence cash/spot price, cash/spot market (i.e. one for immediate delivery and payment).

cash settlement
In the case of those futures and options contracts where it is impossible or impractical to effect physical delivery; open positions are closed out on the last day of trading at a price determined by the spot/cash market price of the underlying instrument. This is how the IPE Brent Index works.

Classical Decomposition Method
This entails the decomposition of a time series into a cyclical, seasonal, trend and random element to be individually analysed and forecast before recombination into an overall forecast.

clearing
The process of registration, position maintenance, settlement and provision of the guarantee of an exchange-cleared transaction.

clearing house
An organization which, in the USA and Europe, guarantees performance and settlement of exchange traded contracts for those exchanges which do not clear for themselves such as those in Japan.

close out
The buying of an equivalent amount of futures to those already sold or vice versa in order to establish a zero net position in the market and hence no financial exposure to it.

coefficient of determination
A measure of the degree to which two variables are correlated, ranging between -1 and +1. +1 is perfect correlation; -1 is perfect inverse correlation; 0 entails no correlation at all. The closer *R* is to 1 or -1, the closer the relationship between the two variables.

commission
A fee charged by a broker to a customer for executing a futures or options transaction. Usually, it is a round-turn fee that covers both the initiation and liquidation of the contract.

commission house
An organization which trades commodities and/or futures and options contracts for clients in return for a fee, but which does not trade on its own account. In the UK often used synonymously with brokerage house.

contango
A market whereby the nearby month is trading at a premium to the deferred months.

contract
A contract is an agreement to buy or sell a specified amount of a specified commodity at a specified price of a specified grade within a specified time period in the future. The purchase of a futures contract binds the buyer to accept delivery of the commodity unless closed out or the contract is cash settled (q.v.)

contract grade
The grade of the commodity selected for the contract.

contract month
One of the months selected for the contract in which delivery can be made or accepted.

convergence
The process whereby the futures price moves towards the equivalent price of the underlying instrument as delivery or cash settlement approaches.

correlation
The degree of relationship between variables. It is measured through the coefficient of determination.

cost of carry
See **fair value**.

D

day trading
Refers to establishing and closing out positions during one day's trading and hence not holding risks overnight.

debenture
A formal written acknowledgement of debt. For eurobonds or US domestic issues, this can be a synonym for bond. In the UK domestic market, bonds tend only to be called debentures if they are secured by a mortgage or charge over specified assets; hence property companies often issue 'first mortgage debentures', a bond with first charge over property. Other companies may issue debentures with a fixed and floating charge over their assets.

declaration date
The last day on which an option taker must state his or her intention to exercise. Also known as exercise or expiry date. If an option is not exercised by this date, it is automatically abandoned.

default
Failure to perform any contract. Can be caused by failure to meet a futures margin call or failure to deliver a physical commodity.

degrees of freedom
The number of data items that are independent of one another. Given a sample of data and a statistic, e.g. the mean, the degrees of freedom are defined as (number of observations included in the formula) minus (number of parameters estimated using the data).

delivery
Settlement of a futures contract during delivery month, or at expiry, by receipt or tender of a commodity or by cash settlement (q.v.) Hence delivery month or day, delivery notice, delivery points (where delivery is acceptable).

Delphi Method
A qualitative forecasting method that seeks to use experts' judgements systematically to produce a forecast. It brings together a group of experts with access to each others' opinions, but without disclosure of the majority opinion.

delta
The amount by which an option premium changes relative to a change in the price of the underlying futures contract. Deltas are positive for bullish option positions and negative for bearish option positions. Deltas of deep in-the-money options are equal to one; deltas of at-the-money options are around 0.5; and deltas of deep out-of-money options are zero. Delta is an instantaneous rate of change and varies by a factor, *gamma*, with respect to the underlying futures price.

dependent variable
A variable whose value is for forecasting purposes said and computed to be dependent on the values of other variables and constants in some identifiable relationship.

depth (of market)
i) The number of contracts available at the current bid and offer price.
ii) The number of contracts (orders placed) available at one, two and more ticks either side of the current bid and offer price.

deseasonalized data
Removal of the seasonal pattern in a data series.

discount
The amount by which a future or option is priced below its theoretical, or fair value, or below the price of the underlying instrument.

discretionary account
An account over which any individual or organization, other than the person whose name the account is carried, exercises trading authority or control.

dummy variable
Often referred to as a binary variable, with a value either 1 or 0, this is frequently used to quantify qualitative or categorical events. For example, peace/war, tariff on/off.

Durbin-Watson Statistic
A summary measure of the amount of autocorrelation in the error terms of the regression. By comparing the computed DW with that in a table of values, the significance can be determined.

E

econometric forecasting
A forecasting method that uses a set of equations intended for simultaneous calculation to capture the way in which endogenous and exogenous variables are interrelated.

electronic trading system
A networked system of PCs in exchange members' offices with a central control at the exchange for the trading of futures and options contracts.

equivalent/equated yield
The total annual return to be received from a reversionary investment assuming no change in the property's rental value.

error term
Deviation of the actual value of an observation from the regression line.

European-style options
Options that are only exercisable at expiration.

ex-ante forecast
Using only the data available at the time at which the actual forecast is prepared.

exchange of futures for physicals (EFPs)
Also known as *against actuals* (AAs). In this deal, one party buys the physical commodity and simultaneously sells, or gives up, a long futures contract while the other party sells the physical commodity and simultaneously buys, or receives, a long futures contract. The price of the exchanged futures position, the quantity of the futures and cash commodity to be exchanged, the price of the cash commodity, and other terms are privately negotiated by the parties rather than being competitively executed in the pit.

exercise
The action taken by the holder of a call if he or she wishes to purchase the underlying futures/shares or the holder of a put if he or she wishes to sell the underlying futures contract/shares.

expiration date
See **declaration date**.

exponential smoothing
A forecasting technique that uses a weighted moving average of past data as the basis for a forecast. Exponential smoothing gives the most weighting to more recent information and less to observations further in the past. It is useful for short-run forecasting when there is randomness and no seasonal fluctuations and has less relevance to commodity forecasting than many other techniques. Exponential smoothing adjusted for trend, also called *Holt's two-parameter exponential smoothing,* adds a trend adjustment to the single smoothed value. Seasonal exponential smoothing, also called *Winter's three-parameter method,* is an extension of the Holt method by including an additional equation used to adjust the smoothed forecast to reflect seasonality.

ex-post forecast
Using some information beyond the period for which the forecast is made.

F

F-test
In statistics, the ratio of two mean squares (variances) can often be used to test the significance of some item. In regression, the ratio of mean square due to the regression to mean square due to error compared to F-table values can be used to test the overall significance of the regression model.

fair value
The level at which a futures contract should trade to be at a level economically equivalent to the underlying instrument, taking into account the net financing costs related to that contract. For options, the fair value premium is calculated using a mathematical option pricing model, e.g. Black-Scholes.

first notice day
The first date, varying according to commodities and exchanges, on which notices of intentions to deliver actual commodities against futures are made.

floor broker
A member who executes orders for the account of one or more clearing members.

floor trader
A trader who executes trades either on his or her own behalf, or for his or her firm, on the physical trading floor of an exchange.

forecast
A projection or estimate of anything, in the context of commodities, usually of price, produced, supplied, consumed quantity or stocks.

forward contract
A cash market agreement in which a seller agrees to deliver a specific cash commodity to a buyer sometime in the future for a predetermined price.

fundamental analysis
Analysis of future (price) trends based on economic factors (as opposed to technical analysis, q.v.)

futures contract
A legally-binding agreement on a nationally-recognized exchange to make or take delivery of a specified instrument, at a fixed date in the future, at a price agreed upon at the time of the agreement.

G

gamma
The rate of change of the delta of the option relative to the asset price. It measures how much the delta will change if the market price of the underlying instrument changes; it corresponds to the acceleration rate of the option premium.

gearing ratio
A means of expressing the relative proportions of a company or group's total financing met by debt (or borrowings) and equity.

give up
(i) At the request of the customer, a brokerage house that has not performed the service is credited with the execution of an order.
(ii) On the floor of an exchange (or on an electronic trading system), a broker gives up the name of the firm for which he or she was acting to another member with whom a transaction had just been completed.

goodness of fit
A degree to which a model fits the observed data. In regression analysis this is demonstrated by the coefficient of determination (R2 statistic).

guarantee
The primary role of the clearing house is to guarantee contract performance. It becomes the actual counterparty to all contracts registered in the name of its clearing members. This removes bilateral obligations and counterparty risk between the original counterparties, as the clearing house becomes the buyer to every seller and vice versa, and permits netting of positions.

H

hedge
The buying and selling of offsetting positions in order to provide protection against adverse change in price. A hedge may involve one or more of positions in the cash, futures or options markets.

hedge ratio
The ratio of a position's exposure to that of an individual long futures contract. The term is usually applied to aggregate positions and individual options contracts (where it is identical to delta).

hedger
An individual, company or institution that owns or plans to own a cash commodity, for example a property, and which (i) is concerned that the price, or some other aspect, of the asset may change before buying or selling it in the cash market, and which (ii) acts to protect against that risk by holding a futures or options position which is opposite to the cash asset position. Adverse movement in one is balanced by favourable movement in the other.

homoscedasticity
One of the assumptions required in a regression in order to make valid statistical inferences about population relationships, also known as constant variance. It requires that the standard deviation and variance of the error terms is constant for all dependent variables, and that the error terms are all drawn from the same population. This indicates that there is a uniform scatter, or dispersion, of data points about the regression line. If the assumption does not hold, the accuracy of the beta coefficient is to be doubted.

I

implied volatility
The volatility of the underlying instrument implied by current options prices.

independent variable
A variable that may take on a value, used to forecast another variable which is said to be dependent on it. In $Y = f(X)$, X is the independent variable.

initial margin
The returnable collateral deposited when initiating an open position. This is required by the clearing house from clearing members as protection against default of a futures or options contract. The exchange requires the level of initial margin set by the clearing house to be the minimum required by (clearing) members from their clients. This level is subject to changes in line with market conditions (and most importantly the volatility of the contract).

initial yield
The gross initial annual income from a property (or other investment) divided by the gross acquisition cost.

intermarket spreads
The price relationship between different futures contracts.

in-the-money
For call options, where the exercise price is below the price of the underlying instrument and for put options, vice versa. Exercise of an in-the-money option results in the realization of its intrinsic value, i.e. the amount that the option is in-the-money.

intramarket spreads
The relationship between different expiration months in the same contract.

intrinsic value
The intrinsic value (in-the-money) for call options is the amount by which the market price for the share exceeds the exercise price and vice versa for put options.

L

last trading day
The final day for dealing in a futures or options contract for a particular delivery or expiry month.

Least-Squares Method
A statistical technique for fitting a straight line through a set of points so that the sum of the squared distances from the data points to the line is minimized.

limit
The maximum permissible up/down movement in price from the previous session's settlement price for a given commodity for any one day's trading. Not usual in UK contracts, but common in the USA. Also called *maximum price fluctuation.*

linear regression
A regression that deals with a straight line relationship between variables, i.e. of the form $Y = aX + b$.

liquidation
A transaction that closes an open futures or options position. There are two means of closing an open futures position:
i) offsetting the initial sale/purchase by a purchase/sale of the same number of contracts for the same delivery month, or
ii) taking or making delivery.
Open options positions can be liquidated by a) offsetting the initial sale or purchase, b) exercising the option, or (c) allowing the option to expire unexercised.

liquidity
The ability to buy and sell an asset, including a derivative contract. A perfectly liquid contract is one in which an infinite amount of buy orders

does not affect the price. Liquidity is a relative concept—there may be sufficient buyers in the market at the current price for one seller to dispose of his or her position, but not for another seller with a position twice as large to sell.

logistic curve
This has the typical S-shape, and is frequently used in connection with long-term curve fitting as a technological forecasting method.

long
The position that is established by the purchase of a futures contract—benefitting from a rise in futures prices.

lot
The standard unit of futures trading in a commodity, e.g. a fixed quantity of money for an index contract or x tonnes of a commodity for a physical delivery contract.

M

mark to market
The process whereby futures contracts are revalued daily for the calculation of variation margins (q.v.).

Markov analysis
A method of analysing the current behaviour of some variable to predict the future behaviour of that variable.

margin
See **initial margin** and **variation margin**.

margin calls
Additional funds that a holder of a futures position must deposit to meet variation margins or increases in initial margins announced whilst the position is open.

maturity
The date on which a bond is redeemed, or the time to go until the redemption date.

maximum price fluctuation
See **limit.**

mean absolute deviation
The mean or average of the sum of all the forecast errors including their signs.

mean absolute percentage error
The mean or average of the sum of all the percentage errors for a given set taken without regard to sign. It is one measure of accuracy (q.v.) commonly used in quantitative methods of forecasting.

mean squared error (MSE)
A measure of accuracy computed by squaring the individual error item in a data set and then finding the average or mean value of the sum of those squares. The mean squared error gives greater weight to large errors than to small errors because the errors are squared before being summed.

minimum price fluctuation
See tick size.

moving average
For a time series this is an average that is updated as soon as new data is entered. The most recent observation is used to calculate an average, used as the forecast for the next period. In Box-Jenkins modelling, the MA in ARIMA stands for moving average and means that the value of the time series at time t is influenced by a current error term and possibly weighted error terms in the past.

multicollinearity
The condition that exists when independent variables are highly correlated with each other. The estimated regression coefficients may be unreliable. The presence of multicollinearity can be tested by investigating the correlation between the independent variables.

multiple regression analysis
A statistical procedure that attempts to assess the relationship between the dependent variable and two or more dependent variables.

N

naive forecast
Forecasts obtained with a minimal amount of effort and data manipulation, and based solely on the most recent information available. One such naive

method would be to use the most recent data available as the forecast for the next period.

naked option
An options position (for the writer) with no offsetting options, futures or cash position. Known also as uncovered option.

nearby basis
The price differential between the current cash price and the nearby month (q.v.) futures price.

nearby/front month
The closest (in terms of expiry date) available month for trading.

notice day
A day on which notices of intent to deliver pertaining to a specified delivery month may be issued.

O

offer/ask price
The price at which a trader or market-maker is willing to sell a contract.

offset
Liquidate a futures or options position by taking another market position equal and opposite. Options can be offset at any time until expiration.

open interest
The sum of futures contracts in one delivery month or one market that has been entered into and not yet liquidated by an offsetting transaction or fulfilled by delivery.

open position
A long or short position that has not been offset and that, at the end of a day's trading, is therefore still maintained at the clearing house.

opening price
The price for a given commodity that is generated through open outcry (q.v.) at the opening of daily trading; more generally, the first sale price.

open outcry
A method of public auction for making verbal bids and offers for contracts in the trading pits or rings of commodity (and financial) exchanges. Still the main method of trading futures and options.

option
The right to buy (a call option) or sell (a put option) stock, bonds, currency or a commodity (including property) in the future at a mutually-agreed price (called the strike price). Options can be for physical or cash equivalent. Sellers of options are sometimes called option writers.

out-of-the-money
An option which has no intrinsic value. See also in-the-money.

over-the-counter option (OTC)
Not traded on an exchange but between individual buyer and seller: specialized bespoke terms, but a risk of default.

P

physical delivery
Settlement of a futures contract by receipt or tender of a financial instrument or a commodity.

premium
The price to buy a call or a put option. It will depend on the strike price, the current futures price, volatility of the underlying futures contract, prevailing interest rates, and the time to maturity of the option.

Q

qualitative forecasting
A forecasting method that brings together, in an organized way, personal judgements about the process being analysed.

R

range
The difference between the highest and lowest prices recorded during a given trading session.

Recognized Investment Exchange (RIE)
An exchange authorized by the Securities and Investments Board (SIB) and conforming to Section 4 of the Financial Services Act 1986. LIFFE, LCE, LME, OMLX and IPE are all RIEs.

risk-management strategy
A trading strategy which uses futures/options to reduce or eliminate the price risk associated with a position in the cash market. Also referred to as a hedging strategy.

roll over
The transfer of a futures or options position from one delivery/expiry month to another—always involving the purchase/sale of the nearby month and the simultaneous corresponding sale/purchase of a farther out delivery month.

round trip
The purchase/sale and subsequent sale/purchase of a futures or options contract, leaving no net exposure to the market; transactions costs are usually expressed on a round trip basis.

S

short
The position created by the sale of a futures contract.

speculation
A trading strategy using a futures or options contract without a corresponding cash market position in order to obtain profit. Speculators assume price risk and add liquidity and capital to the marketplace.

spread
The purchase/sale of one futures/options contract and the simultaneous sale/purchase of a different but related contract. The objective is to benefit from a change in the price relationship between them. Hence, spread margin, the reduced initial margin sometimes available to those holding spread positions as their risk is limited.

strike price
The price at which the holder of a put/call option may exercise the right to sell/purchase the underlying futures contract.

synthetic futures and options
Futures and options positions combined so that they form risk/reward characteristics resembling other futures or options positions.

T

taker
The buyer of an option.

technical analysis
Forecasting and explicative analysis concerned with (usually) price data rather than economic factors.

theoretical value
The fair value of a futures or options contract.

tick size
The standardized minimum price movement of a futures or options contract.

time decay
The time premium (q.v.) is a wasting asset in the hands of the option buyer/holder.

time premium/value
Equal to the price of the option less the intrinsic value, it is a combination of volatility and time to maturity. The longer the time to expiry, ceteris paribus the higher the time premium, and the rate of decline accelerates as the expiry date approaches.

traded options
Options traded on an exchange like LIFFE and which are backed with a clearing house guarantee.

U

underlying instrument
The specific quantity and quality of a commodity or financial instrument or currency, or the index, on which a future or an option is based.

V

variation margin
Actual losses and gains arising from the mark to market process on a daily basis and posted as variation margins. If the price moves adversely, the position holder's broker will call for the additional funds required to cover the realized loss; and realized profits are similarly returned daily by the clearing house.

volatility
How much the asset price is expected or has (historic volatility) fluctuated over a given period of time. Normally measured by the annual standard deviation of daily price changes. Called implied volatility when estimated from the market price of options. Hence, volatility trade, a trade based on expectations as to the level of implied volatility of a futures market rather than the direction of price movement.

volume of trading
The number of contracts traded in a specified period of time. Sometimes quoted in terms of the number of physical units traded, rather than the number of contracts, e.g. 1000 lots or with a contract size of 50 tonnes, 50,000 tonnes traded.

Appendix 1: Commodity organizations & software providers

The list below details some of the more important trading and forecasting software packages and their producers, together with the most important organizations in commodity forecasting. Clearly there are many more such organizations, and probably the best place to start for econometric, time series and fundamental forecasting is either the United States Department of Agriculture or the national equivalent. For technical analysis, a broker specializing in financial, not commodity, trading and a specialized charting service are the right place to start.

Australian Commodities/OUTLOOK Conference

ABARE
GPO Box 1563
Canberra ACT 2601
Australia
Tel: 00 616 272 2000
Fax: 00 616 272 2001

Cambridge Futures Charts

Investment Research of Cambridge Ltd
28 Panton Street
Cambridge CB2 1DH
UK
Tel: 00 44 1223 356251
Fax: 00 44 1223 329806

Fibnodes

Coast Investment Software Inc
358 Avenida Milano
Sarasota FL 34242-1517
USA
Tel: 1 813 346 3801

Futures Pro

Essex Trading Co Ltd
24 West 500 Maple Avenue
Suite 108, Naperville Il 60540
USA
Tel: 708 416 3530
Fax: 708 416 3558

Futures Truth Co

815 Hillside Road
Hendersonville
NC 28739
USA
Tel: 1 704 697 0273
Fax: 1 704 692 7375

Geneva Statistical Forecasting

Pizzano & Co
800 W. Cummings Park
Woburn MA 01801
USA
Tel: 1 617 935 7122

Metastock

Equis International Inc
3950 South 700 East
Suite 100
Salt Lake City
UT 84107
USA
Tel: 1 801 265 8886

Nature's Pulse

Kasanjian Research
PO Box 4608
Blue Jay
CA 92317
USA
Tel: 1 909 337 0816

SmartForecasts Version 3

Smart Software Inc
4 Hill Road
Belmont MA 02178
USA
Tel 0800 762 7899 & 1 617 489 2743
Fax 1 617 489 2748

STAMP: Structural Time series Analyser and Predictor

Department of Statistics
London School of Economics
Houghton Street
London WC2A 2AE
UK
Tel: 00 44 171 955 6725
Fax: 00 44 171 955 7416

StatPlan IV

Lotus Selects
PO Box 9172
Cambridge Mass 02139-9946
USA
Tel: 800 635 6887 & 1 617 693 3981

Swing Catcher

Trend Index Trading Company
Rural Route 10
Eau Claire
WI 54701-9077
USA
Tel: 1 715 833 1234
Fax: 1 715 833 8040

3D for Windows

MESA
PO Box 1801
Goleta CA 93116
USA
Tel: 800 633 6372

Forecast Plus

StatPac, Inc.
3814 Lyndale Avenue South
Minneapolis
MN 55409
USA
Tel: 1 612 822 8252

Forecast Pro

Business Forecast Systems
68 Leonard Street
Belmont
MA 02178
USA
Tel: 1 617 484 5050
Fax: 617 484 9219

Option Master

Institute for Options Research Inc
PO Box 6586, Lake Tahoe
NV 89449
USA
Tel: 702 588 3590
Fax: 702 588 8481

Right Time

TBSP Inc
610 Newport Ctr Dr
Suite 630, Newport Beach
CA 92660
USA
Tel: 714 721 8603
Fax: 714 721 8635

Ganntrader 2

Gannsoft Publishing Company
11670 Riverbend Drive
Leavenworth, WA 98826-9305
USA
Tel: 1 509 548 5990
Fax: 1 509 548 4679

Sibyl/Runner

Applied Decision Systems
510 South Street
Lexington MA
USA
Tel: 1 617 424 9820

Strategist

Optionomics Corp
2835 East 3300 South, Suite 200
Salt Lake City
Utah 84109
USA
Tel: 1 801 466 2111
Fax: 1 801 466 7320

Tomorrow

Isogon Corp
330 Seventh Ave
New York, NY 10001
USA
Tel: 1 212 967 2424

Micro TSP/ EViews

Quantitative Micro Software
4521 Campus Drive
Suite 336, Irvine
CA 92715
USA
Tel: 1 714 856 3368
Fax: 1 714 856 2044

Appendix 2: Bibliography

There are hundreds of books on technical analysis and a similar number, especially articles in economic journals, on the econometric modelling of commodity markets. The Society of Technical Analysts and the World Bank/USDA are useful initial contact points for each respectively. The list below is a selection of a few relatively recent representative works from each discipline outlined in this book together with a few all-time classics drawn not only directly from commodities but from financial markets literature. Traders and policy-makers are unlikely to wish to consult particular original articles in econometrics such as those in the International Journal of Forecasting and these have been omitted however significant their impact on the development of forecasting techniques has been.

- *Volume Cycles in the Stock Market*, R. Arms, Dow Jones -Irwin, NY 1983
- *The Handbook of Commodity Cycles: A Window on Time*, J. Bernstein, John Wiley and Sons 1982 NY
- *The Methodology of Economic Model Building*, L.A. Boland, Routledge, London 1989
- *Nonlinear Dynamics, Chaos and Instability: Statistical Theory and Economic Evidence*, W.A. Brock, D.A. Hsieh and B. LeBaron, MIT Press 1991
- *An Agricultural Model for the UK*, M.P. Burton et al, Avebury 1992
- *On the Behaviour of Commodity Prices*, A.S. Deaton and G. Laroque, Review of Economic Studies, 59, 1-24
- *Market Forecasting*, Fakir Chandra Dutt, Gannsoft Publishing Co, Orig. Pub. 1949
- *Technical Analysis of Stock Trends*, R.D. Edwards, J. Magee, John Magee Inc., Boston Mass, 6th edition 1992
- *Co-integration and Error Correction: Representation, Estimation and Testing*, R.F Engle and C.W.J. Granger, Econometrica 55, pp251-176 1987

- *Merging Short and Long Term Forecasts.* R.F. Engle, C.W.J. Granger and J.J. Hallman, Journal of Econometrics 40, pp45-62, 1989
- *Income Elasticities of Demand for Agricultural Products,* FAO Rome 1972
- *How to Make Profits in Commodities,* W.D. Gann, Pomery Washington Lambert-Gann Publishing reprinted 1976
- *The Adjustment of US Oil Demand to the Price Increase of the 1970s,* D. Gately and P. Rappoport, Energy Journal 9, pp 93-108, 1988
- *Economic Evaluation of Commodity Price Forecasting Models,* M.E. Gerlow, S.H. Irwin and Liu Te-Ru, International Journal of Forecasting 9 (1993) pp 387-397
- *A Rational Expectations Price Model for a Continuously Produced Primary Commodity,* C.L. Gilbert, Paper presented at the World Congress of the Econometric Society, Cambridge MA, 1985
- *Rational Expectations and Efficiency in Futures Markets,* B.A. Goss - Ed, Routledge London 1992
- *Forecasting Economic Time Series,* C.J. Granger and P. Newbold, Academic press, New York, 2nd edition 1986
- *Econometric Modelling of Agricultural Commodity Markets,* D. Hallam, Routledge, London 1990
- *Advanced Commodity Trading Techniques*, J.D. Hamon, Brightwaters NY Windsor Books 1981
- *Technical Analysis in the Options Market,* R. Hexton, 1982
- *Policy Options for Stabilising Earnings in a Speculative Market: A Structural Analysis,* A.J. Hughes-Hallett, Draft Paper 1994
- *Time Series: Forecasting, Simulation, Applications,* G. Janacek and L. Swift, Ellis Horwood, London 1993
- *Commodity Price Forecasting with Large Scale Econometric Models and the Futures Market,* R.E. Just and G.C. Rausser, American Journal of Agricultural Economics 63 197-208 1981
- *Commodity Trading Systems and Methods,* P.J. Kaufman, NY John Wiley and Sons 1978

- *Recent Developments in Commodity Modelling: a World Bank Perspective,* W.C. Labys, WPS 119, Washington DC 1988
- *Commodity Models for Forecasting and Policy Analysis,* W.C. Labys, P.K. Pollak, Croon Helm, London 1984
- *Cyclical Market Forecasting: Stocks and Grains,* J.M. Langham, Gannsoft Publishing Co., Orig. Pub. 1938
- *A Semi-strong Form Evaluation of the Efficiency of the Hog Futures Market,* R.M. Leuthold and P.A. Hartmann, American Journal of Agricultural Economics 63 482-9 1979
- *An Evaluation of the Forward-pricing Efficiency of Livestock Futures Markets,* R.M. Leuthold and P.A. Hartmann, North Central Journal of Agricultural Economics 3: 71-80
- *Forecasting Methods for Management,* S. Makridakis and S.C. Wheelwright, John Wiley, NY 1989
- *Sliding Simulations: A New Approach to Time Series Forecasting,* S. Makridakis, Management Science 36 1990, 505-512
- *The M2-Competition: A Real Time Judgementally Based Forecasting Study,* S. Makridakis et al, IJF 9 1993 5-22
- *Statistics for Business and Economics: Methods and Applications,* E. Mansfield, W H Norton & Co NY and London, 4th edition 1991
- *CandlePower,* G. Morris, Probus Publishing, NY 1992
- *The Theory of Commodity Price Stabilization,* D.M. Newberry and E. Stiglitz, OUP, Oxford 1981
- *Japanese Candlestick Charting Techniques,* S. Nilson, NY Institute of Finance NY 1986
- *Learning Japanese-style 'Candlesticks' Charting,* S. Nison, Futures, December 1989
- *A Japanese Candleabra of Price Chart Patterns,* S. Nison, Futures, April 1990
- *Forecasting With Dynamic Regression Models,* A. Pankratz, John Wiley, New York 1991

- *The Major Works of R N Elliott*, Prechter, R A - Ed., New Classics Library, New York, 1980

- *Forecasting Financial Markets*, T. Plummer, Kogan Page, 2nd edition, London 1993

- *New Directions in Econometric Modelling and Forecasting in US Agriculture*, G.C. Rausser, North-Holland, Amsterdam 1982

- *Estimation and Analysis of a State Natural Gas Econometric Model*, A. Rose, W.C. Labys and T. Witt, Proceedings of the American Statistical Association, 1986, pp 380-385

- *Megamistakes: Forecasting and the Myth of Technological Change*, S.P. Schnaars, The NY Free Press 1989

- *Strategic Business Forecasting*, J.K. Shim, J.G. Siegel and C.J. Liew, Probus Publishing, Chicago 1994

- *Trading in Futures*, Stewart, T H - Ed., Woodhead Faulkner, Cambridge, 1989

- *A Quarterly Forecasting Model of the US Egg Sector*, R. Stillman, TB 1729, ERS, USDA, Washington DC 1985

- *Automatic Forecasting Software: A Survey and Evaluation*, L.J. Tashman and M L Leach, IJF 7 1991 209-230

- *Disarray in World Food Markets: A Quantitative Assessment*, R. Tyers and K. Anderson, Cambridge University Press, 1992

- *Modelling International Cotton Prices*, C. Valderrama, in Proceedings of the Beltwide Cotton Conferences, NCC, 1993, Vol 3 p 449

- *Incorporating Expectations into a Model of the Cotlook A Index*, C. Valderrama, in *Cotton: Review of the World Situation* July-August 1993, ICAC, Washington pp 12-20

Appendix 3: World commodity contracts

i) Metals

ii) Softs

iii) Energy

iv) Others

WORLD COMMODITY CONTRACTS

i) METALS

Exchange	Contract Name	Type[1]	Contract Size	Tick Size	Months	Sett.[2]
Bolsa Brasileira de Futuros	Gold	F	250g	CR$1	All months	P
Bolsa Brasileira de Futuros	Gold	O	250g	CR$1	Jan/Mar/May/Jul/Sep/Nov	
Bolsa de Mercadorias & Futuros	Gold	F	250g	CR$2.5	All months	P
Bolsa de Mercadorias & Futuros	Gold	O	250g	CR$2.5	Odd months	P
Toronto Futures Exchange	Silver	O	100 troz	US$0.01	2 nearest months and next 2 quarters from Mar/Jun/Sep/Dec cycle	P
Vancouver Stock Exchange	Gold	O	10 troz	US$1	Feb/May/Aug/Nov	C
Shenzhen Metal Exchange	Copper	F	50 tonnes	n/a	All months	P
Shenzhen Metal Exchange	Tin	F	2 tonnes	n/a	All months	P
Shenzhen Metal Exchange	Lead	F	10 tonnes	n/a	All months	P
Shenzhen Metal Exchange	Zinc	F	10 tonnes	n/a	All months	P
Shenzhen Metal Exchange	Aluminium	F	50 tonnes	n/a	All months	P
Shenzhen Metal Exchange	Nickel	F	2 tonnes	n/a	All months	P
Shenzhen Metal Exchange	Antimony	F	10 tonnes	n/a	All months	P
Shenzhen Metal Exchange	Magnesium	F	2 tonnes	n/a	All months	P
Hong Kong Futures Exchange	Gold	F	100 troz	US$0.1/oz	Even months, spot and following two months	P
Kuala Lumpur Comm. Exchange	Tin	F	5 tonnes	US$25	Current, plus the next 3 succeeding, plus alternate to 12 mths fwd.	P
Si ngapore Int'l Monetary Exch. (SIMEX)	Gold	F	100 troz	US$5	Feb/Apr/Jun/Aug/Oct/Dec	C
Johannesburg Stock Exchange	All Gold Index	O	R10 x index level	R1-2	Nearest 4 months plus nearest 3 months of cycle Mar/Jun/Sep/Dec	C
South African Futures Exchange (SAFEX)	All Gold Index	F	R10 x index level	1 point	n/a	
South African Futures Exchange (SAFEX)	Gold Price	F	R100 x US price of gold	US$0.01	n/a	
South African Futures Exchange (SAFEX)	All Gold Index	O	1 futures contract		Mar/Jun/Sep/Dec	
South African Futures Exchange (SAFEX)	Gold Price	O	1 futures contract		Mar/Jun/Sep/Dec	
London Metal Exchange (LME)	Primary Aluminium high grade (99.7%)	F[3]	25 tonnes	$12.5	Daily to 3 months, weekly to 6 months, monthly to 27 months	P
London Metal Exchange (LME)	Aluminium Alloy D125, 226 or A380.1	F[3]	20 tonnes	$10	Daily to 3 months, weekly to 6 months, monthly to 15 months	P

London Metal Exchange (LME)	Standard Lead 99.97%	F[3]	25 tonnes	$12.5	Daily to 3 months, weekly to 6 months, monthly to 15 months	P
London Metal Exchange (LME)	Copper Grade A	F[3]	25 tonnes	$12.5	Daily to 3 months, weekly to 6 months, monthly to 27 months	P
London Metal Exchange (LME)	Primary Nickel 99.8%	F[3]	6 tonnes	$6	Daily to 3 months, weekly to 6 months, monthly to 15 months	P
London Metal Exchange (LME)	Tin 99.85%	F[3]	5 tonnes	$5	Daily to 3 months, weekly to 6 months, monthly to 15 months	P
London Metal Exchange (LME)	Zinc special high grade (99.995%)	F[3]	25 tonnes	$12.5	Daily to 3 months, weekly to 6 months, monthly to 27 months	P
CBOT	Gold (100oz)		100 troz	$10	current, two following and Feb/Apr/Jun/Aug/Oct/Dec	P
CBOT	Gold (kg)		32.15troz	$3.22	current, two following and Feb/Apr/Jun/Aug/Oct/Dec	P
CBOT	Silver (1000oz)		100troz	$1	current, two following and Feb, Apr, Jun, Aug, Oct, Dec	P
CBOT	Silver (5000oz)		5000troz	$5	current, two following and Feb, Apr, Jun, Aug, Oct, Dec	P
CBOT	Silver (1000oz)	F	100troz	$1	Feb/Apr/Jun/Aug/Oct/Dec	FP
COMEX	Copper		25,000lbs	$12.5	Jan/Mar/May/Jul/Sep/Dec	
COMEX	Gold		100 troz	$10	Feb/Apr/Jun/Aug/Oct/Dec	
COMEX	Silver		5000 troz	$25	Jan/Mar/May/Jul/Sep/Dec	
COMEX	Gold	F	100 troz	$10	All months	
COMEX	Silver	F	5 000 troz	$5	All months	
COMEX	Copper	F	25,000lbs	$	Feb/Mar/May/Jul/Sep/Nov/Dec	
COMEX	5 day Gold	F	100 troz		Every business day based on the non-spot cycle month (except Oct)	
COMEX	5 day Silver	F	5,000 troz		Every business day based on the non-spot cycle month (except Jan)	
COMEX	5 day Copper	F	25,000lbs		Every business day based on nearest of 5 cycle months - Mar, May	
NYMEX	Platinum		50 troz		3 consecutive months and 4 quarterly on a Jan/Apr/Jul/Oct cycle	
NYMEX	Palladium	F	100 troz		3 consecutive months and 4 quarterly on a Mar/Jun/Sep/Dec cycle	
NYMEX	Platinum	F	50 troz		3 consecutive, plus 2 quarterly	

[1] *Type: F=Futures; O= Options*
[2] *Sett.: P= Physical delivery; C= Cash settlement; FP = Assignment of futures position*
[3] *OTC options are avilable on a number of LME contracts*

ii) SOFTS

Exchange	Contract	Type[1]	Contract Size	Tick Size	Months	Sett.[2]
Bolsa de Comercio de Buenos Aires	Cattle Index	F	5000kg	Pesos 0.002	Odd + October	-
Bolsa de Comercio de Buenos Aires	Cattle Index	F	5000kg	US$0.002	Odd + October	-
Bolsa de Comercio de Buenos Aires	Cattle Index	O	5000kg	Pesos 0.002	Odd + October	-
Bolsa de Comercio de Buenos Aires	Cattle Index	O	5000kg	US$0.002	Odd + October	-
MERFOX (Mercado de Futuros y Opciones SA)	Live Cattle (US $)	F	5000kg	US$.002	Jan/Mar/May/Jul/Sep/Oct/Nov	C
MERFOX (Mercado de Futuros y Opciones SA)	Live Cattle (Pesos)	F	5000kg	$0.002	Jan/Mar/May/Jul/Sep/Oct/Nov	C
MERFOX (Mercado de Futuros y Opciones SA)	Live Cattle (DMK)	F	5000kg	DMK0.002	Jan/Mar/May/Jul/Sep/Oct/Nov	C
MERFOX (Mercado de Futuros y Opciones SA)	Live Cattle (US $)	O	1 futures contract	US$.002	Jan/Mar/May/Jul/Sep/Oct/Nov	
MERFOX (Mercado de Futuros y Opciones SA)	Live Cattle (Pesos)	O	1 futures contract	$0.002	Jan/Mar/May/Jul/Sep/Oct/Nov	
MERFOX (Mercado de Futuros y Opciones SA)	Live Cattle (DMK)	O	1 futures contract	DMK0.002	Jan/Mar/May/Jul/Sep/Oct/Nov	
Sydney Futures Exchange	Wool	F	2500kg	A$25	Feb/Apr/Jun/Aug/Oct/Dec up to 18 months ahead	C
Sydney Futures Exchange	Live Cattle	F	10000kg	A$10	Each successive calendar month up to 12 months ahead	C
Bolsa de Mercadorias & Futuros	Live Cattle	F	330 net arrobas	US3.3/CR$50	Feb/Apr/Jun/Aug/Sep/Oct/Nov/Dec	p/c
Bolsa de Mercadorias & Futuros	Arabica Coffee	F	100 bags	US$1	Mar/May/Jul/Sep/Dec	p/c
Bolsa de Mercadorias & Futuros	Robusta Coffee	F	100 bags	US$5	Jan/Mar/May/Jul/Sep/Nov	p/c
Bolsa de Mercadorias & Futuros	Cotton	F	28,108.65 pounds	US$281.0865	Mar/Apr/May/Jul/Oct/Dec	p/c
Bolsa de Mercadorias & Futuros	Feeder Cattle	F	33 feeder steers	US$3.3	All months	p/c
Bolsa de Mercadorias & Futuros	Soybeans	F	30 metric tonnes	US$5	Jan/Mar/Apr/May/Jul/Aug/Sep/Nov	p/c
Bolsa de Mercadorias & Futuros	Arabica Coffee	O	100 bags	US$1	Feb/Apr/Jun/Aug/Nov	p/c
Winnipeg Commodity Exchange	Canola	F	20/100 tonnes	C$0.1	Sep/Nov/Jan	P
Winnipeg Commodity Exchange	Flaxseed	F	20/100 tonnes	C$0.1	Oct/Dec/Mar	P

Winnipeg Commodity Exchange	Barley (Domestic Feed)	F	20/100 tonnes	C$0.1	Dec/Mar	P
Winnipeg Commodity Exchange	Barley Western (Domestic Feed)	F	20 tonnes	C$0.1	Feb/May/Aug/Nov	P
Winnipeg Commodity Exchange	Canadian Barley (Domestic Feed)	F	20/100 tonnes	C$0.1	Sep/Dec/Mar/May/Jul	P
Winnipeg Commodity Exchange	Oats	F	20/100 tonnes	C$0.1	Oct/Dec/Mar	P
Winnipeg Commodity Exchange	Wheat (Domestic Feed)	F	20/100 tonnes	C$0.1	Oct/Dec/Mar	P
Winnipeg Commodity Exchange	Rye	F	20/100 tonnes	C$0.1	Oct/Dec/Mar	P
Winnipeg Commodity Exchange	Canola (Cash Call)	F	1 railcart lot	C$0.1	any calendar month named at time of sale	P
Winnipeg Commodity Exchange	Canola (American Style)	O	20/100 tonnes	C$0.1	Sep/Nov/Jan/Mar/Jun	FP
Winnipeg Commodity Exchange	Canadian Barley (Domestic Feed)	O	20/100 tonnes	C$0.1	Sep/Dec/Mar/May/Jul	FP
Winnipeg Commodity Exchange	Barley (Western Domestic Feed)	O	20 tonnes	C$0.1	Feb/May/Aug/Nov	FP
Winnipeg Commodity Exchange	Feed Wheat (American Style)	O	20/100 tonnes	C$0.1	Jun/Sep/Nov/Feb	FP
Winnipeg Commodity Exchange	Flaxseed (American Style)	O	20/100 tonnes	C$0.1	Oct/Dec/Mar/May/Jul	FP
MATIF	Coffee Robusta	F	5 tonnes	FF 50	Jan/Mar/May/Jul/Sep/Nov (up to 14 months)	P
MATIF	White Sugar	F	590 tonnes	US$5	Mar/May/Aug/Oct/Dec (up to 16 months)	P
MATIF	Potatoes 50mm	F	20 tonnes	FF 50	Nov/Feb/Apr/May (up to 15 months)	
Hokkaido Grain Exchange	Potato Starch	F	2500kg	Y100	3 months	P
Hokkaido Grain Exchange	Red Beans	F	2400kg	Y80	6 months	P
Hokkaido Grain Exchange	Soyabeans (Domestic)	F	2400kg	Y40	3 months	P
Hokkaido Grain Exchange	Soyabeans (Imported)	F	15,000kg	Y250	alt 6 months	P
Hokkaido Grain Exchange	White Beans	F	2400kg	Y40	6 months	P
Kanmon Commodity Exchange	Refined White Soft Sugar	F	9000kg	10 sen/kg	6 months	P
Kanmon Commodity Exchange	Raw Sugar	F	20,000kg	10 sen/kg	9 months	P
Kanmon Commodity Exchange	White Beans	F	2400kg	Y10/60kg	6 months	P

Kanmon Commodity Exchange	Soya Beans	F	30,000kg	Y10/1000kg	6 months	P
Kanmon Commodity Exchange	Potato Starch	F	2500kg	Y1/25kg	3 months	P
Kanmon Commodity Exchange	Red Beans	F	2400kg	Y10/30kg	6 months	P
Kanmon Commodity Exchange	Yellow Corn	F	100,000kg	Y10/1000kg	6 months	P
Kansai Agric. Commodities Exchange	Azuki beans	F	80 bags of 30kg	Y10 per 30kg	6 months	P
Kansai Agric. Commodities Exchange	Imported Soya Beans	F	30 tonnes	Y10 / tonne	6 even months up to 12 months ahead	P
Kansai Agric. Commodities Exchange	Raw Sugar	F	20 tonnes	Y0.1 per kg	9 months	P
Kansai Agric. Commodities Exchange	Raw Sugar	O	20,000kg	Y0.05 per kg	3 months	FP
Kobe Raw Silk Exchange	Raw Silk	F	150kg	Y1	six months	P
Kobe Rubber Exchange	No3 Ribbed Smoked Sheet Rubber	F	5000kg	Y0.1	current and following five months	P
Maebashi Dried Cocoon Exchange	Dried Cocoon	F	300 kg	Y1 per kg	6 months	P
Nagoya Grain and Sugar Exchange	Red Beans	F	2400kg	Y80	six months	P
Nagoya Grain and Sugar Exchange	Soyabeans (Domestic)	F	2400kg	Y40	n/k	P
Nagoya Grain and Sugar Exchange	Soyabeans (Imported)	F	15,000kg	Y250	alt six months	P
Nagoya Grain and Sugar Exchange	White Beans	F	2400kg	Y40	6 months	P
Nagoya Grain and Sugar Exchange	Sweet Potato Starch	F	2500kg	Y100	3 months	P
Nagoya Grain and Sugar Exchange	Potato Starch	F	2500kg	Y100	3 months	P
Nagoya Grain and Sugar Exchange	Refined White Soft Sugar	F	9000kg	Y900	6 months	P
Nagoya Textile Exchange	Cotton Yarn	F	4000lb	Y400	6 months	P
Nagoya Textile Exchange	Woolen Yarn	F	500kg	Y500	6 months	P
Nagoya Textile Exchange	Staple (Synthetic) Fibre Yarn	F	5000lb	Y500	6 months	P
Osaka Textile Exchange	Cotton Yarn (20s)	F	2000 lbs	Y200	6 months	P
Osaka Textile Exchange	Cotton Yarn (30s)	F	2000lbs	Y200	Current and following five months	P
Osaka Textile Exchange	Cotton Yarn (40s)	F	4000lbs	Y400	6 months	P
Osaka Textile Exchange	Staple (Synthetic) Fibre Yarn	F	5000lbs	Y500	6 months	P
Osaka Textile Exchange	Woolen Yarn	F	500kg	Y500	6 months	P
Tokyo Commodity Exchange	Cotton Yarn	F	1814.36kg	Y0.1 per pound	6 consecutive months	W

Tokyo Commodity Exchange	Woolen Yarn	F	500kg	Y1 per kg	6 consecutive months	W
Tokyo Grain Exchange	US Soyabeans	F	30 tonnes	Y10/ tonne	Apr/Jun/Aug/Oct/Dec/Feb within 12 months	W
Tokyo Grain Exchange	Azuki Beans	F	2.4 tonnes	Y10/ 30kg	6 consecutive months	W
Tokyo Grain Exchange	Corn	F	100 tonnes	Y10/ tonne	Jan/Mar/May/Jul/Sep/Nov	W
Tokyo Grain Exchange	Raw Sugar	F	20,000kg	Y0.1/kg	Odd numbered months within 20 month period	W
Tokyo Grain Exchange	Refined White Soft Sugar	F	9000kg	Y0.1/kg	Nearby six consecutive calendar months	W
Tokyo Grain Exchange	US Soybeans	O	30 tonnes	Y5/tonne	Apr/Jun/Aug/Oct/Dec/Feb within 12 months	FP
Tokyo Grain Exchange	Raw Sugar	O	1 raw sugar futurss contract	Y0.05/ kg	Nearest six odd numbered months within 15 month cycle	FP
Toyohashi Dried Cocoon Exchange	Dried Cocoon	F	300kg	Y300	6 months	P
Yokohama Raw Silk Exchange	Raw Silk	F	150kg	Y200	6 months	P
Kuala Lumpur Commodity Exchange	Crude Palm Oil	F	25 tonnes	M$25	Current month and five following then alternate up to 12 months forward	P
Kuala Lumpur Commodity Exchange	Crude Palm Kernel Oil	F	25 tonnes	US$10	Current month and five following then alternate up to 12 months forward	P
Kuala Lumpur Commodity Exchange	Cocoa	F	10 tonnes	US$25	Jan/Mar/May/Jul/Sep/Nov/Dec	P
Kuala Lumpur Commodity Exchange	Tin	F	5 tonnes	M$25	Current month,the next 3 succeeding, plus alternate months up to 12 months forward	P
Kuala Lumpur Commodity Exchange	Rubber	F	10 tonnes	M$75	Current and 3-5 following then two distant quarters	P
Kuala Lumpur Commodity Exchange	SMR 20	F	30 tonnes	M$75	Current and 3-5 following then two distant quarters	P
Agricultural Fut. Mkt. Amsterdam (ATA)	Live Hogs	F	10,000kg	DFl 0.005	12 forward	P
Agricultural Fut. Mkt. Amsterdam (ATA)	Potatoes	F	25,000kg	DFl 0.1	Nov/Feb/Mar/Apr/may/Jun	P
Agricultural Fut. Mkt Amsterdam (ATA)	Piglets	F	100 pieces	DFl 0.25	12 forward	C
New Zealand Futures and Options Exch.	NZ Wool (WFC)	F	2500c/kg x indicator	NZ$25	bi-monthly	C
Manila International Futures Exchange	Sugar	F	112,000lbs	0.2 centavo	consecutive nearest six months	P
Manila International Futures Exchange	Coffee	F	5000kg	5 centavos	consecutive nearest six months	P
Manila International Futures Exchange	Copra	F	20,000kg	1 centavo	consecutive nearest six months	P
Manila International Futures Exchange	Soyabeans	F	500 bags of 60kg	50 centavos	consecutive nearest six months	P
Manila International Futures Exchange	Dry Cocoon	F	300kg	50 centavos	consecutive nearest six months	P
RAS Commodity Exchange	RSS 1	F	5 tonnes (mth)/15 tonnes (qtr)	S$12.5/S$37.5	single months followed by quarters	P
RAS Commodity Exchange	RSS 3	F	5 tonnes (mth)/15 tonnes (qtr)	S$12.5/S$37.5	single months followed by quarters	P

RAS Commodity Exchange	TSR 20 Award	F	20 tonnes (mth)/60 tonnes (qtr)	S$50/S$150	single months followed by quarters	P
RAS Commodity Exchange	RCS Index	F	1 lot (5000 x RCS Index)	US$5	9 consecutive months	C
London Commodity Exchange	Robusta Coffee	F	5 tonnes	US$1	Jan/Mar/May/Jul/Sep/Nov (7 months quoted)	P
London Commodity Exchange	No 7 Cocoa	F	10 tonnes	#1	Mar/May/Jul/Sep/Dec (10 months quoted)	P
London Commodity Exchange	No 5 White Sugar	F	50 tonnes	$0.1	Mar/May/Aug/Oct/Dec	P
London Commodity Exchange	No 7 Premium Raw Sugar	F	50 long tons	0.01 US cents per pound	Jan/Mar/May/Jul/Oct	P
London Commodity Exchange	EC Wheat	F	100 tonnes	#0.05	Jan/Mar/May/Jul/Sep/Nov (7 months quoted)	P
London Commodity Exchange	EC Barley	F	100 tonnes	#0.05	Jan/Mar/May/Sep/Nov (6 months quoted)	P
London Commodity Exchange	Potatoes	F	20 tonnes	#0.1	Mar/Apr/May/Jun/Nov (8 months quoted)	P
London Commodity Exchange	Robusta Coffee	O	5 tonnes	US$1	Jan/Mar/May/Jul/Sep/Nov (7 months quoted)	FP
London Commodity Exchange	No 7 Cocoa	O	10 tonnes	#1	Mar/May/Jul/Sep/Dec (10 months quoted)	FP
London Commodity Exchange	No 5 White Sugar	O	50 tonnes	$0.1	Mar/May/Aug/Oct/Dec	FP
London Commodity Exchange	EC Wheat	O	100 tonnes	#0.05	Jan/Mar/May/Jul/Sep/Nov (7 months quoted)	FP
London Commodity Exchange	EC Barley	O	100 tonnes	#0.05	Jan/Mar/May/Sep/Nov (6 months quoted)	FP
London Commodity Exchange	Potatoes	O	20 tonnes	#0.1	Mar/Apr/May/Jun/Nov (8 months quoted)	FP
Chicago Board of Trade	Corn	F	5000bu	$12.5	Mar/May/Jul/Sep/Dec	P
Chicago Board of Trade	Oats	F	5000bu	$12.5	Mar/May/Jul/Sep/Dec	P
Chicago Board of Trade	Soyabeans	F	5000bu	$12.5	Jan/Mar/May/Jul/Aug/Sep/Nov	P
Chicago Board of Trade	Soyabean Oil	F	60,000lbs	$6	Jan/Mar/May/Jul/Aug/Sep/Oct/Dec	P
Chicago Board of Trade	Soyabean Meal	F	100 tonnes	$10.00	Jan/Mar/May/Jul/Aug/Sep/Oct/Dec	P
Chicago Board of Trade	Wheat	F	5000bu	$12.5	Jul/Sep/Dec/Mar/May	P
Chicago Board of Trade	Corn	O	5000bu	$6.25	Mar/May/Jul/Sep/Dec	FP
Chicago Board of Trade	Oats	O	5000bu	$6.25	Mar/May/Jul/Sep/Dec	FP
Chicago Board of Trade	Soyabeans	O	5000bu	$6.25	Jan/Mar/May/Jul/Aug/Sep/Nov	FP
Chicago Board of Trade	Soyabean Oil	O	60,000lbs	$5	Jan/Mar/May/Jul/Aug/Sep/Oct/Dec	FP
Chicago Board of Trade	Soyabean Meal	O	100 tonnes	$3	Jan/Mar/May/Jul/Aug/Sep/Oct/Dec	FP
Chicago Board of Trade	Wheat	O	5000bu	$6.25	Jul/Sep/Dec/Mar/May	FP
Chicago Mercantile Exchange	Pork Bellies	F	40,000lbs	$10	Feb/Mar/May/Jul/Aug	P
Chicago Mercantile Exchange	Live Cattle	F	40,000lbs	$10	Feb/Apr/Jun/Aug/Oct/Dec	P
Chicago Mercantile Exchange	Feeder Cattle	F	40,000lbs	$12.5	Jan/Mar/Apr/May/Aug/Sep/Oct/Nov	C
Chicago Mercantile Exchange	Live Hogs	F	40,000lbs	$10	Feb/Apr/May/Jun/Jul/Aug/Oct/Dec	P

WORLD COMMODITY CONTRACTS

iv) OTHERS

Exchange	Contract Name	Type[1]	Contract Size	Tick Size	Months	Sett.[2]
London Commodity Exchange	Baltic Freight Index (BIFFEX)	F	US$10 per index point	1 index point		C
London Commodity Exchange	Baltic Freight Index (BIFFEX)	O	US$10 per index point	1 index point		C
CBOT	National Catastrophe Insurance	F	Qtrly: L/P x $25,000	0.1 point ($25)	Mar/Jun/Sep/Dec	C
CBOT	Eastern Catastrophe Insurance	F	Qtrly: L/P x $25,000	0.1 point ($25)	Mar/Jun/Sep/Dec	C
CBOT	Midwestern Catastrophe Insurance	F	Qtrly: L/P x $25,000	0.1 point ($25)	Mar/Jun/Sep/Dec	C
CBOT	National Catastrophe Insurance	O	One futures contract		Mar/Jun/Sep/Dec	C
CBOT	Eastern Catastrophe Insurance	O	One futures contract		Mar/Jun/Sep/Dec	C
CBOT	Midwestern Catastrophe Insurance	O	One futures contract		Mar/Jun/Sep/Dec	C
CBOT	Anhydrous Ammonia	F	100 tons	10c per ton	Mar/Jun/Sep/Dec	P*
CBOT	Diammonium Phosphate	F	100 tons of contract grade DAP in bulk	$10	Mar/Jun/Sep/Dec	P

[1] *Type: F=Futures; O= Options*

[2] *Sett.: P= Physical delivery; C= Cash settlement; FP = Assignment of futures position; * Shipping certificate*

WORLD COMMODITY CONTRACTS

iii) ENERGY

Exchange	Contract	Type[1]	Contract Size	Tick Size	Months	Sett.2
SIMEX (Sing)	High Sulphur Fuel Oil	F	100 tonnes	US$10	9 consecutive months	P
SIMEX (Sing)	Gas oil	F	1000 barrels	US$10	6 consecutive months	C
IPE	Gas Oil	F	100 tonnes	US$25	18 months incl current	P
IPE	Brent Crude	F	1000 barrels	US$10	9 months incl current	C
IPE	Unleaded Gasoline	F		US$25	6 months incl current	P
IPE	Gas Oil	O	100 tonnes	US$5	6 months incl current	C
IPE	Brent Crude	O	1000 barrels	US$10	6 months incl current	C
NYMEX	NY Harbor Heating Oil	F	42,000 gals	US$4.2	18 consecutive	P
NYMEX	NY Harbor Gasoline	F	42,000 gals	US$4.2	18 consecutive	P
NYMEX	Gulf Coast Gasoline	F	42,000 gals	US$4.2	18 consecutive	P
NYMEX	Propane Gas	F	42,000 gals	US$4.2	15 consecutive	P
NYMEX	Light Sweet Crude Oil	F	1000 barrels	US$10	18 consecutive, plus 2 quarterly, plus 2 semi-annual	P
NYMEX	Sour Crude Oil	F	1000 barrels	US$10	18 consecutive	P
NYMEX	Natural Gas	F	10,000 MMBtu	US$10	18 consecutive	P
NYMEX	Crude Oil	O	1000 barrels	US$10	6 consecutive plus 2 quarterly	FP
NYMEX	Heating Oil	O	42,000 gals	US$4.2	6 consecutive plus 2 quarterly	FP
NYMEX	Gasoline	O	42,000 gals	US$4.2	6 consecutive plus 2 quarterly	FP
NYMEX	Natural Gas	O	10,000 MMBtu	US$10	12 consecutive	FP

[1] *Type: F=Futures; O= Options*

[2] *Sett.: P= Physical delivery; C= Cash settlement; FP = Assignment of futures position*

Mid America Commodity Exchange	Corn	O	1000bu	$1.25	Mar/May/Jul/Sep/Dec	FP
Mid America Commodity Exchange	Rough Rice	O	2000cwt	$5	Jan/Mar/May/Jul/Sep/Nov	FP
Minneapolis Grain Exchange	Hard Red Spring Wheat	F	5000bu	$12.5	Mar/May/Jul/Sep/Dec	P
Minneapolis Grain Exchange	Oats	F	5000bu	$12.5	Mar/May/Jul/Sep/Dec	P
Minneapolis Grain Exchange	White Wheat	F	5000bu	$12.5	Mar/May/Jul/Sep/Dec	P
Minneapolis Grain Exchange	Frozen Shrimp	F	5000lbs	$12.5	Mar/Jun/Sep/Dec	P
Minneapolis Grain Exchange	Hard Red Spring wheat	O	5000bu	$6.25	Mar/May/Jul/Sep/Dec	FP
Minneapolis Grain Exchange	Oats	O	5000bu	$6.25	Mar/May/Jul/Sep/Dec	FP
Minneapolis Grain Exchange	White wheat	O	5000bu	$6.25	Mar/May/Jul/Sep/Dec	FP
Minneapolis Grain Exchange	Frozen shrimp	O	5000lbs	$6.25	Mar/Jun/Sep/Dec	FP
New York Cotton Exchange	Cotton	F	50,000lb	$5	Mar/May/Jul/Oct	P
New York Cotton Exchange	Cotlook World Cotton	F	50,000lb equivalent of index	$5	7 from the Mar,May,Aug/Oct/Dec cycle, plus nearest two from the Jan/Feb/Apr/Sep/Nov cycle	P
New York Cotton Exchange	Orange Juice	F	15,000lb	$7.5	Jan/Mar/May/Jul/Sep/Nov	P
New York Cotton Exchange	Cotton	O	50,000lb	$5	Mar/May/Jul/Oct	FP
New York Cotton Exchange	Cotlook World Cotton	O	50,000lb equivalent of index	$5	7 from the Mar,May,Aug/Oct/Dec cycle, plus nearest two from the Jan/Feb/Apr/Sep/Nov cycle	FP
New York Cotton Exchange	Orange Juice	O	15,000lb	$7.5	Jan/Mar/May/Jul/Sep/Nov	FP

[1] *Type: F=Futures; O= Options*

[2] *Sett.: P= Physical delivery; C= Cash settlement; FP = Assignment of futures position; W = Warrant*

Chicago Mercantile Exchange	Broiler Chicken	F	40,000lbs	$10	Feb/Apr/May/Jun/Jul/Aug/Sep/Oct	P
Chicago Mercantile Exchange	Pork Bellies	O	40,000lbs	$10	Feb/Mar/May/Jul/Aug	FP
Chicago Mercantile Exchange	Live Cattle	O	40,000lbs	$10	Feb/Apr/Jun/Aug/Oct/Dec	FP
Chicago Mercantile Exchange	Feeder Cattle	O	40,000lbs	$12.5	Jan/Mar/Apr/May/Aug/Sep/Oct/Nov	FP
Chicago Mercantile Exchange	Live Hogs	O	40,000lbs	$10	Feb/Apr/May/Jun/Jul/Aug/Oct/Dec	FP
Chicago Mercantile Exchange	Broiler Chicken	O	40,000lbs	$10	Feb/Apr/May/Jun/Jul/Aug/Sep/Oct	FP
Coffee, Sugar and Cocoa Exchange	Coffee C	F	37,500lbs	$18.75	Mar/May/Jul/Sep/Dec	P
Coffee, Sugar and Cocoa Exchange	Brazil Differential Coffee	F	37,500lbs	$18.75	Mar/May/Jul/Sep/Dec	P
Coffee, Sugar and Cocoa Exchange	Cocoa	F	10 tonnes	$10	Mar/May/Jul/Sep/Dec	P
Coffee, Sugar and Cocoa Exchange	No 11 Sugar	F	112,000lbs	$11.2	Mar/May/Jul/Oct	P
Coffee, Sugar and Cocoa Exchange	No 14 Sugar	F	112,000lbs	$11.2	Jan/Mar/May/Jul/Sep/Nov	P
Coffee, Sugar and Cocoa Exchange	White Sugar	F	50 tonnes	$10	Jan/Mar/May/Jul/Oct	P
Coffee, Sugar and Cocoa Exchange	Non-fat Dry Milk	F	44,000lbs	$22	Feb/May/Jul/Sep/Nov	P
Coffee, Sugar and Cocoa Exchange	Cheddar Cheese	F	40,000lbs	$20	Feb/May/Jul/Sep/Nov	P
Coffee, Sugar and Cocoa Exchange	Coffee C	O	One futures contract	$3.75	Mar/May/Jul/Sep/Dec	FP
Coffee, Sugar and Cocoa Exchange	Cocoa	O	One futures contract	$10	Mar/May/Jul/Sep/Dec	FP
Coffee, Sugar and Cocoa Exchange	No 11 Sugar	O	One futures contract	$11.2	Regular options: Mar/May/Jul and Oct plus Jan option on March; Serial options: Feb/Apr/Jun/Aug/Sep/Nov and Dec	FP
Coffee, Sugar and Cocoa Exchange	Non-fat Dry Milk	O	One futures contract	$4.4	Feb/May/Jul/Sep/Nov	FP
Coffee, Sugar and Cocoa Exchange	Cheddar Cheese	O	One futures contract	$4	Feb/May/Jul/Sep/Nov	FP
Kansas City Board of Trade	No 2 Red Wheat	F	5000bu	$12.5	Mar/May/Jul/Sep/Dec	P
Kansas City Board of Trade	No 2 Red Wheat	O	5000bu	$6.25	Mar/May/Jul/Sep/Dec	FP
Mid America Commodity Exchange	Corn	F	1000bu	$1.25	Mar/May/Jul/Sep/Dec	P
Mid America Commodity Exchange	Oats	F	1000bu	$1.25	Mar/May/Jul/Sep/Dec	P
Mid America Commodity Exchange	Soyabeans	F	1000bu	$1.25	Jan/Mar/May/Jul/Aug/Sep/Nov	P
Mid America Commodity Exchange	Soyabean Meal	F	20 tons	$2	Jan/Mar/May/Jul/Aug/Sep/Oct/Dec	C
Mid America Commodity Exchange	Wheat	F	1000bu	$1.25	Mar/May/Jul/Sep/Dec	P
Mid America Commodity Exchange	Cattle	F	20,000lbs	$5	Feb/Apr/Jun/Aug/Oct/Dec	P
Mid America Commodity Exchange	Hogs	F	20,000lbs	$5	Feb/Apr/Jun/Jul/Aug/Oct/Dec	P
Mid America Commodity Exchange	Rough Rice	F	2000cwt	$10	Jan/Mar/May/Jul/Sep/Nov	P
Mid America Commodity Exchange	Soyabeans	O	1000bu	$1.25	Jan/Mar/May/Jul/Aug/Sep/Nov	FP
Mid America Commodity Exchange	Wheat	O	1000bu	$1.25	Mar/May/Jul/Sep/Dec	FP

Forecast Plus

StatPac, Inc.
3814 Lyndale Avenue South
Minneapolis
MN 55409
USA
Tel: 1 612 822 8252

Forecast Pro

Business Forecast Systems
68 Leonard Street
Belmont
MA 02178
USA
Tel: 1 617 484 5050
Fax: 617 484 9219

Option Master

Institute for Options Research Inc
PO Box 6586, Lake Tahoe
NV 89449
USA
Tel: 702 588 3590
Fax: 702 588 8481

Right Time

TBSP Inc
610 Newport Ctr Dr
Suite 630, Newport Beach
CA 92660
USA
Tel: 714 721 8603
Fax: 714 721 8635

SmartForecasts Version 3

Smart Software Inc
4 Hill Road
Belmont MA 02178
USA
Tel 0800 762 7899 & 1 617 489 2743
Fax 1 617 489 2748

STAMP: Structural Time series Analyser and Predictor

Department of Statistics
London School of Economics
Houghton Street
London WC2A 2AE
UK
Tel: 00 44 171 955 6725
Fax: 00 44 171 955 7416

StatPlan IV

Lotus Selects
PO Box 9172
Cambridge Mass 02139-9946
USA
Tel: 800 635 6887 & 1 617 693 3981

Swing Catcher

Trend Index Trading Company
Rural Route 10
Eau Claire
WI 54701-9077
USA
Tel: 1 715 833 1234
Fax: 1 715 833 8040

3D for Windows

MESA
PO Box 1801
Goleta CA 93116
USA
Tel: 800 633 6372

Ganntrader 2

Gannsoft Publishing Company
11670 Riverbend Drive
Leavenworth, WA 98826-9305
USA
Tel: 1 509 548 5990
Fax: 1 509 548 4679

Sibyl/Runner

Applied Decision Systems
510 South Street
Lexington MA
USA
Tel: 1 617 424 9820

Strategist

Optionomics Corp
2835 East 3300 South, Suite 200
Salt Lake City
Utah 84109
USA
Tel: 1 801 466 2111
Fax: 1 801 466 7320

Tomorrow

Isogon Corp
330 Seventh Ave
New York, NY 10001
USA
Tel: 1 212 967 2424

Micro TSP/ EViews

Quantitative Micro Software
4521 Campus Drive
Suite 336, Irvine
CA 92715
USA
Tel: 1 714 856 3368
Fax: 1 714 856 2044

Index

The Publisher....

Probus Publishing is a leading international business and finance publishing company, committed to excellence. Our books and information products are known worldwide for their quality and clarity. We are proud to be the publishers of acknowledged experts in the subjects of investments, banking, trading, the capital markets, accountancy, taxation, property, insurance, sales management, marketing and healthcare.

Why not forward us your contact information to allow us to send you information about our full range? In addition, we are always interested to hear from potential authors. If you have a project that you believe would compliment our list, then please get in touch.

You can contact Probus Publishing at:

1333 Burr Ridge Parkway
Burr Ridge
IL 60521
USA
Tel: (708) 789-4000
Tel [Sales]: 800-634-3966 [USA only]
Fax: (708) 789-6933

OR

Lynton House
7-12 Tavistock Square
London WC1H 9LB
England
Tel: (0171) 388-7676
Fax: (0171) 391-6556

The World's Futures & Options Markets

Nick Battley (Ed.)

1029pp, 1994. ISBN 1 55738 513 0

Where in the world can you trade euroyen futures? Is there a Finnish interest rate contract available? Which is the most heavily-traded of the world's five eurodollar futures contracts? The answers to all these questions—and more—can be found in this fully classified directory, making it **the** essential reference work for everyone with a professional or personal interest in futures and options. This major publication features detailed information on over 550 contracts, categorized by type and listed alphabetically for ease of reference. Of course, in addition to the contracts, the 51 exchanges on which they are traded are covered in full detail.

For those with an appetite for statistics, the appendices contain 7-year historical volume figures, not only for almost every contract, but also for each exchange.

Dictionary of Futures & Options: Over 1,500 International Terms Defined and Explained

Alan Webber

240pp, 1994. ISBN 1 55738 595 5

The *Dictionary of Futures and Options* is a comprehensive source of essential information for anyone involved in futures and options markets throughout the world. Both the complete beginner and the seasoned professional will find this book full of indispensable facts. It contains all the basic terminology used throughout the international arena, as well as substantial descriptions of options strategies, the 'Greek' letters, position exposure to certain measures and more. With the growth and innovation in the futures market, even seasoned veterans sometimes find it difficult to keep up with all the new developments. This book is an enduring reference work that helps practitioners stay abreast of this constantly changing field.

The Global Investor: Opportunities, Risks and Realities for Institutional Investors in the World's Markets.

Gavin Dobson

300pp, 1994. ISBN 1 55738 556 4

Global investment is booming! The amount of money invested overseas by institutional investors has increased dramatically in recent years. With so many opportunities available, it's clear that investors can no longer afford to focus on their domestic market alone. Author Gavin Dobson, a top international fund manager, describes the theory, methods and practices of international investing. Insightful and captivating, *The Global Investor* takes the reader inside the fascinating and sometimes mysterious world of international investing. For all financial professionals, this book will prove to be both a good read and an enduring reference.

North South: An Emerging Markets Handbook

Robert Lloyd George

360pp, 1994. ISBN 1 55738 873 4

A book that addresses one of today's hottest investment topics, *North South* provides a timely, comprehensive and much-needed country-by-country guide to 60 emerging markets around the world. A highly practical handbook designed for the sophisticated investor, this book assesses the opportunities as well as the risks associated with the developing markets. Each market is examined both individually and in relation to the global economy, looking at the question of possible political instability, the health of the currency, and legal and financial regulation. Coverage is not only of East and South Asia but also of Latin America, the Middle East, Africa, Eastern Europe and Russia.

The European Currency Crisis: What Chance Now for a Single European Currency?

Paul Temperton (Ed.)

350pp, 1993. ISBN 1 55738 560 2

With the continuing uncertainty within Europe's foreign exchange markets, what is the likelihood of a single currency for the European Union before the end of the millennium? Editor Paul Temperton has assembled a host of key figures to write this seminal work. Within the pages of this book, central bank governors, financial advisors, economists, pundits and politicians debate the central issue for Europe that refuses to go away.

Does the Maastricht Treaty still provide a viable plan for a move to a single currency? And if not, what alternative plans might be considered? Is there a rapid route to forming monetary union? Or, if central banks had greater independence would that be a solution? All of these critical questions are addressed by contributors including Sir Alan Walters (former economic advisor to Margaret Thatcher), Robin Leigh-Pemberton (former governor of the Bank of England), Graham Bishop (Salomon Brothers), Dr Martin Seidel (legal advisor to German Federal Ministry of Economics), as well as many others.

The Reuter Guide to Official Interest Rates

Ken Ferris **and** *Mark Jones*

200pp, 1994. ISBN 1 55738 560 2

The money markets are truly international. To succeed in today's fast-moving 24-hour markets, traders and investors must understand how monetary authorities around the world control money supply and set interest rates. Failure to do so can lead to big losses. Covering 20 industrialized countries, this book provides a thorough explanation of how official interest rates are set, how central banks control money markets and the relationship between official interest rates and market rates. Armed with this knowledge, traders and investors can anticipate central bank actions and profit from the big swings in the stock, bond and currency markets that frequently result from changes in official interest rates.

Look out for the new paperback edition of this invaluable reference tool - coming soon!

Option Volatility and Pricing:
Advanced Trading Strategies and Techniques

Sheldon Natenberg

Revised edition. 200pp, 1994.
ISBN 1 55738 486 X

A financial classic revised! The first edition of this bestseller helped to educate an entire generation of options traders. Written by renowned options expert Sheldon Natenberg, *Option Volatility and Pricing* explains the factors behind the pricing of options and illustrates how options prices change in response to new market conditions. The author reveals a wide range of strategies which capitalize on option mispricings and traders' volatility expectations. Completely revised and updated, this new edition reflects the products and strategies of today's markets and will be of great value to veteran and neophyte traders alike.

The 'ALL ABOUT' Series

This popular series of books, each one written by an expert in their field, covers all aspects of finance and investing, and is ideal for both beginners and veterans.

Titles include:

All About Stocks: From the Inside Out

Esme Faerber

225pp, 1995. ISBN 1 55738 806 7

All About Real Estate Investing: From the Inside Out

William Benke & Joseph M. Fowler

200pp, 1995. ISBN 1 55738 882 2

All About Mutual Funds: From the Inside Out

Bruce Jacobs

250pp, 1994. ISBN 1 55738 807 5

All About Bonds: From the Inside Out

Esme Faerber

250pp, 1993. ISBN 1 55738 437 1

All About Options: From the Inside Out

Russell Wasendorf & Thomas McCafferty

250pp, 1993. ISBN 1 55738 434 7

All About Futures: From the Inside Out

Russell Wasendorf & Thomas McCafferty

250pp, 1992. ISBN 1 55738 296 4

All About Commodities: From the Inside Out

Russell Wasendorf & Thomas McCafferty

250pp, 1992. ISBN 1 55738 459 2

Winner Take All: Inside the Mind of a Top Commodity Dealer

William R. Gallacher

Revised edition. 200pp, 1994.

ISBN 1 55738 533 5

A trader's classic. *Winner Takes All* takes you inside the mind of William Gallacher, an expert trader who transformed a small.stake into a large fortune in the commodity markets. In this well-written and wonderfully witty book, Mr Gallacher satirizes the commodity industry establishment and explains his unique philosophy of trading. Along the way, he illustrates why most traders lose money and what it takes to win. Topics include: The deceptive claims of self-appointed trading gurus; Why technical systems work in theory but not in practice; The importance of imagination, independent-thinking and discipline to trading success; How to make decisions under conditions of great uncertainty; How to trade apart from the crowd.

An Introduction to Commodity Futures and Options

Nick Battley

Second edition. 146pp, 1995.
ISBN 1 55738 920 9

A complete introduction to the industry, this book takes you from the basic principles right through to trading techniques, with all the necessary technical terms fully explained in a straightforward and easily understood manner. It includes:

- The basic principles of futures trading
- How the markets operate and who are the players
- The clearing of futures and options
- Differential and basis trading
- The vital issues of regulation and malpractice
- The principles and application of option trading
- An invaluable fully-illustrated guide to trading floor hand signals